Contemporary Barbie™

Barbie Dolls

1980 and Beyond

Bob Mackie's
Neptune Fantasy Barbie

Contents

ACKNOWLEDGEMENTS

Out of the proverbial blue, I received a call from a cable TV host planning a show on collecting Barbie® dolls. He needed someone to sit in the hot seat. That host was Harry Rinker, who has subsequently become my collectibles honesty broker (I was the one selected for the hot seat). Harry is perhaps the only person on the planet whose mission in life is to keep collectibles markets flowing and free, defending the rights and expanding the knowledge of collectors. It is fair to say that without Harry, this book would never have been written as it was he who said, "You've *got* to write a book." And it was his son, Harry Rinker, Jr., who has created some of the most beautiful photographs of the Barbie doll ever published.

Thanks, too, to Sandi Holder of the The Barbie Attic. Sandi embodies the model of what good dealers provide collectors: access, good information and loads of fun. She is a real-life example of how you can make true friends through a hobby.

Barbie doll's family at Mattel generously assisted me in gathering research and unearthing interesting stories about Contemporary Barbie. Lisa McKendall and Judy Schizas provided valuable counsel and direction. I thank Paulette Bazerman, Kitty Black-Perkins, Kim Burkhardt, Ann Driskill, Abbe Littleton, Larry Morgan, Anne Parducci and Cynthia Young for spending time with me. Danny Palumbo ably and patiently responded to my numerous requests for information.

At Antique Trader Books, Art Director Jaro Šebek designed the book and provided artistic inspiration throughout its development. Allan Miller, my editor, helped make my words sing.

I am blessed with a circle of wonderful friends. They challenge me, support me, and give me so much joy. I thank them: Constanza Erdoes Low, Betsy Jackson, Dave Peterson, Susan Steele, and the Wright Family. Carey Preston gets the Devon clotted cream award for finding the Franco-Italianate country house in England where I completed the manuscript for this book, overlooking sheep, the ruins of a magnificent manor home and spectacular gardens. Barbie never had it so good, even in her original Dream House! I also thank Jennifer Wayne, Internet Surfer Exceptionelle, who assisted me in my research. My circle of e-friends on the Internet, America Online, Compuserve and Prodigy also provided virtual collegiality.

Thanks to my sisters, Nancy and Margie, for letting me be number three in the line of "magnificent daughters." Because I was the baby, I was, to quote Paul Simon, "Born at the Right Time" to be in the first generation of Barbie doll consumers. To Polly Sarasohn, I owe my love of life and my love of play, along with abundant affection, my first two Barbie dolls and a trunk full of 900-series outfits. She must be having one great giggle from her heavenly perch, watching me still playing with these vintage toys. To Charles Sarasohn, I owe my senses of integrity, intellectual curiosity and social justice.

Finally, to my life partner and best friend, Robert Kahn, I extend loving gratitude and never-ending hugs. He continually encourages me to do anything and everything I believe in. He really makes me feel that I can do anything.

JS-K, 31 August 1995
Stevenstone
St. Giles-in-the-Wood
Devon, United Kingdom

INTRODUCTION

When Mattel began life in 1945 as a small giftware business, the company had $100,000 in sales in its first year. In 1980 (fiscal year ended January 31, 1981), Mattel had net sales of $916 million. By 1994, net sales reached $3.2 billion—Barbie® dolls represent over one-third of the company's sales, more than the company's 1980 total sales figure.

Festival Dolls. *Mattel gave these reproduction Barbie dolls to participants at the Barbie Festival in 1994. The highlight was this titian-haired ponytail, unavailable in the mass market.*

Barbie doll, a billion dollar baby to Mattel, celebrated her 35th anniversary in 1994. Mattel now sells over one billion dollars in Barbie dolls and accessories each year, representing one of the most powerful brands in the global economy. As overseas sales of the Barbie doll expand beyond the 100 countries in which she is already sold, the market promises to double—perhaps even triple—in the years ahead.

The average American girl has an estimated eight-plus Barbie dolls in her collection. Barbie dolls already reside in 99 percent of young Americans' homes. However, Mattel recognizes that both children and adults are consumers of Barbie dolls and related products. The adult market has become so important that Mattel sponsored a Barbie Festival at Walt Disney World in September, 1994. Thousands of collectors showed up for the event. This was not surprising: Adult collectors spent $65 million on Barbie dolls in 1993.*

While a number of books have been published about Barbie dolls and accessories, none cover the Barbie doll comprehensively after 1980. The first generation of Barbie doll collectors played with the doll between 1959 and 1967. Many of these (mostly) women have become collectors of the dolls of their childhood. However, since the celebration of Barbie's 35th anniversary in 1994, legions of new Barbie collectors have entered the collecting fray—many with young children of their own, and they are sharing their childhood memories, and making new ones, in parallel.

These Barbie doll collectors, unless surnamed Rockefeller, Winfrey (as in Oprah) or Perot, have one thing in common: They cannot afford to buy every new Barbie doll issued by Mattel. In fact, if one wished to own every Barbie doll manufactured for the U.S. market since 1980 alone, in never-removed-from-the-box condition, a sizable cash sum approaching $60,000 would need to be invested.

A quick review of the comprehensive list in the Appendix illustrates that the roster of new Barbie dolls issued each year since 1980 gets longer and deeper; longer due to the sheer numbers of new dolls, and deeper in the broadening of market segments that Mattel is targeting. It is too simple to say that Mattel recognizes that there are two markets for Barbie dolls—children and adults. Even within those macro segments there are sub-segments of collectors. Some adults collect the high-end Bob Mackie dolls and porcelain examples; others specialize in bride and holiday dolls. Still others acquire every "career" Barbie doll and costume.

*Source: *Brandweek,* December 12, 1994, p. 18

So whether specialist in "vertical" collections or dabbler across all types of doll themes, the contemporary Barbie doll collector must allocate available financial resources carefully.

My interest in writing this book is driven by my professional persona: I am an economist with a passion for information. As an economist by profession, I have two fundamental beliefs regarding markets:

1. A healthy, "perfect" market is based on the presence of a multitude of buyers and sellers.
2. A healthy market requires the free flow of information. More (good) information means a healthier market.

Prior to the Barbie doll's 35th year, the Barbie and associated collectibles market was highly imperfect. The vintage Barbie doll market was represented by relatively few sellers, lots of buyers, and relatively few sources of reliable information. Much of the information that was available was in fact written by dealers themselves, who can have conflicts of interest.

Through the years, Barbie has adapted her bathing suit styles to her times. From left: ***Baywatch Barbie*** *(1995),* ***Malibu Barbie*** *(1971),* ***Bubblecut Barbie*** *(1961),* ***Sun Sensation Barbie*** *(1993).*

Then, in 1994, when the Barbie doll's 35th anniversary was celebrated, several things happened in parallel:

- Mattel explicitly recognized and rewarded the Barbie doll collector with the company's first-ever national convention in Orlando, at Walt Disney World.
- Madison Avenue, the news media and daytime talk shows based content and hype on the Barbie doll and related topics, raising the profile of the 35th anniversary of the doll.
- The number of new Barbie doll collectors doubled (some say tripled). Some had rediscovered their baby boom childhoods; other, non-baby boomers, began new collections with "pink box" and/or mass merchandise Barbie dolls.

*From American Airlines Stewardess (above) to **Astronaut Barbie** (below) in 35 years.*

This book seeks to fill a gap in the Barbie doll collecting literature that tends to focus on the early vintage era of the doll. The intent is to provide collectors, both long-standing and new entrants into the arena, with a baseline of information on contemporary Barbie: those dolls produced after 1980. A primary objective is to provide this information with an eye toward freeing-up the collecting market, creating more informed consumers and more responsible dealers. Only in the balance of well-informed supply and demand can a healthy market exist. This will enhance collective enjoyment of the hobby for all of us in the long run.

Contemporary Barbie? Hasn't the Barbie doll always been contemporary since she was unveiled at Toy Fair in 1959? The fact is that it has always been the intention of Mattel's Barbie doll designers to have the doll reflect her times. Appearing as Barbie first did, so very pale and blonde in her zebra-striped bathing suit, the doll was a quintessential Fifties conception. But over time, Sorority Girl and Junior Prom outfits were joined by American Airlines Stewardess in 1960. We sweated with Great Shapes Barbie aerobicizing in 1980; went to the moon when Astronaut Barbie flew into space in 1974; and voted when Barbie [ran] for President in 1992. Since introduced, the Barbie doll has reflected the contemporary society in which she lived (or was played with). This was and still is art imitating life. "Art?" you say. Yes, art! Andy Warhol painted her, and the Museum of Modern Art, London's Victoria and Albert Museum, the Smithsonian Institution and the Oakland Museum all exhibited her. She has even had her own Hall of Fame in Palo Alto, California. And in December, 1995, the Liberty Art Gallery in New York City celebrated "Art and Barbie"—assembling works by some 50 prominent contemporary artists such as John Baldessari, Kenny Scharf, Andy Warhol and William Wegman; and architects Robert A.M. Stern and Emilio Ambasz.

This book provides a context of social history for *Contemporary BARBIE* and the colorful, sometimes twisted, ofttimes paradoxical, contemporary history within which the dolls were introduced in the United States. In the modern period of the Barbie doll, her global presence grew and she is well represented in both developed and emerging economies. However, the scope of this book is limited to U.S. domestic Barbie dolls in the contemporary period, leaving the Barbie dolls manufactured for non-U.S. consumption for another book. In addition, this book does not cover the prototypes or convention dolls that many *Contemporary BARBIE* collectors covet. Only dolls available on the mass market through national distribution (for the great bulk of collectors) are covered in this book.

One of the most limited Barbie dolls of the contemporary era, Gold Jubilee Barbie *was issued in 1994 to commemorate the 35th anniversary of the* Barbie *doll. She was designed by Carol Spencer and was reportedly limited to 5,000 dolls.*

Chapter 1

CONTEMPORARY BARBIE® HISTORY

This chapter describes the evolution of the modern Barbie doll using a timeline perspective for the *Contemporary BARBIE* era. Key real-world events which have shaped development of the doll are highlighted. These include events in politics, society, demography, the economy, and the arts (both the so-called "fine" and "popular" arts). This timeline should be kept in mind when reading the rest of the book because it sets the stage for understanding *Contemporary BARBIE* in the doll's modern historical and social contexts.

Before exploring the external events that provide a context and influence the modern Barbie doll, it is important to have some understanding of Mattel's corporate culture during the period. This book defines the contemporary era as beginning in 1980 and continuing to the present day. While the decade of the 1990s—when the adult collector market substantially boomed—has contributed to Mattel's success, the earlier years of the period were difficult times for the company.

It is worth first revisiting the 1970s, a period of new social attitudes, some of which did not bode well for Barbie. In 1971, the National Organization for Women began a formal campaign against Barbie with a press release that condemned advertising for the doll as sexist. By the early 1980s, many consumers had written-off the doll as, at a minimum, uninteresting; at the extreme, she was thought to be a sexist, poor example for children. (Such debates continue to the present day, and still appear occasionally expressed in Op-Ed pages, on television talk shows, in feminist manifestos and sociology Ph.D. dissertations).

To make matters worse, Mattel was devastated when the videogame craze of the early 1980s faded. Their venture into videogames had cost Mattel $403 million, and the company found itself headed into 1984 with a $394 million loss. Many Wall Street toy industry analysts believe that Mattel might not have survived the troubling early years of the 1980s if the venture capital firms E.M. Warburg, Pincus & Co. and junk bond king Drexel Burnham Lambert hadn't come together, in 1984, to pitch-in $231 million in capital to rescue Mattel from its videogame woes.

Mattel hit paydirt again in 1985 with its Masters of the Universe action toy line for boys. But the fad was short lived, leaving the firm with excess manufacturing capacity and a bloated corporate payroll.

Further complicating matters, between 1982 and 1987 Mattel underwent two major financial reorganizations and three reconstructed management teams. Sales in the period fell by 23% from their 1982 peak of $1.3 billion, and profits were erratic. In 1985, Hasbro overtook Mattel to become the world's largest toymaker. Between 1985 and 1987, Mattel lost $121 million, reflecting the restructuring, write-offs and some consumer indifference—even hostility—to many of the company's new toys (not just the Barbie doll).

A first generation international doll, from 1980. ***Parisian Barbie*** *wore a Follies Bergere-type costume.*

1988 Happy Holidays Barbie—
one successful experiment.

A re-energized board of directors, including representatives from the financial backers, counted on one man to bring Mattel out of the doldrums. That man was John Amerman, an ace consumer goods marketer who had originally joined Mattel in 1980 after successfully managing various brands including Ajax cleanser, Bromo-Seltzer, Listerine and Rolaids.

Prior to assuming the helm of Mattel as President and Chief Executive Officer in 1986, Amerman was head of Mattel International. During his tenure with that division, sales grew fourfold and, unlike Mattel's domestic operations, the international division had shown solid profitability.

Amerman downsized the company internally and focused on the two brands he believed could save the organization—Barbie and Hot Wheels®—brand names that by 1987 were 28 and 20 years old, respectively. He also established a tie-in with Disney on a toy line for infants and preschoolers; consolidated manufacturing in nine countries with among the lowest labor costs in the world; and convinced his own marketing staff that there was, indeed, a market for Barbie dolls beyond the long-held $10 price point. Finally, Mattel under Amerman developed the "We're into Barbie" advertising campaign for television. Amerman's multi-pronged strategy worked. Following a loss of more than $120 million on sales of $1 billion in 1987, Mattel reported a profit of $36 million on sales of $990 million in 1988, with Barbie ranking as the firm's biggest franchise.

How Holiday Barbie Was Born

John Amerman believed that there was pent-up demand for expanding Barbie dolls beyond a $10 price point. He recalled a staff meeting where he asked, "Why can't we sell a Barbie Doll for more than $9.99?" In response, Amerman said, "Everybody's face turned white. They held their heads for a while, then went to the easel with pointers and graphs and explained all the reasons why you couldn't do that. It all came down to being afraid of the retail buyer. I told our head of design and development to come up with the most elegant Barbie ever. I told the packaging people to develop the best package they could conceive. A week later, they gave me the hard costs. I said, 'Geez, we're gonna have to sell her for $19.99.' And that's how Holiday Barbie was born."

Amerman proceeded cautiously, shipping just 300,000 units in October 1988. "But they never even reached retail shelves," he said. "The clerks in the stores would buy whole cases and take them home for their family and friends or sell them for $50 apiece, so they became black-market items. When we saw that, we knew we had a bright idea."

The next year, the company shipped 600,000 Holiday Barbies retailing for $21.99. The company expanded the line each year, until it became a holiday tradition. In 1994, Happy Holidays Barbie retailed at about $34.99, and as of November 1995, the doll fetched over $100 on the secondary market. Amerman's 1988 intuition paid off for both Mattel and collectors of the Happy Holidays series.

SOURCE: "King Barbie," *Los Angeles*, August 1994, v39, n8, p62

Good reason to smile—Mattel's Jill Elikann Barad and John Amerman.

Beyond his concept for charging more than $10 for a Barbie doll, Amerman and his team had other ideas that ultimately resulted in an expanded marketing strategy to attract even more adult collectors to Barbie dolls. These included working with Bob Mackie, manufacturing a line of porcelain dolls, and creating various themed lines of special edition dolls.

While Amerman is credited with turning Mattel (the corporate entity) around, Jill Elikann Barad played a key role in the resurgence of the Barbie doll line specifically. In the period since Barad took charge of marketing the doll in 1988, annual sales of the Barbie family have increased from $485 million to over $1 billion.

Jill Barad began working at Mattel in 1981 by pitching the sale of cosmetics for children. In 1985, Barad conceived She-Ra, Princess of Power, the first action doll for girls, as a female counterpart for the Masters of the Universe line. She-Ra, while short-lived, gave rise to a growing number of new ideas for the Barbie doll. (Note, some ten years later, the introduction of Flying Hero Barbie, with the look and feel of her predecessor, She-Ra.) Barad has been described as one of the top 50 women in American business. In 1988, *USA Today* dubbed her, "The toy industry's Princess of Power." And that was four years before Barad became Mattel's Chief Operating Officer in 1992.

In a very tangible way, then, this book covers the "Amerman and Barad era" of the Barbie doll. Given where the Barbie doll is in late 1995, collectors owe homage to both: to Amerman for his successful turnaround of Mattel through leveraging the Barbie brand in the latter 1980s; and to Barad for her continued focus on, and interest in, broadening the Barbie doll line.

The Short Life of She-Ra

She-Ra was the sister of the Master of the Universe. Known as the Princess of Power, protector of the land of Etheria, she was among the first fashion/action dolls to have a world of characters to call her own. Her arch-rival, Catra, and fellow companions, winged horses, a unicorn and a comic book, were paraphernalia included in She-Ra's World.

She-Ra's alter-ego was Princess Adora.

SOURCE: *Working Woman,* September, 1985

"I Will Survive" by Gloria Gaynor was the hot disco hit, and the first Black Barbie hit the floor in 1980 doing The Hustle and other popular dances of the time.

Chapter 2

Contemporary Barbie®
Snapshots: 1980-1985

This chapter, and the two that follow, highlight key Barbie doll releases based on annual Mattel Toys catalogs published from 1980 through 1995. As the chapter heading implies, this is a "snapshot" of the available offerings. It is not meant to be an exhaustive inventory of all dolls released each year, but is instead intended to provide a flavor for how the *Contemporary Barbie* doll has evolved since 1980. The descriptive "snapshots" are organized chronologically by year, each with a Barbie-specific anecdote from the Mattel, Inc., Annual Report for that year.

For ease of reading, we have divided the *Contemporary Barbie* period from 1980 through 1995 into three chapters—each covers a five-year period. Readers should note that the dates dividing these three periods have no special significance in Barbie doll history, and they do not define recognized or unique "eras."

1980
Mattel, Inc., says...

"Mattel Toys U.S.A. continued to demonstrate the strength of its principal consumer franchises, Barbie and Hot Wheels, with increased sales and profits in each of those lines.

"The Company's strong consumer franchises in continuing product lines such as the Barbie doll, Hot Wheels® and Preschool toys and the Intellivision™ Intelligent Television videogame/personal computer are more characteristic of branded consumer products than short life cycle or promotional toy products, and thus contribute to Mattel's established leadership positions."

(Source: 1981 Annual Report)

Mattel, Inc.
Annual Report to Shareholders for the year ended January 31, 1981
Mattel
A Multinational Company
Toy Products
Mattel Toys U.S.A.
Mattel Toys International
Mattel Electronics
Publishing and Printing
Western Publishing Company, Inc.
Entertainment
Ringling Bros.-Barnum & Bailey Combined Shows, Inc.
Ice Follies and Holiday on Ice, Inc.
Ringling Bros.-Barnum & Bailey Circus World, Inc.
Hobby Products
Monogram Models, Inc.

1980

◆ First group of female graduates from the nation's service academies include 61 from West Point, 55 from Annapolis and 97 from the Air Force Academy.

◆ The White House confirms a *Time* magazine account that reports First Lady Nancy Reagan continued to borrow expensive gowns from top designers for indefinite periods despite an earlier agreement not to do so. *Time* estimated that the borrowed fashions were worth in excess of $1 million.

The first Black doll named "Barbie" was designed by Kitty Black-Perkins. The doll had short hair and wore a long red lurex dress.

The big news in 1979 and 1980 was the introduction of both the first Black Barbie doll (#1293) and the first Hispanic Barbie doll (#1292). The Mattel catalog from 1980 enthuses about each doll.

"Black is beautiful, and Black Barbie® is a knock-out. She's ready for a night out in her fabulous body suit with a wrap-&-snap disco skirt. Little girls will love to pose Barbie. Her arms move and she twists at the waist. Completing the outfit, she comes with stylish hair comb/pick, stud, hoop & dangle earrings, modern necklace & ring, and shoes."

"Little Hispanic girls can now play with their very own Barbie®. Her pretty face accents her lovely dark eyes and long, dark hair. She has many glamorous poses—her arms move and she twists at the waist. Hispanic Barbie comes with fiesta-style dress and shawl, modern necklace & ring, choker with 'rose' stud, hoop & dangle earrings, and shoes."

The Hispanic Barbie doll's packaging featured both English and Spanish text. Not only was ethnicity being reflected by the advent of the "American" Black and Hispanic Barbie dolls, but the International line was introduced in 1980 as well. This year, the first International Barbie dolls included the Italian Barbie doll (#1601), the Parisian Barbie doll (#1600) and the Royal Barbie doll (#1602). The Italian doll was the first Barbie doll to use the Guardian Goddess face mold first seen in 1979.

The lead glamour doll of 1980 was Beauty Secrets Barbie (#1290). While Mattel did not celebrate the 21st birthday of the Barbie doll with a special issue, many collectors believe that this is the "official" doll of the 21st birthday. Beauty Secrets was promoted as having the longest hair ever on a Barbie doll (a distinction ultimately surpassed in 1993 by the Hollywood Hair Barbie). Beauty Secrets, a very "poseable" doll, continues to be popular with collectors today. The features of this doll included movable wrists and bendable elbows. When her back was pressed, the doll could comb her hair, brush her teeth, powder her face, and put on lipstick. She was therefore marketed as a beauty and hair play doll, and included lipstick, powder puff, hair dryer, toothbrush, two perfume bottles, wash mitt, compact with "mirror," comb, brush and clothing.

Kissing Barbie (#2597) would "kiss" when her back was pressed—tilting her head, puckering her lips, and making a kissing sound. With her special lipstick, she would even leave a tiny lipstick mark. Her pink floor-length dress was adorned

1980

◆ American entrepreneur Ted Turner founds the Cable News Network (CNN). Over the next few years, cable TV stations of many kinds proliferate.

◆ Jacqueline Cochran, the first woman to fly faster than the speed of sound, died at the age of 70.

◆ According to a report from the surgeon general, lung cancer in women is increasing dramatically and soon will overtake breast cancer as the leading cause of cancer fatalities among women.

with "kiss prints." This was the first Barbie doll to use a new face mold, known, appropriately, as the "kissing" face mold.

Pretty Changes Barbie doll (#2598), another hair play doll, came with hair-pieces and a changeable costume that allowed the doll to alter appearances. Her "natural" hair was a chin-length bob, and she was packaged with long blonde and brunette "falls."

The novelty of Sun Lovin' Malibu Barbie and friends were their "peek-a-boo" tans: When the top or bottom of the doll's bathing suit was removed, suntan lines could be seen. Each came with a monogrammed swimsuit and mirrored sunglasses, in the style of the time.

Rollerskating Barbie and Rollerskating Ken were the "king and queen of the roller scene," according to Mattel's promotion. While roller-skating had been a popular sport among children and teenagers for decades, Mattel capitalized on the trendiness of skating featured in popular rink and disco skating films of the time such as *Xanadu*, which starred Olivia Newton-John. The dolls featured plastic wrist straps so Barbie and Ken dolls could skate holding hands.

Other dolls marketed by Mattel this year were the Mork & Mindy™ character dolls, Starr™ and her high school friends, and Guardian Goddesses.

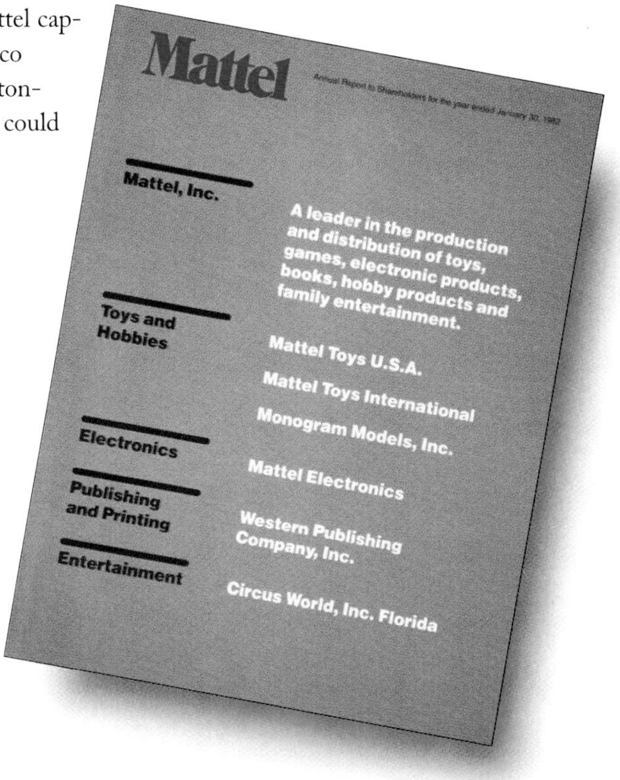
Mattel

Annual Report to Shareholders for the year ended January 30, 1982

Mattel, Inc.

A leader in the production and distribution of toys, games, electronic products, books, hobby products and family entertainment.

Toys and Hobbies

Mattel Toys U.S.A.

Mattel Toys International

Monogram Models, Inc.

Electronics

Mattel Electronics

Publishing and Printing

Western Publishing Company, Inc.

Entertainment

Circus World, Inc. Florida

1981
Mattel, Inc., says. . .

"Barbie, the world's best-known fashion doll, is now in her twenty-third year. More than 135 million Barbie dolls, in various styles and costumes, have been sold worldwide since introduction in 1959, with new unit sales records set in fiscal 1982. . . .

"Mattel also utilizes the established Barbie franchise on non-doll related product introductions to gain more ready customer and consumer acceptance. During the past year, Mattel Toys U.S.A. introduced a line of Barbie Cosmetics intended for use in play by young girls who have traditionally associated with the Barbie name."

(Source: 1982 Annual Report)

1981

◆ President Reagan announces he will nominate Arizona judge Sandra Day O'Connor to serve on the U.S. Supreme Court, making her the first female justice on the high court.

◆ The video game Pac-Man shows up in every nook and corner of the country as the nation finds itself in the grips of Pac-Mania.

◆ MTV, an all-music cable channel, radically changes the face of TV. It takes to the air with its first video—"Video Killed the Radio Star"—by the Buggles.

Factoid

The 1980 New York Barbie collectors convention was the first ever devoted to a single doll, according to Dolls, The Collector's Magazine, *Spring, 1984.*

The lead glamour doll this year was Golden Dreams Barbie (#1874). "She's golden. She's gorgeous. She's got the billion dollar look!" Mattel promoted. The doll came with Quick Curl hair and gold body suit with overskirt. Golden Dreams Barbie was both a glamour and a hair play doll: She came packaged with curling "iron," styling foam, two combs, hair arranger, two barrettes, brush and comb.

New International Barbie dolls were introduced in 1981, including the Oriental (#3262) and the Scottish (#3263). The Oriental Barbie doll was the first to use the new Oriental face mold.

The Barbie World of Fashion booklet illustrated the broadest range of Barbie dolls to date, from the Western Barbie to the glamorous Golden Dream Barbie and Christie dolls.

***Golden Dream** doll: blonde with fur coat (left); blonde (center); and **Christie**–Black (right).*

*This **Golden Dream** variation came with "big hair."*

Western Barbie (#1757), dressed in a silver-trimmed western jumpsuit, cowboy hat and boots, came with a unique "autograph-signing" feature. This was accomplished through an autograph stamp, included with the doll, which attached to her hand. A second special feature was her ability to wink an eye, which she did when her back was pressed. Positioned as a western star, she came with small pictures of herself to "autograph" for her adoring fans. This was the first Barbie doll to use the new "winking" face mold, considered by many collectors to be among the least attractive face molds in all of Barbiedom. Her horse, Dallas, was packaged separately.

The first My First Barbie (#1875) appeared in 1981. She was—and to this day still is—marketed as an entry-level Barbie doll especially easy for younger children to dress. In addition, this doll helped prepare the young Barbie consumer for future hair play dolls since she was

This is the first ***My First Barbie*** *doll, issued in 1981. My First Barbie variation 1 (left), My First Barbie variation 2 (right).*

Western Barbie *winked and signed her autograph.*

designed with long blonde hair simply gathered into a ribbon. Carol Spencer, a Barbie doll designer with Mattel since 1963, developed My First Barbie. Mattel conducted market research in the late 1970s which revealed that the largest group of children playing with Barbie were four to six years old, although some children received their first Barbie as early as age two. Mothers in the focus group said that younger children had trouble dressing Barbie, so a new niche was identified.

Another key introduction in 1981 was the Happy Birthday Barbie (#1922), the first in a very successful themed series for Mattel. "What happens all year long?" Mattel queried. "Birthdays!" the company rightly surmised, and the Happy Birthday dolls have been successful for Mattel ever since. This doll was packaged with a "birthstone" ring and a booklet of party games. To carry the theme through, the Barbie doll also carried a gift box.

Carol Spencer, designer of My First Barbie for Mattel.

"Happy Birthday to you!" the first ***Happy Birthday Barbie*** *sings. She came packaged with gift and birthday story book.*

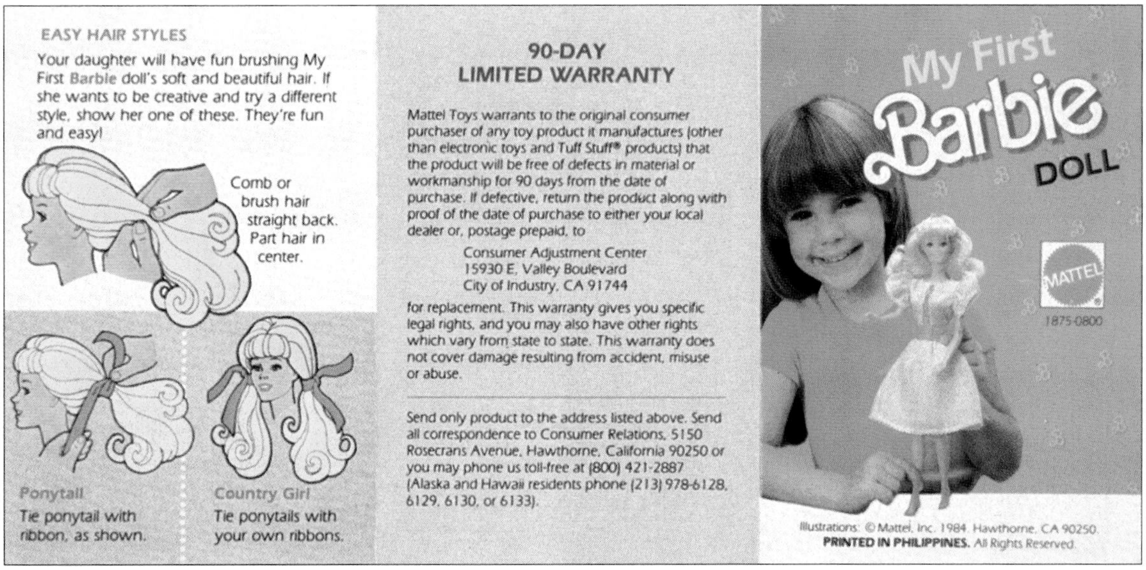

A booklet included with My First Barbie in 1981 introduced and explained the Barbie Experience to new, young Barbie doll consumers.

1982
Mattel, Inc., says. . .

"In the United States, traditional non-electronic toy industry sales declined slightly from $3.87 billion in 1981 to $3.68 billion in 1982. This sales decline—the first in eight years—was attributed to difficult economic conditions and a continuing shift in consumer purchases toward video game products. . . .

"Mattel Toys U.S.A., products offerings. . .include fashion dolls, featuring the Barbie® doll line in its 24th year. . . .

"The Barbie franchise was expanded throughout Japan following the successful 1981 market test by Japanese licensee Takara."

(Source: 1983 Annual Report)

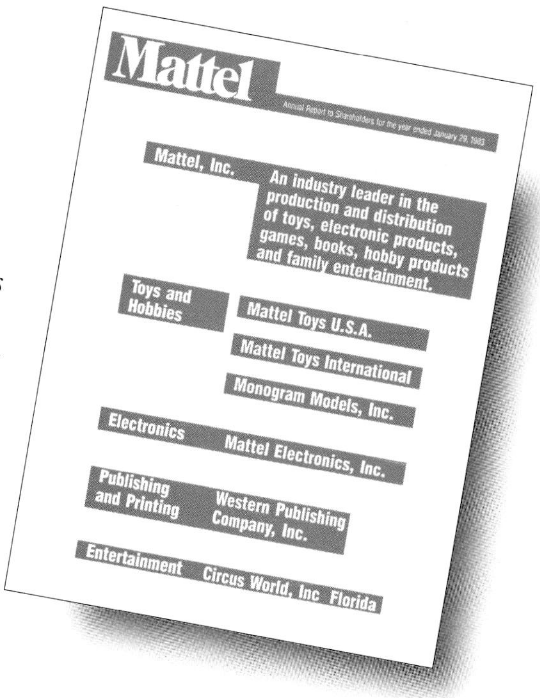

1982

◆ The booming video games industry receives a series of jolts in December, when the price of related stocks fell sharply in trading on the New York Stock Exchange. Issues of Mattel Inc., the industry's No. 2 manufacturer, dropped 2⅛, to 24 points. Mattel reopened trading December 10 and lost nearly one-third of the market value of its issues. Its stock declined by 7¼ to 16¾ on 2.6 million shares traded.

◆ *USA Today* debuts in the Washington-Baltimore area. Calling itself "The Nation's Newspaper," the new entry in American journalism relies on short, punchy articles and the heavy use of color.

Factoid

According to Mattel, a little girl gets her first Barbie about age 3, and is given six more Barbies until she turns about 12.

The lead glamour doll was Magic Curl Barbie (#3856). "Look at Barbie®—she's gone curly! She's got gorgeous hair you can curl, straighten, curl again! And again!" the Mattel ads promoted. Magic Curl Barbie, dressed in a long yellow puff-sleeved dress, had hair with chameleon-like properties: Her hair could go from Dolly Parton style "big hair" to straight, sleek, blonde Christie Brinkley type hair, to a curly style that Tammy Faye Baker had been known to wear in the 1980s. Yet another hair play model, Mattel saw early-on that little girls never seemed to tire of such dolls. The doll also came in Black Magic Curl Barbie doll version (#3989), one of the first Black Barbie-named variations.

New International Barbie dolls in 1982 included the Eskimo Barbie doll (#3898) and the India Barbie doll (#3897). The Eskimo doll used the 1981 Oriental face mold.

Eskimo Barbie, *costumed in warm, furry coat and hood, was added to the International series.*

Magic Curl Barbie *was an early Black Barbie. Her hair could be curled or straightened using Magic Mist™ spray solution.*

The Pink & Pretty Barbie (#3554), new for 1982, wore a pink ensemble that could be magically transformed into over 20 "absolutely dreamy looks." A furry trimmed hat became a cape or peplum, and a fur boa could be used in many ways.

Fashion Jeans Barbie (#5315) mirrored the designer jeans trends of the year. Her back jeans pocket was emblazoned "Barbie" in pink embroidery, and pink

Pink & Pretty Christie *(and Barbie) came with 20 outfit "changes."*

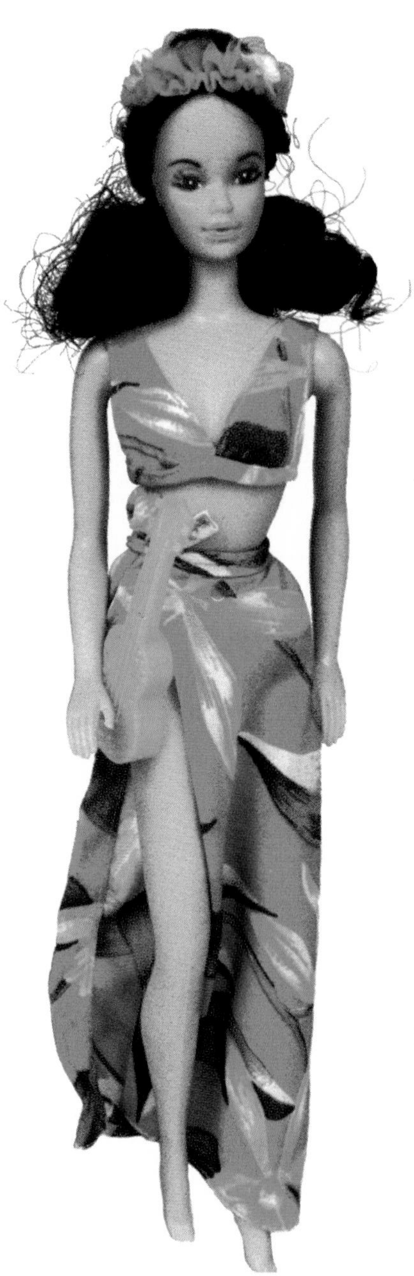

Hawaiian Barbie *was packaged with a windsurfer. She was made with the Steffie face mold.*

stitching accented the legs and pockets. Her fuzzy pink short-sleeved sweater was personalized as well. Her blonde hair was extra-long for the time.

The second My First Barbie doll (#1875) hit the market based on the initial version's "success story that went beyond even our expectations," according to the 1982 Mattel Toys catalog.

Hawaiian Barbie was introduced this year, using the 1972 Steffie face mold with a slight smile and open mouth. She was packed with a ukulele and windsurfer.

1982

◆ Ground is broken for a memorial to honor the 58,022 Americans killed in the Vietnam War. Maya Lin submitted the winning design for the Vietnam Veterans Memorial in Washington, D.C.

◆ Mattel Inc. announces in March that it will sell Ringling Bros. and Barnum & Bailey Combined Shows Inc. back to the unit's managers, for $22.8 million in cash.

1983
Mattel, Inc., says. . .

"Mattel's leadership in the toy industry is dramatically illustrated by the worldwide popularity of the Barbie doll, 25 years after introduction still the world's best-selling toy.

"Barbie, the best known and most successful toy product in history, celebrates her 25th anniversary in 1984.

"More than 200 million dolls in the Barbie family have been purchased around the world since 1959.

"More Barbie dolls were bought in the United States last year than there are little girls—14 million dolls for 11.5 million girls ages 3-9.

"The Barbie dolls, fashions, accessories and playsets stimulate a child's imagination and take her into a special world of her own.

"Mattel is the largest manufacturer of female apparel in the world. More than 20 million Barbie doll outfits are purchased each year."

(Source: 1984 Annual Report, for year ended January 28, 1984)

The lead glamour doll was Twirly Curls Barbie (#5579). Capitalizing on previous successes with hair play dolls, Twirly Curls Barbie came with her own personal beauty parlor which included a special chair, barrettes, and Twirly Curler device. The doll was also available as Black Twirly Curls Barbie doll (#5723) and Hispanic Twirly Curls Barbie doll (#5724) versions.

Angel Face Barbie (#5640), new for 1983, came with makeup in its own case and hair accessories. She wore a Victorian-inspired dress with fuchsia pink skirt and white lace high-necked blouse with cameo brooch—"a perfect blend of yesterday and today," according to the 1983 Mattel Toys catalog. Cheesebrough-Pond's, cold cream king at the time, had a marketing tie-in with this doll.

This booklet covered the Barbie International Collection, the first edition of the International Barbie Dolls. Photos include: Parisian Barbie, Eskimo Barbie, Scottish Barbie, Swiss Barbie, Irish Barbie, Spanish Barbie, Oriental Barbie, Swedish Barbie, and Indian Barbie.

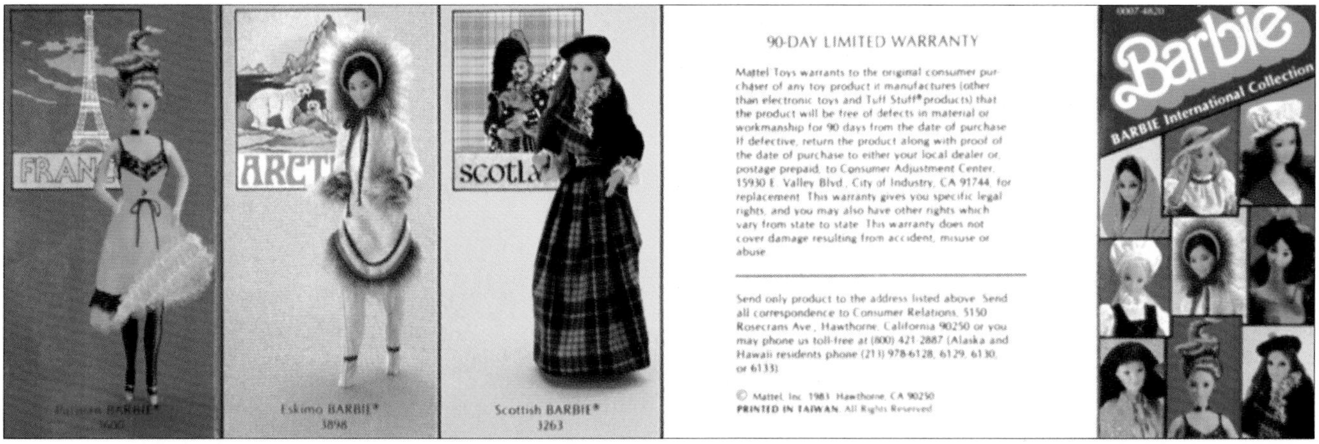

1983

◆ The Cabbage Patch doll creates pre-Christmas pandemonium. In a Pennsylvania store a woman suffered a broken leg in the push to get to the toy counter, where the toy department manager swung a baseball bat for protection.

◆ The final episode of "M*A*S*H," a long-running series on U.S. medics in the Korean War, was seen by the largest television audience to date for a non-sports program: 125,000,000 viewers.

◆ Astronaut Sally K. Ride becomes America's first woman in space as she and four colleagues blast off aboard the space shuttle Challenger.

In 1983, the new International Barbie dolls include the Spanish (#4031) and the Swedish (#4032). The Spanish Barbie doll was the first to use the new Spanish face mold.

Dream Date Barbie (#5868) set the trend for more glamour dolls later in the decade (such as the JC Penney's customized dolls). Her hair was long and sleek, and her red and purple ruffled gown came with a ruffle wrap that changed the look of the outfit. The sequined top of the gown marked an early example of sequins used on a Barbie doll fashion.

Horse Lovin' Barbie (#1757) continued the western fashion fad that persists throughout the *Contemporary BARBIE* era. "Here come the dolls who love to ride horses!" was the introductory line used to promote this doll. Barbie came equipped with leather-like pants and boots, as well as saddlebags. Like the Western Barbie of 1980, Horse Lovin' Barbie also came with an autograph stamp.

Factoid

Barbie's parents, George and Margaret Roberts, were married in San Francisco, but Barbie grew up in Willows, Wisconsin.

Spanish Barbie *wore a lovely black mantilla and red dress.*

1984
Mattel, Inc., says. . .

"The United States toy industry sales in 1984 grew at a higher rate than in any year in recent history. Consumer purchases of traditional non-electronic toys were approximately 18 percent more than in 1983.

"Industry sales in 1985 and beyond will benefit from such demographic factors as the increasing birth rate, the larger percentage of first-born children, the increased disposable family income per child, the increasing incidence of three-parent families and the expanding population of grandparents.

"The popularity of Barbie extends around the world as little girls continue to enjoy role-playing with the Barbie family of dolls and accessories. Since her introduction in 1959, more than 250 million Barbie dolls have been purchased worldwide.

"Mattel's nationally-distributed Barbie and Masters of the Universe magazines are each expected to grow beyond the 1 million circulation mark in 1985."

(Source: Annual Report dated 12/29/84)

Barbie's 25th birthday was in 1984. This marked the last time the word "birthday" would be associated by Mattel with the period elapsed since Barbie's introduction in 1959. The press promoted this as "the year an American Legend turns 25." On Valentine's Day, 1984, Mayor Ed Koch of New York City named Fifth Avenue, "Barbie Boulevard." Tiffany & Co. commemorated Barbie's 25th anniversary with a sterling silver replica of the doll. At Toy Fair that year, hundreds of "Loving You Barbie" dolls adorned the Mattel Gallery.

The lead glamour doll was Crystal Barbie (#4598). The feature of this doll was her gown, made of a silver shimmery new fabric, and sparkly shoes (the companion Ken doll came with glittery socks). The doll was packaged with a child-size necklace for girls to wear, a feature that would be repeated with future dolls. The Crystal Barbie ensemble was the best-selling outfit to date in Barbie's entire ensemble.

Great Shape Barbie (#7025) represented the influence of aerobics and exercise on fashion. In addition to a turquoise spandex-style leotard and headband, she

1984

◆ The first black Miss America, Vanessa Williams, relinquishes her crown two months early after nude photographs of her are published in *Penthouse* magazine. She is the first pageant winner to give up her title.

◆ Democratic presidential candidate Walter Mondale chooses Geraldine Ferraro of New York to be his running mate. Ferraro is the first woman to run for vice president of the U.S. on a major-party ticket.

◆ Mattel gets rescue financing. Shareholders of Mattel Inc. approve a plan by which an investor group would put up $231 million for the ailing toy maker in return for a 45% share in the company.

***Crystal Barbie** was the lead glamour doll of 1984.*

came with a workout bag, striped leg warmers and ballet slippers. Exercises were illustrated on the package.

A new Happy Birthday Barbie (#1922) hit the market. Although numbered the same as the 1981 first version, this doll was dressed differently in a pink confetti-dotted party dress. The gift box packaged with the doll included a child-size, heart-shaped necklace.

New International Barbie dolls in 1984 included the Irish Barbie doll (#7517) and the Swiss Barbie doll (#7541).

1985
Mattel, Inc., says. . .

"Innovation means applying new ideas to concepts that have proven to be successful, a practice that has kept Barbie at the front of the fashion doll market for more than 27 years.

"Times change and so does the Barbie doll. Her ability to keep up-to-date is a key to her continuing success. Girls today can become anything they want to be, from a glamorous personality to astronaut to rock star, just like Barbie. Joining Barbie in her musical group are The Rockers, Diva, Dee Dee, Dana and Derek."

(Source: 1985 Annual Report)

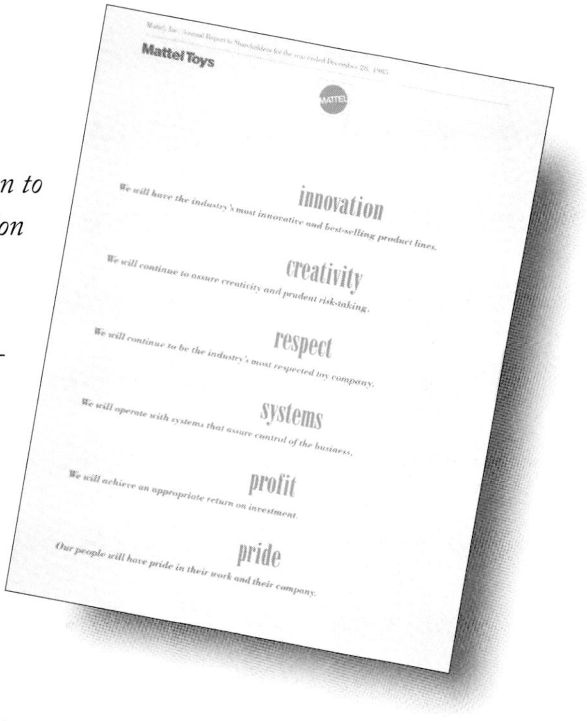

Mattel Toys

innovation
We will have the industry's most innovative and best-selling product lines.

creativity
We will continue to assure creativity and prudent risk-taking.

respect
We will continue to be the industry's most respected toy company.

systems
We will operate with systems that assure control of the business.

profit
We will achieve an appropriate return on investment.

pride
Our people will have pride in their work and their company.

Thanks to Kitty Black-Perkins, the Barbie doll returned to the workplace in 1985 in the guise of one of the most important dolls to emerge in the 1980s: the Day-to-Night Barbie doll (#7929). This doll also came in both Black (#7945) and Hispanic (#7944) versions. She was outfitted in a pink suit with white lapels and wore a hat. Her accessories included a pink attaché case, shoulder bag, Chanel-inspired pink and white spectator pumps, a calculator, business cards, financial newspaper, a credit card, and jewelry. Girls playing at going to work helped to shape the Day-to-Night Barbie doll via focus group research. Her pink daytime suit trans-

1985

◆ Rudi Gernreich, the fashion designer who introduced the topless bathing suit for women in the 1960s, died of cancer at the age of 62. Among his many innovative designs, he was also associated with the miniskirt, knit tank suits, colored stockings, the see-through blouse and unisex outfits.

◆ In a bold move, the Coca-Cola Company announces that it is abandoning its old formula and that Coke is now the "Real Thing." By July, complaints from cola lovers pressure the company to return to the original version, now named Coca-Cola Classic.

◆ Nancy Reagan and Raisa Gorbachev, wife of Soviet leader Mikhail S. Gorbachev, meet for the first time in Geneva, Switzerland. The first ladies, who shared an interest in fashion, met at Maison de Saussure, the 18th-century chateau that was home to the Reagans during their Geneva visit.

suit transformed into evening wear by reversing the skirt and removing the jacket. This marked the beginning of the "We Girls Can Do Anything" theme.

A treat for fans of haute couture fashion was BillyBoy*'s design of a new Barbie doll, the likes of which hadn't been seen since Barbie first hit the market in 1959. Le Nouveau Theatre de la Mode (#6279) Barbie doll exemplified the early era of Barbie doll fashions with a streamlined, tailored fashion that represents the essence of *Contemporary Barbie.* Le Nouveau Theatre de la Mode was developed in concert with BillyBoy*'s wish to commemorate Barbie's 25th anniversary through a special fashion show titled, "The New Theatre of Fashion." (For more insight into the marvels of BillyBoy*, refer to Chapter 5, Pure Couture).

These career dolls, designed by Kitty Black-Perkins, were dressed in tailored suits and came packaged with a nighttime ensemble just in case. Left to right: ***Day to Night****–Black,* ***Day to Night****–Blonde,* ***Day to Night****–Hispanic.*

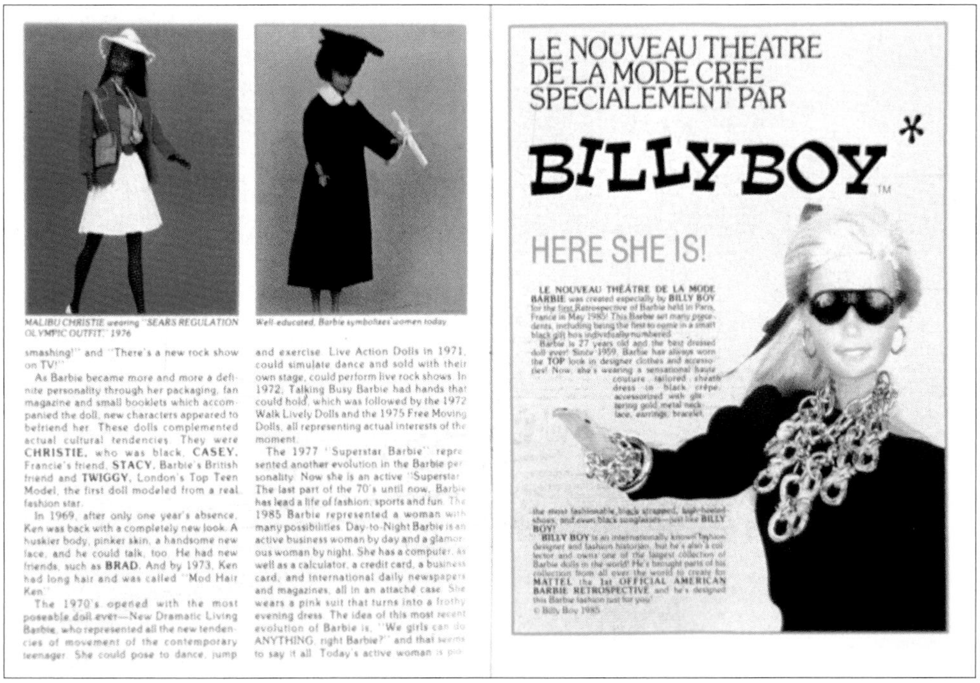

MALIBU CHRISTIE wearing "SEARS REGULATION OLYMPIC OUTFIT," 1976

smashing!" and "There's a new rock show on TV!"

As Barbie became more and more a definite personality through her packaging, fan magazine and small booklets which accompanied the doll, new characters appeared to befriend her. These dolls complemented actual cultural tendencies. They were **CHRISTIE**, who was black, **CASEY**, Francie's friend, **STACY**, Barbie's British friend and **TWIGGY**, London's Top Teen Model, the first doll modeled from a real fashion star.

In 1969, after only one year's absence, Ken was back with a completely new look. A huskier body, pinker skin, a handsome new face, and he could talk, too. He had new friends, such as **BRAD**. And by 1973, Ken had long hair and was called "Mod Hair Ken."

The 1970's opened with the most poseable doll ever—New Dramatic Living Barbie, who represented all the new tendencies of movement of the contemporary teenager. She could pose to dance, jump

Well-educated, Barbie symbolizes women today

and exercise. Live Action Dolls in 1971, could simulate dance and sold with their own stage, could perform live rock shows. In 1972, Talking Busy Barbie had hands that could hold, which was followed by the 1972 Walk Lively Dolls and the 1975 Free Moving Dolls, all representing actual interests of the moment.

The 1977 "Superstar Barbie" represented another evolution in the Barbie personality. Now she is an active "Superstar." The last part of the 70's until now, Barbie has lead a life of fashion, sports and fun. The 1985 Barbie represented a woman with many possibilities. Day-to-Night Barbie is an active business woman by day and a glamorous woman by night. She has a computer, as well as a calculator, a credit card, a business card, and international daily newspapers and magazines, all in an attaché case. She wears a pink suit that turns into a frothy evening dress. The idea of this most recent evolution of Barbie is, "We girls can do ANYTHING, right Barbie?" and that seems to say it all. Today's active woman is pio-

LE NOUVEAU THEATRE
DE LA MODE CREE
SPECIALEMENT PAR

BILLYBOY*

HERE SHE IS!

LE NOUVEAU THÉATRE DE LA MODE BARBIE was created especially by **BILLY BOY** for the first Retrospective of Barbie held in Paris, France in May 1985! This Barbie set many precedents, including being the first to come in a smart black gift box individually numbered.

Barbie is 27 years old and the best dressed doll ever! Since 1959, Barbie has always worn the **TOP** look in designer clothes and accessories! Now, she's wearing a sensational haute couture, tailored sheath dress in black crêpe, accessorized with glittering gold metal necklace, earrings, bracelet, the most fashionable black strapped, high-heeled shoes, and even black sunglasses—just like **BILLY BOY**!

BILLY BOY is an internationally known fashion designer and fashion historian, but he's also a collector and owns one of the largest collection of Barbie dolls in the world! He's brought parts of his collection from all over the world to create for **MATTEL** the **1st OFFICIAL AMERICAN BARBIE RETROSPECTIVE** and he's designed this Barbie fashion just for you!

© Billy Boy 1985

The BillyBoy booklet that accompanied* Le Nouveau Theatre de la Mode *featured a short history of the Barbie doll to 1985, along with many photos of fashions designed for the Barbie doll by BillyBoy*'s legendary couture designer friends.*

The first porcelain doll was introduced for the 1985/86 toy seasons. Known as Blue Rhapsody (#1708), it was made from the Superstar Barbie face mold. This was a milestone, notwithstanding the fact that many collectors "dissed" the doll: It was still the first Barbie doll made strictly for the adult market.

The only new International doll introduced in 1985 was the Japanese Barbie doll (#9481), which used the 1981 Oriental face mold.

The lead glamour doll was Peaches 'n Cream Barbie (#7926). Her peach-toned gown included the change-around ruffled stole successful in previous versions of glamour Barbie dolls. The doll included a "date spinner" which could be dialed to select a date (date themes included going to the theatre, attending the ballet performance or concert, going to a party, and other typically-teenage activities). This doll also came in Black Peaches 'n Cream Barbie doll version (#9516).

Complementing Barbie doll's career looks were fashion playsets such as the Vet Fun Fashion Playset (#9267) and the Travel Fashion Playset (#9264). In addition, the Barbie Home & Office structure was introduced in 1985. This portable case featured an office on one side and a bedroom on the other. The office included a fold-out desk, chair, computer and telephone.

Dreamtime Barbie (#9180) came packaged with a pink stuffed bear named B.B.—the first bear ever included with a Barbie doll.

This year, Barbie also received her first designer wardrobe from Oscar de la Renta. The designer created four gowns for Barbie, including a red satin dress with gold lamé flounce, a black and gold lamé dinner suit, a pink brocade ball gown, and a fuchsia and gold satin ensemble. "Barbie is the ideal customer," said de la Renta. "She looks like a perfect size 6, and she keeps her figure. She's the all-American girl." De la Renta's name would subsequently appear on six more gowns in 1986.

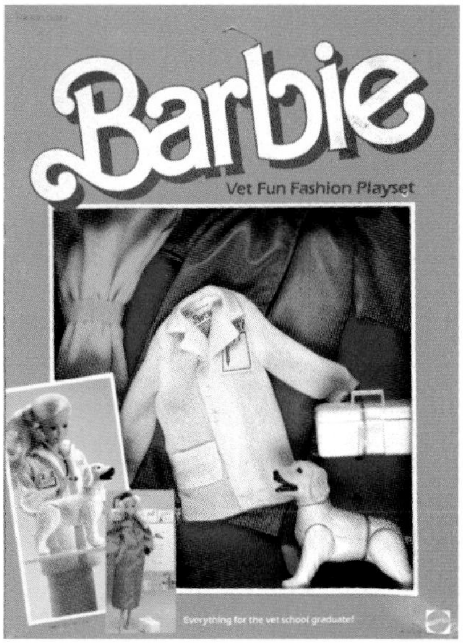

Barbie served the health needs of her legions of pets and horses when she became a veterinarian with this Vet Fun Fashion Playset in 1985.

UNICEF Barbie *promotes global goodwill.*

Chapter 3

CONTEMPORARY BARBIE® SNAPSHOTS: 1986-1990

1986
Mattel, Inc., says. . .

"Our traditional continuing brands will always be an important factor in Mattel's success. Barbie, celebrating her 28th year, continues to set sales records and remains the worldwide standard in the fashion doll segment despite renewed competition.

"The breadth and depth of our product line have greatly improved for 1987. We expect to expand our leadership in the fashion doll market through our established Barbie brand and two new lines introduced in 1987—Spectra, fashion dolls from outer space, and Hot Looks, soft poseable larger dolls with an international fashion model theme.

"The Barbie doll, created in 1959, remains a legend. Having withstood the test of time, she continues to set sales records and remains the standard by which other fashion dolls are measured. More than 300 million dolls in the Barbie family have been sold since her debut. In 1986, Barbie emerged with a brand new look—a star in her own rock band. With her four rock-and-roll superstar friends, Barbie and the Rockers proved to be one of Mattel's most successful product line extensions.

"Mattel introduced the Spectra collection of fashion dolls from outer space early in 1987. Each of these 11.5" dolls has a shiny body and sparkly hair, is fully poseable, and comes dressed in a lacy fashion outfit. Space-age accessories combining beauty and fantasy provide hours of fun fashion play."
(Source: 1986 Annual Report)

1986

◆ Perry Ellis, top U.S. fashion designer who founded the "slouch look" in fashion, died at the age of 46, reportedly due to viral encephalitis. He was a participant in Billy Boy*'s 1985 Barbie fashion show, *Le Nouveau Theatre de la Mode.*

◆ The space shuttle Challenger explodes immediately after take-off from Cape Canaveral, killing all seven astronauts, including Christa McAuliffe, a schoolteacher who was the first private citizen picked to go into space.

The 1986 Mattel Toys catalog began with this introduction:

"This year, Barbie is more exciting than ever! She's doing more things, going more places, taking on new challenges. One minute she's a glamorous movie star, the next she's a rock star. . . and then, she's an astronaut blasting off into space! And whatever she does and wherever she goes, Barbie always looks beautiful and elegant."

The lead glamour doll in 1986 was Magic Moves Barbie (#2126). By means of a switch, this doll moved one or both arms through her hair. Her dramatic outfit

Magic Moves Barbie *could "magically" brush her hair.*

Astronaut Barbie *came in both Black and Caucasian variations.*

was a glittery body suit and belt, long skirt, and fur-trimmed cape that could be fashioned as either a coat or a skirt. Also marketed was the Black Magic Moves Barbie (#2127).

The first career doll of the 1980s that wasn't a ballerina or a generic suited doll was Astronaut Barbie (#2449). This was not the Barbie doll's first venture into space—Barbie had been clad as an astronaut as far back as 1965, a full 20 years before anyone heard of Sally Ride. Designed by Carol Spencer, the 1986 version astronaut "is venturing beyond the world of fashion and glamour to exciting space exploration. She's dressed for first class travel in a glittery space suit that can change to a sparkly skirt and tights." Her accessories included a space helmet,

Greek Barbie *poses amidst classical urns.*

computer, flagpole, and two space maps that could be punched out of the package. The doll was also available as Black Astronaut Barbie (#1207). Additional Astro Fashions were offered for separate sale.

Sears celebrated its 100th anniversary in business in 1986 with the Celebration Barbie doll (#2998).

Also that year, the second porcelain Barbie doll—named Enchanted Evening—was issued.

The International dolls of 1986 included the Greek Barbie doll (#2997) and the Peruvian Barbie doll (#2995).

One of the first special effects Barbie dolls of the 1980s was Dream Glow Barbie (#2250). This doll was outfitted in a pink ruffled tiered gown with parasol—both adorned with stars that glowed in the dark. The ensemble also included glow-in-the-dark shoes. Fans of Dream Glow Barbie could also buy additional Dream Glow fashions. The Dream Glow Bed and Dream Glow Vanity completed the Dream Glow experience. The doll was also available as Black Dream Barbie (#2242).

*This Barbie World of Fashion booklet illustrated **Dream Glow Barbie** wearing various Dream Glow fashions. Note that even Ken's costume glowed!*

Dream Glow Barbie *dolls came in Caucasian (right), Black (below) and Hispanic variations. The costumes glowed in the dark.*

In addition to her demanding job as astronaut, Barbie doll had another career in 1986. She was the lead singer in a rock group, Barbie and the Rockers (#1140). Her eyelids were painted in neon purple and pink, and she was outfitted in a pink-and-silver lurex costume. Her ethnic colleagues in the band included Dee Dee, Dana, redheaded Diva, and Derek, the male member in this otherwise all-female rock group. In 1986, Rocker Barbie faced new competition in the fashion doll marketplace from Jem, Hasbro's "truly outrageous" 12-inch blonde punk goddess. Among several simultaneous vocations, Jem headed a rock group called "The Holograms" [See Sidebar]. It is interesting to note that the new face mold for Diva was also used for the first Native American Barbie doll (#1753) seven years later, in 1993.

By 1986, Mattel got more explicit with an adult-targeted marketing strategy and created a new division called Timeless Creations. The idea was to manufacture a line of higher quality collector dolls for the discriminating collector. These would include the Porcelain Series, the Bob Mackie Collection and others. The sales channels for some of these dolls focused on direct-to-consumer marketing, such as advertisements in mass market magazines (e.g., *Sunday Parade*) as well as specialty doll publications (e.g., *Doll Collector, Barbie Bazaar*).

Tropical Barbie, notable for her exceptionally long hair, appeared in 1986 with a special friend, Tropical Miko (#2056), whose face mold is that of a beautiful Pacific Islander. Tropical Barbie also came in a Black Tropical Barbie version (#1022).

Gift Giving Barbie (#1922) was 1986's version of the Happy Birthday Barbie doll. Wearing a purple and pink ruffled dress, she came with three little boxes and matching stickers that could be used for gift wrapping. In addition, a pink child-sized charm and ribbon were included in the package.

Barbie was an active rock and roller throughout the 1980s. This ***Dancing Action*** *doll was the second Rocker Barbie issued.*

BARBIE VS. JEM — ROCK WARS

The Barbie doll's first serious competitor in some years emerged in 1986. Her name was Jem, and she had a rock band called the Holograms. Jem's manufacturer, Hasbro, Inc., invited little girls to enter a contest by dialing 1-800-ROCKGEM and singing the Jem theme song ("Jem is truly outrageous, truly, truly, truly outrageous . . . "). So many girls called that the phone company had to install extra lines.

By 1986, MTV, the music cable television channel, had grown enormously popular. Rock videos introduced little girls to a whole new way of thinking about fashion: Eight-year-olds were asking their moms if they could dye their hair pink and cut holes in their sweatshirts and do a lot of other things that Barbie didn't do. It occurred to people at Hasbro that there might be a market for a fashion doll that looked less like Barbie and more like the people on MTV.

Hasbro created an entire history for their creation: Jem. By day she was Jerrica Benton, co-owner of Star Light Music Company and benefactor of Starlight House, a shelter for homeless girls. By night, she was rendered Jem, through the magic of "Synergy," a super-holographic computer that filtered power through her Jem Star earrings. As Jem, she was "a truly outrageous rock singing sensation," according to her own press.

Just as Rocker Barbie had a back-up band that included Dee Dee, Dana, Diva and Derek, Jem had the help of her little sister, Kimber, and friends Aja and Shana. Together, they were known as "Jem and the Holograms." Adventures unfolded as Jerrica competed for control of Star Light Music against evil co-owner Eric Raymond; while Jem and the Holograms came up against the mischievous "bad-girl" rock band, "The Misfits."

1987
Mattel, Inc., says. . .

"We're pleased with Mattel's 1988 product line which features innovative breakthroughs in our major toy categories. With Perfume Pretty Barbie, Mattel continues to strengthen its well-established fashion doll line. Barbie remains the highest volume brand in the industry, due in no small part to our ability to reintroduce the product line year-after-year to fit the current life-styles of girls.

"Mattel created the fashion doll toy category 29 years ago with the introduction of the Barbie doll. Today, the World of Barbie is a collection of dolls, fashions and accessories to delight little girls everywhere. Additions to the line this year include Perfume Pretty Barbie doll, and California Dream Barbie Surf 'N Shop playset and Beach Taxi vehicle."

(Source: 1987 Annual Report)

For the first time in the *Contemporary BARBIE* era, the first doll featured in the Mattel Toy catalog was not a Barbie doll: it was Spectra, from the planet Shimmeron. Designed by Kitty Black-Perkins, this doll is actually a precursor to the 1995 Gymnast Barbie. She blends the poseability of the gymnast with outer space themes. Her friends were named Astragold, Ultraviolet, Stylablue and Tom Comet; Spectra's robotic friend was called Spark (who bears a remarkable resemblance to R2D2 of *Star Wars* fame). According to Black-Perkins, Spectra was in fact part of Barbie's world. . . for just one year. Children appreciated the poseability of the doll, and didn't even mind that her joints were exposed. However, Spectra and friends were made from a shiny metallic-like substance that apparently did not find favor with little girls.

In Mattel's 1987 catalog, Barbie dolls do not appear until page 69, well after Popples, Color Clicks, Lady Lovelylocks and the Pixietails, The Heart Family, Princess of Power, and Baby Heather. The positioning of the Barbie and family dolls so far into the catalog suggests that Mattel did not prioritize the Barbie

1987

◆ Nancy Lopez is inducted into the Ladies Professional Golf Association Hall of Fame when she wins her 35th career victory. Her first tournament win came in 1977.

◆ The Supreme Court rules (7-0) that women must be admitted to Rotary Clubs, hitherto all male. On July 4, Lions Club International votes to admit women and on July 7 Kiwanis International followed suit.

◆ Mary R. Stout, a former U.S. Army nurse, becomes the first woman to head a national veterans' organization: the Vietnam Veterans of America. At the time she was elected, the organization had 35,000 members, only about 300 of whom were women.

FROM OUTER SPACE ALIENS TO GYMNAST BARBIE

Kitty Black-Perkins related this interesting piece of Barbie doll design history: "In 1990, we did a doll called Spectra. She was not a part of Barbie's world, but a little outer space doll with friends. She was a resurgence of the poseable dolls, Young Sweethearts, that we previously did. If you look at Spectra, she has poseable knees and elbows. The difference is the vacuum metal on the body. The poseable knees and elbows concerned us, and we wondered whether it would bother kids. With our Barbie doll, we have always been so particular about how she looks. When we did research we found out that kids wanted Barbie to do the things that they could do. So with that in mind, we wanted to give her things to do that would emphasize her new movement. The kids really do think that Gymnast Barbie can do the same things that they can do. She was launched worldwide and she's doing great! Based on her success, we will probably design a poseable doll every year from now on."

SOURCE: Author's interview with Kitty Black-Perkins, August 1995.

Spectra, *from the planet Shimmeron, was an early precursor to Gymnast Barbie.*

brand that year. It was, in fact, a difficult year for Mattel and the company underwent a full-scale reorganization. It was also, according to Mattel's annual report, "one of [the] worst years in [the toy industry's] history" overall.

The lead glamour doll in 1987 was Jewel Secrets Barbie (#1737). This doll came with a 24-page storybook, describing the tale of Barbie and the Jewel Secrets. The skirt of her pink-and-silver shimmery gown was transformed into a little girl's purse. Under the floor-length skirt, Barbie wore a miniskirt with a changeable ruffle. Her choker-style necklace was adorned with "gems" that changed colors at the touch of a dial. The doll also was available as Black Jewel Secrets Barbie (#1756).

Jewel Secrets Barbie *poses with and without her long bag-skirt.*

BillyBoy* designed his second and final Barbie doll this year. The Feelin' Groovy (#3421) doll, subtitled "Glamour-a-Go-Go," was very *au courant*, including a tailored fuchsia and black costume and black aviator-style sunglasses.

The American Beauties collection kicked off with Mardi Gras Barbie (#4930) in 1987.

Funtime Barbie (#1738 blonde wearing blue outfit, #3718 blonde wearing pink outfit, #3717 blonde wearing lavender outfit, #1739 Black wearing pink outfit) came with her own digital watch. Her outfit was a two-piece short set with a clock motif on the top. She also came with pastel-colored sun glasses.

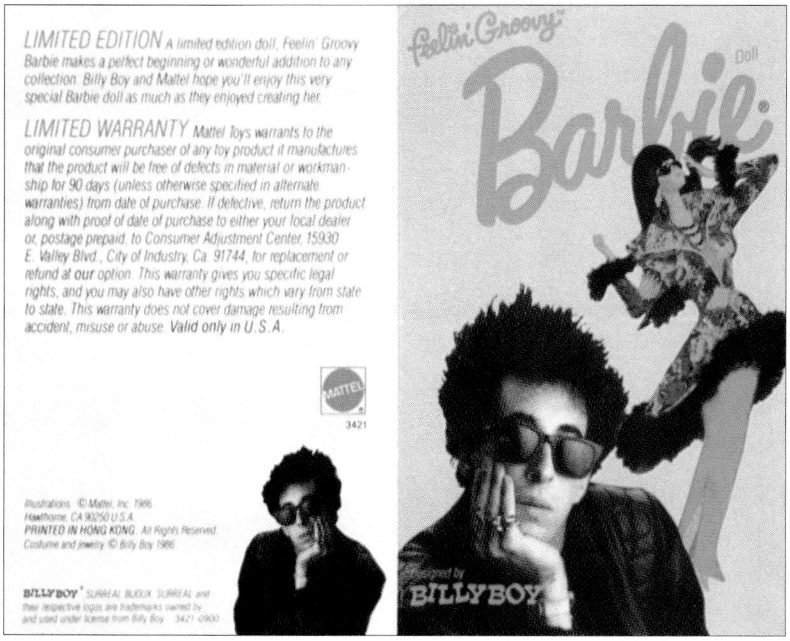

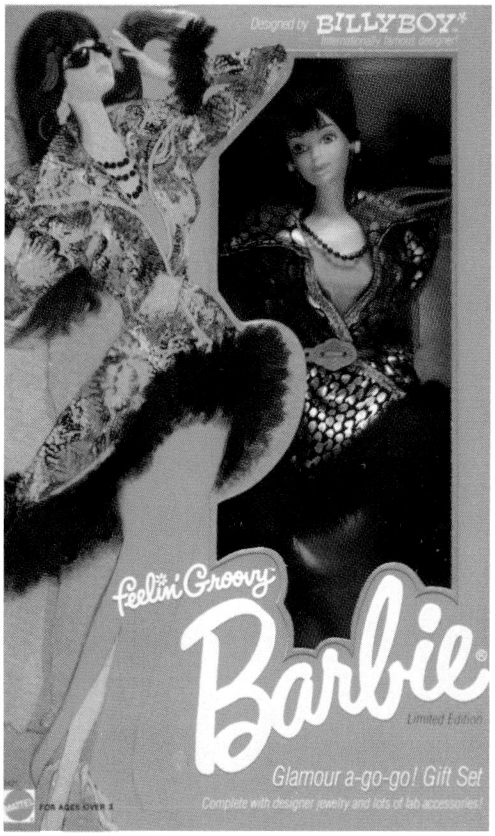

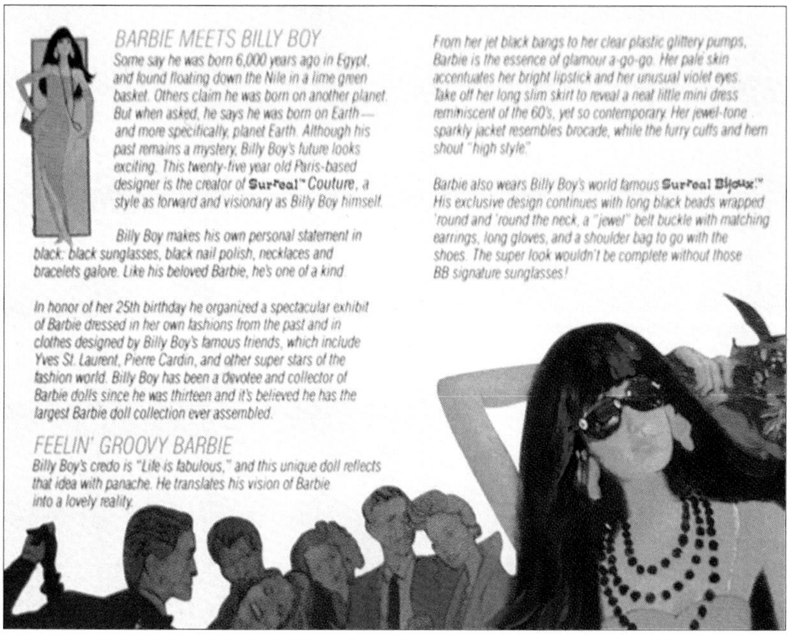

This booklet (top left) came packaged with the ***Feelin' Groovy Barbie*** *doll and featured a photo of BillyBoy* on the front and back covers. The inside of the Feelin' Groovy Barbie booklet (left) described the mystical origins of BillyBoy* along with his credo, "Life is fabulous." Feelin' Groovy Barbie was designed to reflect that attitude.*

The Barbie doll continued rockin' out as a Rocker, but in the form of a hyperactive Dance Action Rocker (#3654). When the doll's waist was tilted, her arms moved up and down, "just like they're really dancin'!" Ken doll (looking much like the actor Richard Dean Anderson of MacGyver fame) joined Derek as the second male in the band. The dolls came packaged with a cassette of their "hit" songs.

Wal-Mart celebrated the company's 25th anniversary with the Pink Jubilee Barbie doll (#4589). She was dressed in a long pink gown with an adjustable pink feather boa and silver accessories.

In 1987, the International dolls included the German Barbie doll (#3188) and the Icelandic Barbie doll (#3189).

1988

Mattel, Inc., says. . .

(On the cover: 1959 Barbie in Solo in the Spotlight and 1989 SuperStar Barbie)

"It was the best year ever for Barbie. Fresh new advertising drove consumers to the stores, where U.S. sales were up by more than 30 percent.

"A 30-year success, she's known worldwide as the most popular doll of all time. More than 500 million Barbie dolls have been produced to date, and 90 percent of all girls age 3 to 11 in the U.S. own at least one.

"Retailers were skeptical in 1959, but consumers left no doubt. . .they loved Barbie. The fashion doll category was created overnight, and she has dominated it since. First there were fashions, then friends, careers, and accessories. She's a new doll every year, and yet she's always glamorous and fun—she's always Barbie. Imagination is the key, the imagination of little girls. They can role-play and rehearse their fantasies and their futures. Even in a world of high-tech and fast pace, it's imagination that makes little girls grow. In 1989, there are more than 250 individual Barbie packages, including 32 different dolls, 153 fashions and 43 accessories. The attention to detail that distinguished the original concept continues to set Barbie apart today. From sculpting and face paint to hair styling, jewelry and wardrobe, she sets the standard."

(Source: 1988 Annual Report)

The biggest news this year actually happened at year's end: The introduction of the 1988 Holiday Barbie doll. First in the series, the doll was fairly limited in number. They quickly disappeared from the toy store shelves. (For more on the background of Happy Holidays Barbie, see sidebar in Chapter 1, *Contemporary BARBIE* History).

*On anyone's list, this **1988 Happy Holidays Barbie** doll is among the treasures issued in the* Contemporary BARBIE *era. By Christmas of 1995, offers as high as $750 for this doll were seen on the Internet.*

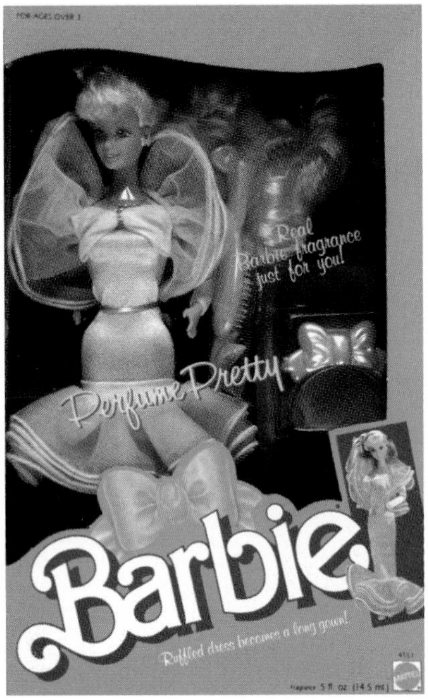

Perfume Pretty Barbie, *designed by Cynthia Young, was packaged with specially-designed perfume created especially for the doll and its customers.*

In Mattel Toys' 1988 catalog, the Barbie doll is brought back to page 1 in a full-head photograph of Perfume Pretty Barbie. Perfume Pretty was designed by Cynthia Young, who received a Doll of the Year award for the doll. Young reminisced: "The very first doll that I designed after joining Mattel was Perfume Pretty. That was our lead glamour doll of the year. She was ultra feminine, a little girl's dream." Young recalled that the doll came with a "real Barbie fragrance," actually designed by a Paris-based parfumier. Once the parfumier mixed the ultimate fragrance, the entire Mattel design team was given full-sized flaçons of perfume. Perfume Pretty also came in a Black version (#4552). The Black doll uses what collectors refer to as the "New Black" face mold first used in the Christie doll of 1988.

No one-hit-wonder pop phenomenon, the Barbie doll succeeded for a third year in a row in the rock star incarnation of Barbie and the Sensations (#4931). Retro fever was hitting the fashion world with Yves St. Laurent's flower power loose floral shirts for evening wear and Jean-Paul Gaultier's adoption of thick-soled Doc Martens shoes. This doll and her all-girl group went retro with '50s-style fashions, including saddle shoes, white ruffled bobby sox, and short skirts with net petticoats (except for Bopsy, who wore pedal pushers). In addition, the dolls wore glasses in a shape reminiscent of the Barbie doll's first pair of "cat's-eye"

Do Ken & Barbie Share a Closet?

"Carina Guillot and her 12-year-old daughter, Jocelyn, stepped into a Tampa, Fla., toy store and picked out a 'My First Ken' doll. It was wearing a purple tank top and lace apron over a turquoise and purple skirt.

"'Oh, my God,' said Guillot, 'Now we have a cross-dressed Ken.'

"Clerks checked this one out, as you can imagine, but could find no tampering with the package.

"Reporters at the scene went straight to the miniature transvestite's birthplace—Mattel Inc.—where spokeswoman Donna Gibbs gave them the strangest look and said, 'I'd guess it slipped through.'

"Then she offered to replace the doll. 'Nothing doing,' answered Guillot: 'This is like a real collector's item.'"

SOURCE: San Jose *Mercury News*, July 23, 1990

1988

◆ The word "Tomboy" is obsolete, according to a Penn State University professor who reported that 82% of young women participate in sports.

◆ After nine years in power, Margaret Thatcher becomes Britain's longest continuously serving prime minister of the twentieth century.

◆ There are now 10,513 McDonald's restaurants world-wide, but Pepsi's combined restaurants (Pizza Hut, Taco Bell and Kentucky Fried Chicken) total 17,373.

◆ America's last Playboy Club, in Lansing, Michigan, closes. The first Playboy club opened in Chicago in 1960, and there were once 22 such establishments throughout the country.

glasses from 1959. Sensations Barbie's colleagues in the band included Belinda (a Black doll) and Becky (an Asian doll). Like Rocker Barbie, Sensations Barbie came packaged with a cassette tape of the group's hit songs.

Doctor Barbie (#3850) emerged in 1988. She carried a kit of 20 medical supplies including a stethoscope, blood pressure gauge, doctor's bag, water pitcher, tumbler and tray for the hospital bedside, and other pieces. Consistent with the Barbie doll's previous careers of the 1980s, Doctor Barbie came outfitted with both a doctor's white coat along with a party dress for evening glamour. No Black Doctor Barbie was issued this year, but Nurse Whitney (undoubtedly Doctor Barbie's right hand in surgery) was Black.

Animal Lovin' Barbie was based on the prevailing themes of environmentalism and animal rights. Barbie came packaged with a panda bear. Zizi Zebra and Ginger Giraffe (each with long, brushable hair) and friends could be purchased separately. In classic Barbie style, Animal Lovin' Barbie wore a leopard-print ensemble accented with golden lurex thread, perfect for those glamorous anthropological outings!

*Echoing environmental and pro-animal rights sentiments, **Animal Lovin' Barbie** was outfitted in a glitzy safari outfit (note the pink high topped hiking boots) and came packaged with her panda bear friend.*

Factoid

During the summer of 1988, the premiere issue of Barbie Bazaar *magazine is published.*

In 1988, the International dolls included the Canadian Barbie doll (#4928), wearing an authentic uniform of the Canadian Mounted Police, and, the Korean Barbie doll (#4929). The Korean doll used the 1981 Oriental face mold.

California Barbie doll (#4439) came with a Beach Boys' record written especially for the doll. Under her colorful clothes, Barbie wore a swimsuit and she came packaged with a comic book, record, sun visor, sunglasses, camera and other accessories.

Canadian Barbie *(above), was dressed as a Royal Canadian Mounted Police woman.* **California Barbie** *(above left) was accompanied by tunes from the Beach Boys which were included in the package. Note the innovative packaging with the two beach chairs and palm tree at the bottom.*

1989

Mattel, Inc., says. . .

"Highlights from the more than 800 toys in the company's 1990 product line demonstrate the innovation and play value which consumers expect from Mattel. A new line each year generates excitement, and produces demand. Western Fun is the theme for a new Barbie line which captures the popular fashion style of the American Southwest. Longtime friend Ken and new friend Nia are outfitted in boots, suede, and big-buckle belts. An Ice Cream Fun set makes real ice cream, and a doll in a gold-sequined gown by designer Bob Mackie is the first in a new Barbie collector series. . . .

"We have a significant number of enduring consumer franchises at Mattel which have sold well over time. These core products provide stability in what can be a volatile industry.

"At the top of the list, of course, is Barbie. Sales for Barbie products have increased $160 million in two years, from $430 million in 1987 to $590 million in 1989–impressive growth for a consumer franchise in its 29th and 30th year."

(Source: 1989 Annual Report)

The year 1989 was a pivotal one for Barbie collecting. It ushered in Barbie's 30th anniversary—an occasion celebrated in grand style with a Thirtieth Anniversary Pink Jubilee party for Barbie at Lincoln Center in New York City in February. Some 1,200 special guests and members of the press were invited by way of a special silver tray with an engraved invitation. The Pink Jubilee doll

1989

◆ The Berlin Wall is opened, and for the next few days hundreds of thousands of East Germans stream into West Berlin. This is taken as evidence that the long Cold War is finally over.

◆ Giorgio di Sant'Angelo, fashion designer noted for avant-garde accessories and clothing styles, died at the age of 56 of lung cancer. He created innovative fashions in the 1960s that included gypsy and Native American styles.

◆ For the first time, compact discs surpass the sales of vinyl albums.

◆ The richest man in the U.S., according to *Forbes* magazine, was Sam Moore Walton, founder of Wal-Mart stores. Walton is said to be worth $8,700,000,000.

Barbie's 30th anniversary magazine featured this comprehensive Barbie family tree.

was packaged in a plain white box with the Barbie/Mattel logo on the face and wrapped with a large pink ribbon. Each doll was numbered, and only 1,200 were ever made. The doll wore a rose-colored gown with a tulle overskirt spangled in silver stars. A pink feather boa and lavish earrings completed the look. One reporter commented that, "No one else in the crowd—which included toy manufacturers, collectors and Barbie fans—looked nearly as ravishing."

Mattel also helped the mass of Barbie collectors celebrate the doll's 30th anniversary. A nostalgic licensing program was launched, and many companies

1989

◆ Rap's big breakthrough comes in January with the debut of "Yo! MTV Raps" on MTV. A rap star, Fresh Prince, gets his own TV sit-com ("The Fresh Prince of Bel-Air"); and a rap duo, Kid 'N' Play, stars in movies such as *House Party* and its sequel, *Class Act.* Rap finally entered advertising jingles for everything from family cars to refrigerated crescent roll dough.

◆ There is a moment, early one morning this year, when the time is 1:23:45-6/7/89.

UNICEF Barbie—*done in Black, Asian, Caucasian, and Hispanic variations—appeals to the universal character of all children. This was the first Barbie doll to be offered in four ethnic versions.*

were granted permission to use the nostalgic image on products. Clay Art made a Barbie mask, picture frame and mug; Leaverly Greetings made greeting cards; American Postcard Company created full color Barbie doll postcards. Life size Barbie doll mannequins were known to welcome customers into department stores where Barbie doll pendants, watches and t-shirts were being sold.

Barbie also went political in 1989. The UNICEF Barbie doll was offered in a record four variations, all called "Barbie." UNICEF Barbie doll was manufactured as Asian (#4774), Black (#4770), Caucasian/blonde (#1920), and Hispanic (#4782).

FAO Schwarz offered its first customized doll in the form of Golden Greetings Barbie (#7734). The chain's entré into Barbie's world would be followed annually by many more, and equally successful, customized Barbie dolls.

The 1989 International dolls included the Mexican Barbie doll (#1917) and the Russian Barbie doll (#1916)—the latter doll reflecting the softening of Cold War era tensions.

The American Beauties collection issued its second and final in the series, the Army Barbie doll (#3966).

American Beauties Army Barbie *(left) was the last in the series. The first* ***Russian Barbie*** *doll (right) was issued when "Russia" was still a synonym for the entire Soviet Union.*

HOT DATE: BARBIE AND G.I. JOE

"Anniversaries honor an American love affair. When the first generation of Barbie doll consumers was playing with Barbie, they were also playing with Tressy and boys were playing with G.I. Joe. The 1970s were not the best of times for Barbie and G.I. Joe; too many people burning bras and draft cards. Barbie's sales dropped. Mattel learned that parents of that era wanted more creative, less commercial toys, like paint sets or clay. Hasbro, manufacturers of G.I. Joe, took him off the market completely in 1978. They said he was being "furloughed" because of the rising price of oil, a major component of plastic. But the real problem may have been the still-fresh memory of soldiers coming home in body bags. War toys weren't fun.

"But by 1989, all that changed. Barbie and G.I. Joe were back on the list of all-time toy best sellers. Barbie turned 30 in February 1989, and Mattel went all-out with a black-tie birthday bash at Lincoln Center in New York. The invitations were shocking-pink paper affixed to a silver platter."

SOURCE: *Newsweek,* February 20 1989, p 59

1990
Mattel, Inc., says. . .

"Barbie is the preeminent brand of the toy industry, and one of the most universally recognized consumer products in the world today. Ongoing changes keep Barbie in step with the latest trends. In 1990, for instance, the doll hosted an international Children's Summit where children from 28 countries discussed issues relevant to them. Their deliberations identified world peace as a principal concern, and Mattel donated funds to this cause.

"Worldwide, Barbie gross revenues in the product's 31st year reached $740 million, up from $600 million in 1989, $485 million in 1988 and $430 million in 1987. This growth of more than 70 percent in three years demonstrates the success of our efforts to further expand a toy franchise that is second to none.

"Mattel today has marketing organizations in 23 countries around the world. . . . Eastern Europe presents a new growth opportunity. New Mattel offices were opened in Berlin, Budapest and Prague during 1990, and Mattel was the first toy company to advertise when the barriers fell.

"There are 71 million children from birth through age 10 in Europe, versus 40 million in the United States.

"At the company's principal Barbie manufacturing plant in Kuala Lumpur, for instance, Barbie dolls are produced on an automated production line which integrates assembly, hair rooting, grooming, sewing and packaging."

(Source: 1990 Annual Report)

1990

◆ Halston, top American fashion designer in the 1970s, died of AIDS at the age of 57. He became famous as the milliner who created the pillbox-style hat worn by former first lady Jacqueline Kennedy for her husband's inauguration in 1961.

◆ The 1990 Census reports that the population of the U.S. in 1990 is 249,632,692—a 10.2% increase over 1980.

◆ Between 1980 and 1990, women's earnings increased from 64 cents per male dollar to 72 cents per male dollar. However, the narrowing of the female-male earnings ratio is in part accountable to a drop in male earnings during the period.

◆ For the first time ever, the top five positions in the U.S. singles record chart are held by female artists. The hitmakers include Madonna, Heart, Sinead O'Connor, Wilson Phillips, and Janet Jackson.

These two ***Freudenschaft Barbie*** *dolls were developed for the global market. They commemorated the fall of the Berlin Wall. At left is Berlin Wall #1 (1990) with friendship heart theme. Berlin Wall #2 (1991) is at right.*

By 1990, Barbie dolls were commanding increasing shelf space at retail stores, particularly in giant retailers such as Toys 'R Us, Kmart and Wal-Mart Stores. As important, Barbie began to make a big splash in a new pond. Friendship "Freudenschaft" Barbie (#5506) made her debut in East Berlin, Budapest and emerging Central European markets. Priced at around $5, she did not contribute much to Mattel's bottom line, but she did help make the point to the industry that Mattel was committed to overseas expansion in new markets.

Back on home turf, Dance Magic Barbie (#4836) was the lead glamour doll in this anniversary year. Her ball gown could be detached to reveal a ballerina tutu, or it could be attached in the back for a salsa train, capitalizing on the dance trend of the moment. Her lip color changed from pink to rose with ice water,

Barbie Beats Brinkley

People magazine reported that models Christie Brinkley, Beverly Johnson and Cheryl Tiegs approached Matchbox Toys to create a line of dolls called the Real Model Collection. "I'd been approached many times about becoming a doll," Brinkley said, but she had always turned down the offer.

The dolls were unveiled at the 1990 annual toy fair in New York City. The dolls were Barbie-doll-sized, priced at $13.99 each, and had available additional outfits, a mini-photo studio and a 35-inch limousine complete with a whirlpool bath.

To help create vinyl doll models of the real-life personalities, Matchbox enlisted the advice of Joyce Christopher, who crafted the original Barbie doll.

Cheryl Tiegs is reported to have said: "It's strange having something look so much like you."

SOURCE: *People,* Feb 12, 1990 v33 n6 p116(2)

and changed back with warm water. The doll was also available as Black Dance Magic Barbie (#7080) version.

Flight Time Barbie doll (#9584) had flight wings. Serving her first stint as a pilot, the Barbie doll could also double as a flight attendant by changing her tie into a scarf. Her third costume variation was a ruffly skirt for parties. The package included doll-sized luggage and a child-size set of airline wings. Also available were Black Flight Time Barbie (#9916) and Hispanic Flight Time Barbie (#2066).

Summit Barbie doll, like the 1989 UNICEF Barbie doll, was featured in four variations. They included the Asian (#7029), Black (#7028), Caucasian-blonde (#7027) and Hispanic (#7030). Mattel designed the Summit Barbie doll as part of the Barbie Children's Summit, which brought 40 youngsters from 28 countries together to discuss the most important issues facing the world's children.

The Wet 'n Wild Barbie doll (#4103) had a special effect swimsuit that changed color in icy water. All 1990 dolls had extra-long hair. There was no Black Wet 'n Wild Barbie doll; the Black Christie Wet 'n Wild doll was #4121.

A popular doll with young girls—Ice Capades™ Barbie doll (#7365)—came adorned in lace skating skirt, glittery leotard and headdress, and ice skates. The doll's costume was transformed into human-size proportions by the Ice Capades touring company and was featured in road performances throughout the country.

1990 was yet another year of rock stardom for Barbie doll and friends. In 1990, Barbie and the Beat hit the top of the charts. Beat Barbie (#2751) came with a leather-look outfit, guitar and cassette tape with Beat music. Her clothes glowed in the dark, depending on the amount of light used. Midge and Christie joined Barbie doll in the Beat trio.

Barbie doll cruised the skies in 1961 as an American Airlines flight attendant. Now, here she is piloting the plane as ***Flight Time Barbie****.*

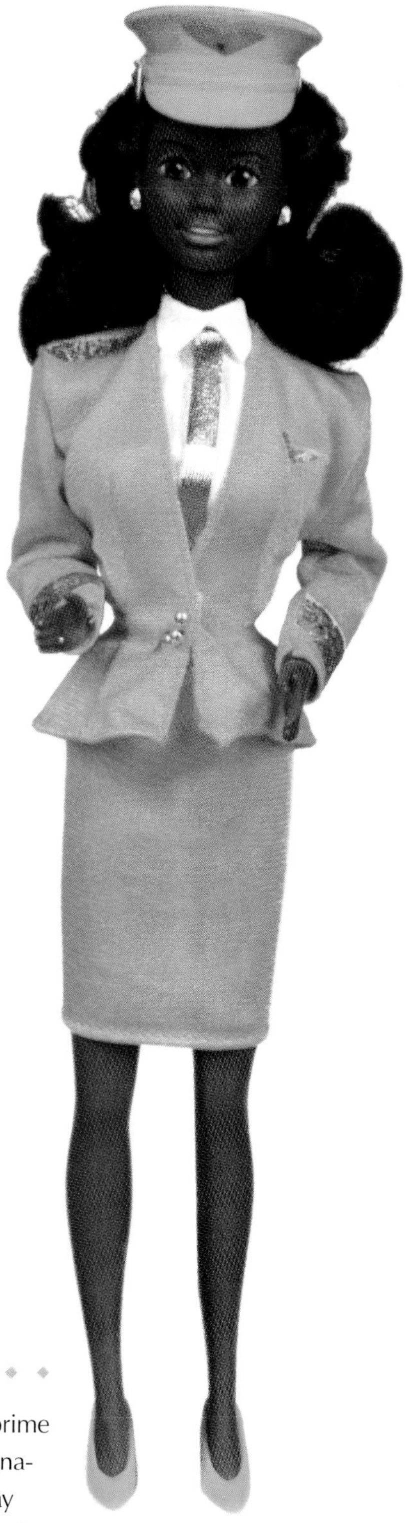

1990

◆ Following a heated controversy, the Professional Golfers Association announces that it will not hold tournaments at clubs that have exclusionary policies based on race or sex.

◆ Margaret Thatcher, the longest-serving British prime minister of the 20th century, announces her resignation. She had been elected prime minister in May 1979. Her term in office—more than 11 years and 29 weeks—was the fifth-longest consecutive term in British history and the seventh longest overall.

Summit Barbie

In late November, 1990, Mattel invited 40 children from 28 countries as far away as the Philippines, South Africa and the Soviet Union to the first Barbie Summit. Held in New York's Waldorf-Astoria Hotel, the conference featured tots as young as 6 years old discussing world hunger, degradation of the environment, and war and peace issues.

Televised advertising for the event—based on the theme "Together we can do it"—was launched November 9, 1990, in both 30- and 60-second versions tied in with Barbie Summit Month promotions. Mattel contributed a percentage of the profits from every Barbie doll sold in November 1990 to charity, with the minimum contribution set at $500,000.

Throughout the month of November, ballots were available at toy stores throughout the U.S. for children to express their opinion on what they felt was the most pressing issue facing the world. The ballots were tallied, and the results were reported to children attending the November 19 Barbie Summit.

Mattel's idea for creating the Barbie Summit and the accompanying television ad campaign was an indirect result of the fall of the Berlin Wall. Mattel's management team was impressed with photos of Anika Polzin, a six-year-old whose first goal after crossing into West Germany was to buy a Barbie doll. Polzin was invited to the Barbie Summit as an honorary delegate.

The other 40 delegates—including the eight-member delegation from the U.S.—were selected by the editors of Scholastic Inc., a New York based educational publishing company. The firm judged original artwork entries depicting a better world which were submitted by first- through fourth-grade students worldwide.

All delegations to the Summit rode on a float in the 1990 Macy's Thanksgiving Day parade.

Mattel hosted a children's summit in 1990 to air issues relevant to children from around the world. This was clearly one way of many that Mattel could "give back" to its global community.

Dance Club Barbie doll (#3509) was said to be a dancer on the latest TV dance show, á la "Soul Train." This Barbie doll and her Dance Club compatriots (Ken, Kayla and Devon) each came packaged with their own audio cassettes. The Hot Dancin'™ Set (#4841) was offered separately and it included a VHS videotape, dance lessons on doing "The BARBIE" dance, and a guest appearance by Paula Abdul. A special Child World limited edition of Dance Club Barbie (#4917) included a blue cassette player with a strap and working karaoke-type microphone. An audio cassette included in the package featured "Barbie" singing "Doin' the Barbie," "Our Game," and "Dreamin'."

Continuing the Great Shape aerobics theme established in 1984, the Barbie and the All Stars (#9099) Barbie doll of 1990 came ready to work out in exercise gear. The doll carried an exercise bag for sports gear, along with an appropriate post-exercise party fashion. All Stars fashions, sold separately, provided various sporting attire including tennis, weight-training, skateboarding and skiing.

Dance Club Barbie *from 1990 was packaged with an audio cassette.*

Factoid

In December's Ebony *magazine this year, the Barbie doll appeared as part of a new advertising campaign to promote Black and Hispanic Barbie dolls.*

Finally, Barbie Doll Ads Go Ethnic

"For more than 30 years, Mattel's Barbie has been one of the best-selling dolls in the country. There are Hispanic Barbies, Black Barbies, Asian Barbies and, of course, White Barbies. Yet the only doll featured in its print and TV ads is a fair-skinned, blue-eyed lass who tools around in a fancy sports car and changes her designer clothes faster than you can say Oscar de la Renta.

"Starting Fall, 1990, Barbie ads went ethnic. Mattel announced it would launch an ad campaign for the Black and Hispanic versions of the popular doll. With an eye toward capitalizing on ethnic spending power, Mattel featured multicultural Barbies in such outlets as *Essence* magazine and on 'Pepe Plata,' a children's show. It also included Barbie's ethnic sisters in some network spots.

"Why the slowness in integrating Barbie's dollhouse? Whatever the reason, the company can no longer ignore ethnic markets. Hispanics buy about $170 billion worth of goods each year, and Blacks spend even more."

SOURCE: *Newsweek*, August 13, 1990

What can you say about a doll designed by the guy who outfitted Cher, Carol Burnett, and countless Broadway casts? You say, "Bob Mackie," you think, "glitz and glamour," and you count the Bob Mackie Gold Barbie doll among your all-time favorites!

Chapter 4

Contemporary Barbie® Snapshots: 1991-Present

1991
Mattel, Inc., says. . .

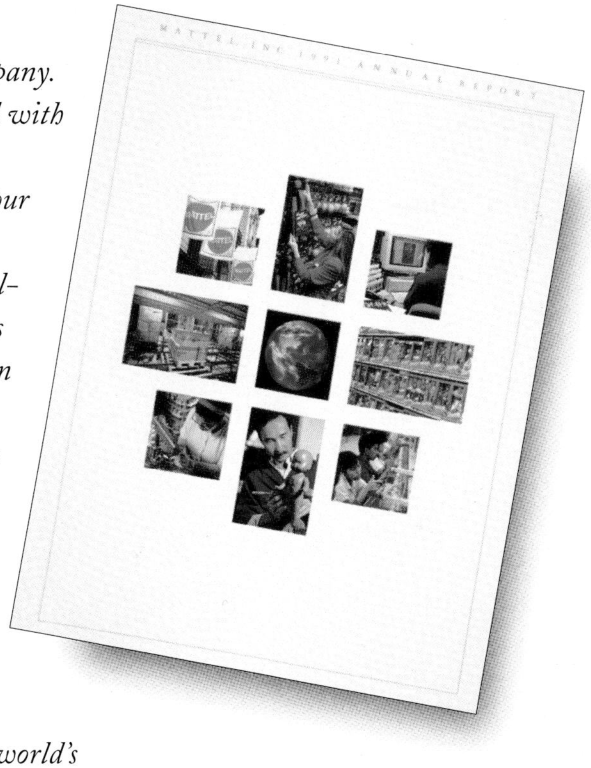

"1991 turned out to be the best year in the history of our company. Our belief that the Barbie doll was an undermarketed brand with tremendous growth potential has proven to be correct. We've nearly doubled our Barbie sales volume to $840 million in four short years.

"Barbie products reached $840 million in Mattel sales volume during 1991, nearly doubling the $430 million in sales that this principal core brand generated just four years ago in 1987. More than 50 million doll units were produced in 1991, ranging from low-cost dolls starting at about $6 each to holiday and birthday dolls retailing for about $30 and collector dolls selling for more than $200. Fashions and accessories also contribute to the success of this 33-year-old brand franchise, as do new "Barbie for Girls" consumer products including everything from shoes and clothing to linens, backpacks and furniture. A cosmetics and work-out videotape take Barbie to new dimensions, and in 1992 the world's favorite doll will even speak.

"A 1991 Mattel/McDonald's Happy Meal promotion was a great success. More than 45 million Barbie and Hot Wheels premiums were distributed in three weeks, along with coupons for dollars off on Mattel products. . . ."

(Source: 1991 Annual Report)

1991

◆ Almost 66% of married women are working or looking for work this year, as compared with 46% in 1973.

◆ The first world championship of women's soccer is won in Guangzhou, China, by the U.S., which defeats Norway, 2-1.

◆ Jack Ryan, an inventor who worked for Raytheon Co. and for Mattel Inc., died. He designed the best-selling Barbie doll, as well as the Chatty Cathy doll and Hot Wheels toy cars, and was at one time married to actress Zsa Zsa Gabor.

This year signified a major transition in Mattel's Barbie doll marketing strategy: Several key lines were introduced that were explicitly targeted to adult collectors, emphasizing John Amerman's belief that the doll was previously "undermarketed."

The most significant event in 1990/91 Barbie doll history was the introduction of Bob Mackie Designer Barbie® dolls—the first vinyl collection of Barbie dolls explicitly designed for the adult collector. By late 1991, three glamorous Mackie designs were introduced: the Gold Barbie doll (#5405), the Platinum Barbie doll (#2703) and the Black Barbie doll (#2704), which was also known to collectors as Starlight Splendor. Janet Goldblatt, veteran Barbie doll designer, worked directly with Mackie in 1990 to help bring his series to market. While Mattel had introduced porcelain Barbie dolls in the latter 1980s, the Bob Mackie Barbie dolls ushered in a truly new level of Barbie doll glamour. They continue to be among the most highly prized dolls on the secondary market. (See Chapter 5, Pure Couture, for a further discussion of Mackie and his importance in the world of *Contemporary BARBIE*).

The second crucial Barbie collecting event in 1991 was the introduction of the Barbie Porcelain Treasures™ Collection. These limited edition dolls reproduced classic Barbie dolls "from over three decades of Barbie fashion leadership." The first doll in the series was Gay Parisienne Barbie (#9973). Based on a very rare outfit from the introduction of Barbie in 1959, the doll was an exact replica of the original, complete with satin lined "fur" stole and bubble skirt hem. Even the gold velveteen clutch purse was lined in silk. Her light blue lingerie replicated a 1959 undergarment set with 1991 additions of garters and seamed stockings. The entire Porcelain Treasures line came with certificates of authenticity. A porcelain 30th Anniversary Ken doll (#1110) was simultaneously introduced, wearing the 1961 Tuxedo ensemble. His 1991 additions included striped boxer shorts, undershirt, and knee socks complete with garters.

The Swan Lake Barbie doll (#1648) was the first in a series of Barbie prima ballerina dolls that some collectors call the Music Box series. Designed after the Swan Queen from Tchaikovsky's ballet, the doll wore a white shimmery tutu, tights, and feather headdress, and her arms are newly sculpted to hold a graceful ballet pose. She came in a display case with the look of etched glass and stood on a rotating music box that plays ballet music. Her hair was done in elaborate braids gathered up into the headdress, which was accented by tiny pearls.

*The second in the Bob Mackie series, the **Platinum Barbie** (left) doll, was a successful followup to the initial **Gold Mackie**. Her pearlized white sequins sparkle with a silvery glow.*

*Every Bob Mackie Barbie doll comes packaged with a copy of Mr. Mackie's sketch of the doll. Many collectors frame these sketches and exhibit them behind the dolls. Shown are sketches for Mackie's **Gold** (facing page) and **Platinum Barbie** (below) dolls.*

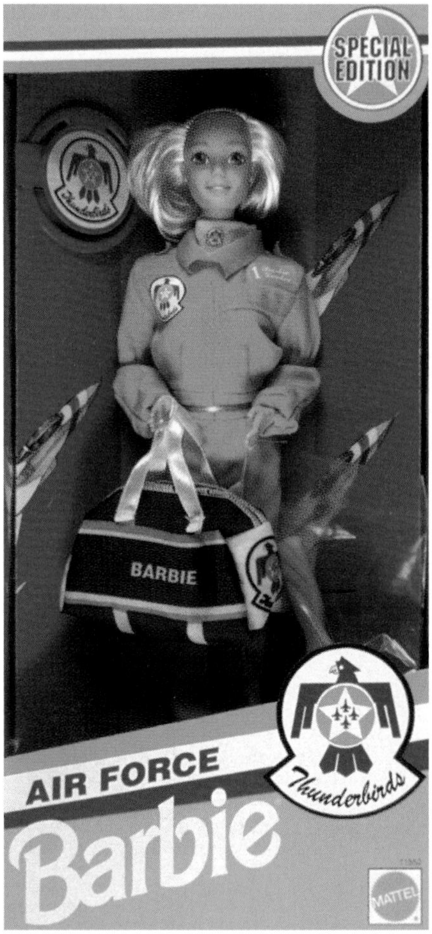

Air Force Barbie *(right) was packaged with her flight bag and official uniform from the flying Thunderbirds.* ***Stars 'n Stripes Navy Barbie*** *(above, left to right) came in both Black and Caucasian versions. Note the packaging variations.*

1991 also ushered in two important new career dolls: the Navy Barbie doll (#9693 and #9694 in the Black version) and Air Force Barbie doll (#3360). Navy Barbie doll was outfitted in a replica of the official new uniform worn by enlisted women in the U.S. Navy, including a white jumper blouse with authentic insignia, t-shirt, skirt, tie, hat and high heel shoes. She also came with uniform pants, flat shoes and a nautical map. Air Force Barbie doll was similarly authentically dressed in a one-piece flight suit and the official A-2 flight jacket issued to front line Air Force pilots and crew. A blue flight cap and scarf completed the ensemble.

The lead glamour doll, Costume Ball Barbie (#7123), wore a costume that changed from a pink tiered ruffled gown into a butterfly with shimmering wings or fantasy flower. In addition, the Barbie doll skirt doubled as a child-size mask. She was also available as Black Costume Ball Barbie (#7134).

Hawaiian Fun Barbie doll (#5940) was a typical bathing suit Barbie doll with long blonde hair, a hula skirt and sunglasses. The doll was packaged with a child-size "friendship bracelet" filled with fruit-scented fragrance for girls to wear. The significance of this doll is that her Hawaiian Ice Party Playset™ was used to make shaved ice confections flavored with Kool-Aid® Brand Tropical Punch unsweetened Soft Drink Mix. A packet of Kool-Aid Tropical Punch mix was included with the set. This was Barbie doll's first alliance with Kool-Aid, which would be repeated in 1994 in the form of the Wacky Warehouse Kool-Aid Barbie doll premium.

The Ice Capades Barbie (#9847) was reprised in 1991. This year, the doll included a transformable purple and glitter costume, along with ice skates.

All American Barbie (#9423) came outfitted in a denim skirt and vest with American flag motif, along with two pair of Reebok® Hi-Tops. Barbie doll's companions in the line included Christie, Ken, Teresa and Kira, and all of their denim outfits were also studded with metallic stars.

Another important fashion tie-in of 1991 was with Benetton's United Colors of Benetton™ label. Benetton Barbie doll (#9404) wore brilliantly-colored and patterned clothing in the style of the Italian casual fashion line. Additional Benetton outfits were sold separately. The use of the Benetton brand helped to further build the global Barbie brand as Benetton shops are found in select retail districts and in shopping malls around the world.

Lead glamour doll, ***Costume Ball Barbie's*** *outfit was changeable, and her skirt doubled as a child-sized mask.*

The ***All American Barbie*** *doll Christie (far left), came appropriately packaged with an American flag and wearing the All American fabric: denim. The* ***United Colors of Benetton Barbie*** *(left), the first issue, came fully accessorized with colorful hat, slouchy hobo bag, leg warmers and belt.*

Volley of the Dolls

"Indignantly claiming that she has been cloned, Barbie starts a heavyweight bout with Miss America. Miss America is a line of dolls developed by Kenner Products under license from the Miss America Organization. Mattel believed that Miss America's head is too similar to Barbie's copyrighted cranium. In March 1991, Mattel complained to the U.S. Customs Service, and shipments of Miss America (who is manufactured in China) were intercepted. "We detained Miss America," says a Customs spokeswoman "pending a decision on whether she infringed on [Mattel's] copyright." In fact, Customs blocked the entry of three of the five Miss America models. Raquel and Justine, who had a different head shape, were allowed in. The other detainees—Devon (a blonde dance major), Tonya (a Black aspiring veterinarian) and Blair (an Olympic gymnast in training) sat in a government warehouse. Kenner was found guilty by Customs officials."

COMPARING BARBIE DOLL TO MISS AMERICA DOLL

	Barbie	*Miss America*
Height	11.5"	11.5"
Weight	5 oz.	5.5 oz.
Chest	5.5"	5.5"
Waist	2.75"	2.75"
Reach	3.5"	3.5"

SOURCE: *People*, 36:95, September 9, 1991

__Nigerian Barbie__ (right), was dressed in a gold topped dress with animal print skirt. __Czechoslovakian Barbie__ (far right) is a favorite among adult collectors of the International Barbie dolls. She signalled the opening of eastern European markets. The doll might better have been named "Czech Republic" Barbie, but forecasting border changes is not an easy business for anyone, even Barbie!

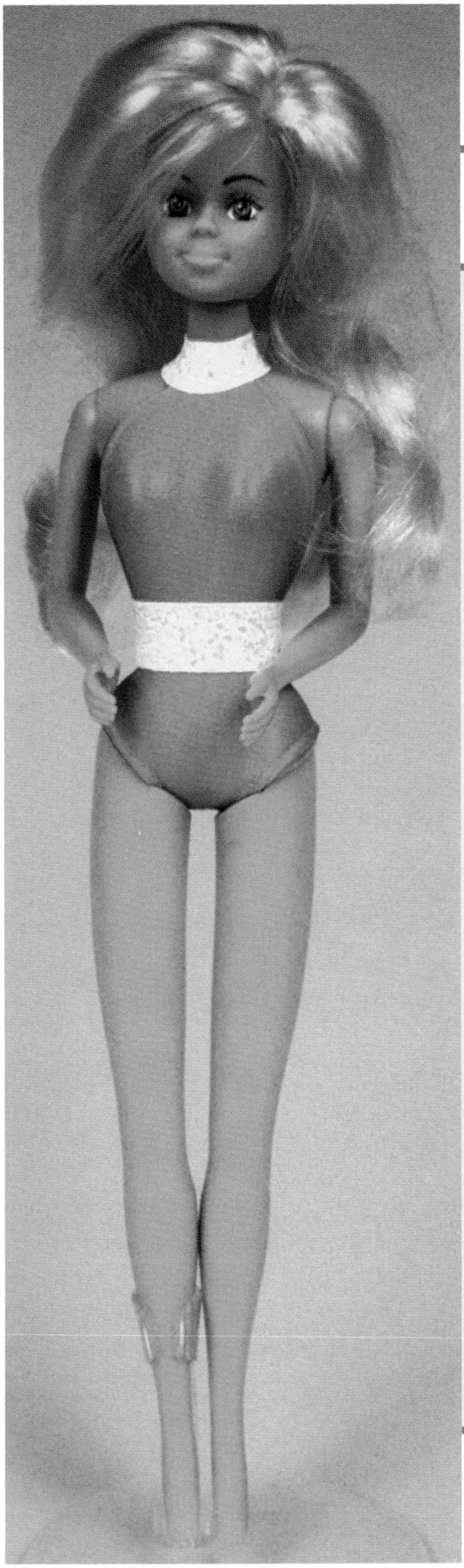

1991 Doll Wars: Happy to be Me, Miss America and Petra Pose No Competition

Several dolls were introduced this year under the banner of political correctness, but ended up posing no lasting competitive threat to the Barbie doll. Happy to Be Me, a red-headed doll with a so-called more "realistic" figure was promoted to bash Barbie as a terrible role model for girls. The news about Happy generated headlines the world over lauding Happy as a doll that would help young girls accept their less-than-ideal bodies.

The doll, in fact, had a sold-out launch in Minneapolis. The Barbie-hating prophecy was fulfilled when thousands of Happys sold out in Byerly's supermarkets in the Twin Cities over Thanksgiving. Forecasters thought Happy would rival the Cabbage Patch Kids phenomenon.

It simply didn't happen!

Then Kenner introduced the Miss America Fashion Doll Collection, an officially-licensed line of nine beauty pageant dolls and accessories. The 11-inch, Barbie-doll-sized creations had flexible bodies (like Barbie doll), painted faces (like Barbie doll), combable hair (ditto), authentic Miss America insignia, and evening gowns or talent outfits that stripped down to a swimsuit. The dolls also came with a cassette tape featuring Bert Parks singing, "Here She Comes, Miss America."

As a competitive response to the Kenner doll, Mattel's American Beauty Queen Barbie was introduced. The Barbie version wore a gown that transformed to a bathing suit and then to a ballerina costume.

Finally came Petra, an 11-inch Swedish doll, popular in Europe, that entered the U.S. market. To introduce the doll into the U.S., Lundby of Sweden—which markets the Petra dolls—had produced a 30-second television commercial that opened with a little girl, Petra in hand, telling a friend: "She came from Europe to play with your Barbie doll. I hope they'll be good friends." Mattel sought a restraining order to prohibit Lundby of Sweden from airing the commercial.

U.S. District Judge David Kenyon issued a restraining order barring Lundby from airing the ad.

Petra was one of Barbie's most formidable competitors in European markets.

In 1991, Mattel changed the name of the International doll series to the Dolls of the World (DOW) series. The new DOW dolls this year were the Brazilian Barbie doll (#9094), Czechoslovakian Barbie doll (#7330), Malaysian Barbie doll (#7329) and the Nigerian Barbie doll (#7376). Second editions of the Internationals were offered in the DOW line, including the Eskimo Barbie doll (#9844) (a second edition of the 1982 doll), the Parisian Barbie doll (#9843) first introduced in 1980, and the Scottish Barbie doll (#9845) which was first introduced in 1981. The Malaysian doll used the 1981 Oriental face mold.

In 1991, Janet Goldblatt designed Mermaid Barbie and received Mattel's Creative Excellence Award for Bathtime Barbie, creating a new foam-fashions-in-the-bathtub play pattern.

This year, the Barbie doll was packaged with computer software for the first time. The Earring Magic/Radio Shack Barbie doll (#25-1992, Radio Shack stock number) included a software pack with the Barbie Design Studio program and a manual from Hi Tech Expressions.

*Darryl Hannah was perhaps Janet Goldblatt's model for the **Mermaid Barbie** doll.*

1991

◆ "Baseball caps are the new t-shirts," the *New York Times* announces, billing them as going from "home plate to fashion plate."

◆ *Beauty and the Beast,* a Disney Studios animated film featuring the voice of Angela Lansbury and the music of Howard Ashman and Alan Menken, becomes the first animated movie to be nominated for an Oscar for Best Picture.

1992
Mattel, Inc., says. . .

(Hollywood Hair Barbie shares the cover of the annual report with the Genie from Disney's *Aladdin*, "Big Bones" from the Hot Wheels "Attack Pack" line and "Baby Walk 'n Roll").

"With revenues that approached $1 billion in 1992, the 34-year-strong Barbie doll is the leading product of the toy industry, having grown almost $500 million over the past four years. She is a big sister and a role model to girls around the world, and through her, girls play out their fantasies.

"Fashions, cars, houses and playsets all have contributed to the growth of Barbie. 'Barbie for Girls' products ranging from girls' clothing and shoes to skates, backpacks, cosmetics and furniture also take Barbie beyond the doll. The Barbie doll itself, however, remains the core of our business, and the average American girl, three to ten years old, now owns eight.

"The key is to make Barbie fresh and new every year, to develop multiple doll segments based on established play patterns, and to drive sales through effective advertising, promotion and merchandising."

(Source: 1992 Annual Report)

Direct mail emerged in the 1990s as a key marketing distribution channel for a broad range of consumer and commercial markets. So Mattel, in tune with leading-edge marketing strategies, initiated direct mail sales of the Barbie doll in 1992 with the Crystal Rhapsody Barbie, the first in the Presidential Porcelain Collection. (See sidebar, How Life Imitates Art in Barbie's World)

In 1992 Mattel also opened a Barbie boutique in New York City toy store FAO Schwarz and a toy shop at Disneyland. The latter move gave Mattel outlets for its products at all three Disney theme parks, which attract some 50 million visitors each year.

1992

◆ Four women are elected to the Senate, bringing the total to six, the most ever. Among the newly elected is the first Black female Senator.

◆ Donna Redel is elected the first woman chairperson of the New York Commodity Exchange. The 39-year-old Redel was an executive vice president of the Redel Trading Company.

◆ By August of this year, Mattel had completely automated its trade transactions for goods entering the U.S. West Coast. Mattel earned the distinction of being the largest shipper to go paperless.

◆ Martina Navratilova wins her 158th tennis title—surpassing every other player, male or female. She took her first championship in Czechoslovakia in 1973.

Factoid

By 1992, placed head to toe, the 700 million Barbie dolls and family members sold since 1959 would circle the earth over 3.5 times.

*Some collectors' favorite Mackie—**Neptune Fantasy Barbie**—poses on a Delaunay-inspired background.*

The Classique Collection's Benefit Ball Barbie, designed by veteran Barbie doll designer Carol Spencer, excited collectors. With her "foil" effect turquoise gown, and red hair, the doll continues to be a favorite with collectors as the first in an exciting series aimed at adult collectors.

Bob Mackie had major hits with two magnificent, highly detailed dolls: Empress Bride (#4247) and Neptune Fantasy (#4248). These have had significant staying power on the secondary market with collectors.

Featured on the evening news in 1992 was the introduction of the Teen Talk™ Barbie doll (#5745). The news wasn't so much the doll itself: it was what the doll "said" when her voice chip was activated by a push of the button in the doll's back. Each doll featured four so-called "fun phrases," randomly selected from approximately 270 sayings. One of the 270 sayings was, "Math class is tough!" This caused a furor among women's special interest groups ranging from the American Association of University Women (who attacked the math comment in a report on how schools shortchange girls) to radical feminist organizations. Mattel offered to make exchanges for the so-called offensive doll. It is not known how many of the dolls were actually returned.

Collectors who yearn to collect rare variations of Barbie dolls should be challenged by this fact: Teen Talk dolls were packaged wearing a range of different fashions, with different hair colors in straight and curly styles. According to Mattel, based on the scores of different sayings and voice chips, the number of Teen Talk Barbie doll variations mathematically computes to over 6,400 dolls. Another collector reality is that of the (reportedly) 350,000 talking Barbie dolls produced, only about one percent—or about 3,500—of the dolls contain the sound chip with the controversial phrase. The doll also was packaged as Black Teen Talk Barbie doll (#1612).

Barbie not only talked in 1992—she also took on a new appearance. New facial sculpting gave Barbie several different looks. Among the new face molds were the "New Smile", found in Teen Talk Barbie, Rappin' Rockin' Barbie, and Snap 'N Play Barbie; "The Neptune," found in Bob Mackie's Neptune Fantasy Barbie (#4248), Barbie as Scarlett in red, and other Mackie dolls; and, the "New Hispanic" face mold used in Teresa and the second issue of the Italian Barbie doll (#2256).

Barbie was also tied in to the United Colors of Benetton brand in 1992 with the Benetton Shopping Barbie, which was packaged with a (cut-out) Benetton logo shopping bag.

United Colors of Benetton Shopping Barbie, *the second Benetton Barbie, was dressed in brightly colored clothes typical of the United Colors of Benetton style.*

Honey, They Blew Up Barbie!

"Mattel has just created My Size Barbie, a three-foot mannequin. Touted as, 'A girl's best friend' and, 'the first Barbie little girls can actually share clothes with!' the $100 My Size, which makes her debut this fall, comes with a maillot, a tutu and a long skirt made from glittery elastic that will stretch to fit a normal three-foot kid.

"Bob Mackie has made two limited edition Barbie's: The $250 Empress Bride wears an antebellum tulle skirt, a beaded tiara and a floor-length veil that could double as My Size Barbie's hankie. Neptune's Fantasy Barbie is a miniature Vegas diva. For $170, she comes wrapped in green sequins and a teal velvet cloak whose spiked collar frames her head like a claw. She could be the headline act at a Lilliputian Tropicana."

SOURCE: *Newsweek,* July 27, 1992, 120:42

Crystal Rhapsody *porcelain Barbie, designed by Cynthia Young, was done with Swarovski crystals and inspired by Botticelli's* Birth of Venus.

How Life Imitates Art in Barbie's World

Cynthia Young, Barbie doll designer, tells a wonderful story about how the design for the Crystal Rhapsody Barbie doll evolved. Overall, the doll was inspired by the beauty of Swarovski® crystals. Jill Barad challenged Barbie doll designers to create a gown for Barbie using the radiant crystals. The gown's silver bodice shimmered with the reflected light of 75 Swarovski crystal rhinestones, combining multi-colored aurora borealis crystals and clear silver crystals. The bodice flowed into a straight skirt of black silk velvet. Framing the entire gown was pearly white, Fortuny pleated satin.

But where did the idea for this pleated design come from? Young relates: "The doll's white satin Fortuny pleated skirt fanned out behind her with a black velvet silhouette. The inspiration for this came from a painting by Botticelli, the *Birth of Venus*. I was trying to think of a theme for a new doll, and I have an art book at home on which the *Birth of Venus* is on the cover. I just happened to look at the image and thought, 'the shell that Venus is coming out of, you could move it behind her and that could become her skirt. . .'." Now, that's life imitating art!

Continuing on the thread of designers receiving clues for Barbie designs from great art, Young recalled another such flash of inspiration. "Super Power Barbie, released in 1995 as Flying Hero Barbie, was inspired in a similar way. Debby Meyer, one of the designers with whom I work on my team, had an inspiration that came from *The Creation of Adam* by Michelangelo. You can see on the doll's costume that there are lights. These are touch-sensitive. We did not use these in production. Instead, we translated this into a toy with lights that sparkle and shine on the back of the cape. . . ."

And you thought the Sistine Chapel was a complicated project!

The Creation of Adam, *by Michelangelo (top);* Birth of Venus *by Botticelli (bottom).*

FAO Schwarz's customized Barbie dolls changed in tone with this ***Madison Avenue Barbie*** *doll in 1992. Prior to 1992 the FAO Schwarz dolls were all dressed in long glitzy gowns. This tailored day suit became a rave with collectors. The outfit came complete with fuchsia undergarments as well as an FAO Schwarz shopping bag.*

Customized Barbie dolls for retail stores made a particular impact on collectors in 1992. The FAO Schwarz Madison Avenue Barbie doll (#1539) was a collector favorite. Designed by Ann Driskill, whose fashion designs often reflect the kind of tailoring present in the earliest Barbie doll costumes, Madison Avenue Barbie was clad in a fuchsia and lime green suit with all of the important accouterments for a Manhattan shopping trip.

Another customized doll for a retail outlet—the Toys 'R Us Barbie for President doll—came in both Caucasian and Black versions (#3722 and #3940, respectively). While Barbie doll had been involved with political causes before (such as the UNICEF and Summit Barbie dolls), this was the first time in her career that she had made a run for the White House. Did Geraldine Ferraro's Vice Presidential nomination in 1988 influence Barbie doll designers? Perhaps so. . . .

In 1992, George Bush, William Clinton and Ross Perot were greeted by a fourth major candidate: Barbie. There were two box variations for the ***Barbie for President*** *doll: The initial box was printed with the presidential seal across the top (above), and the second box was decorated with stars (left).*

Factoid

This year, Toys 'R Us doubled the amount of shelf space per store dedicated to Barbie and friends.

It was a case of art imitating life once again when the Stars and Stripes Army Barbie doll (#1234 Caucasian, #5618 Black, also available in gift sets with Ken) appeared quickly on toy store shelves in 1992. Dubbed by collectors "Desert Storm Barbie," this doll wore the uniform of a soldier serving in the Gulf War, complete with beret and camouflage fatigues. The doll's box also refers to the event as "Rendezvous with Destiny."

Rappin' Rockin' Barbie Doll (#3248) and her ethnic friends, Christie and Teresa, were based on the hip music trend that went mainstream by 1992. Barbie doll and friends each came with a boom box that played a rap beat sound. When played together, they sounded like a rap group. They came outfitted in hip-hop costumes and each wore a long gold chain, a style popular with rap artists of the time.

*Capitalizing on the trend in music, **Rappin' Rockin' Barbie** and friends came packaged with boom boxes. Their black and neon colored outfits and caps reflected the street styles of the time.*

The Stars and Stripes series offered ***Army Barbie*** *and she quickly became known as "Desert Storm Barbie."*

Another trend doll—Rollerblade™ Barbie doll (#2214)—took a cue from the "hottest skating trend sweeping the nation," Mattel wrote. This doll straddles trend and licensed dolls, as Barbie wore skates with the Rollerblade trademark advertising the product. Each doll came with an officially licensed set of Rollerblade skates. Different from people-sized Rollerblades, Barbie's Rollerblade skates flickered and flashed as they rolled.

The lead glamour doll in 1992 was Sparkle Eyes Barbie (#2482) which had blue "rhinestone" eyes that sparkle. The Black Sparkle Eyes Barbie doll (#5950) came

__Rollerblade Barbie__ (below) tied in with the brand-named in-line skates. Barbie's skates had the special effect of flickering when they rolled. An ophthalmologist's dream patient, glamour doll __Sparkle Eyes Barbie__ (right) had "rhinestone" implanted eyes.

TOTALLY HAIR BARBIE: A $100 MILLION SUCCESS

Totally Hair Barbie is the most successful Barbie doll segment ever, generating $100 million in worldwide sales during 1992.

The Totally Hair Barbie doll makes the most of a popular play feature, with hair so long it reaches her toes. Styling gel comes packed with the doll for added fun, and for the first time in 20 years this Barbie is available with a choice of blonde or brunette hair. To maintain the momentum of Totally Hair Barbie, a Hollywood Hair doll has been introduced for 1993. The new doll again has special extra-long hair, but this time with the added unique feature of a hair mist that turns her blonde hair to pink, in patterns or all over.

SOURCE: 1992 Mattel Annual Report

Totally Hair Barbie *was packaged with Dep styling gel.*

1992

◆ Judit Polgar, the youngest person ever to earn the rank of chess grandmaster, celebrates her 16th birthday. She achieved this ranking the previous December. There were only 401 active grandmasters in the world at the time.

◆ In an advance for women in professional sports, Manon Rheaume becomes the first woman to play in one of the four major professional sports (baseball, football, basketball, and ice hockey) when she appears as goal tender for the Tampa Bay Lightning in an exhibition ice hockey game.

◆ Anita Colby, the first "super model" and beauty writer, died at 77.

with green rhinestone eyes. Like most glamour dolls of previous years, Barbie's pink costume transformed into several looks: a floor-length ball gown, a silvery mini dress, and a dress with pink sparkle train.

Totally Hair Barbie doll (#1112) came with the longest Barbie hair ever at ten inches, reaching her ankles. She wore a Pucci-style knit dress, her hair was tied back in a pink scarf, and she came packaged with a tube of Dep® Styling Gel. Totally Hair Barbie doll also came in a Black version (#5948) and a Brunette version (#1117).

The 1992 Dolls of the World included the English (#4973), Jamaican (#4647) and the Spanish (#4963) Barbie dolls.

English Barbie *(left) was one of the Dolls of the World offered in 1992. This was the second British Barbie, following up the Royal Barbie International of 1980, the first year the Internationals were offered.* ***Jamaican Barbie*** *(center) had a multi-print cotton ensemble which caused some discussion amongst collectors who questioned whether the outfit was consistent with the International Barbie doll image of earlier years. This same year a second* ***Spanish Barbie*** *doll (right) followed the first issued in 1983.*

1993
Mattel, Inc., says. . .

(Cover: Disney® characters, Barbie dolls, Hot Wheels® and other toys)

Big news: Merger with Fisher-Price Toys, resulting in Mattel's best sales and earnings in company history.

"Barbie sales have more than doubled in five years, increasing from $485 million in 1988 to over $1 billion in 1993. In 1994, Barbie celebrates her 35th anniversary year, and also becomes a doctor, or—more specifically—a pediatrician. To help provide access to basic health care for all children, Mattel will donate $1 million in proceeds from Barbie products to children's health care organizations."

(Source: 1993 Annual Report)

In 1993, Barbie brought in nearly half of Mattel's $2.1 billion revenue. This year, Totally Hair Barbie generated $100 million alone, and helped to increase sales 20% annually for five years. By this year, the average American girl owned eight Barbie dolls.

The Classique Evening Extravaganza Barbie doll (#11622 Caucasian, #11638 Black) was the third in the series, introduced in 1992. The popularity of the doll with collectors was in part attributable to Mattel's first infomercial designed for a Barbie doll, hosted by Pam Dawber of "Mork and Mindy" fame. The infomercial introduced the audience, many of whom were first-time adult buyers of a Barbie doll, to Barbie doll designers including Kitty Black-Perkins (the designer of Evening Extravaganza), Janet Goldblatt (the designer of Opening Night Barbie and City Style Barbie, the second in the Classique series) and Carol Spencer (the designer of Benefit Ball Barbie, the first Classique doll).

1993

◆ Mattel agrees to buy rival Fisher-Price Inc. in a stock swap worth about $1.1 billion. The merged company would rival Hasbro Inc. as the world's largest toy company.

◆ Julie Krone wins the 125th running of the Belmont Stakes, riding Colonial Affair—a 13-1 longshot—in the third leg of the U.S. Triple Crown. She thus becomes the first woman to win a U.S. Triple Crown race.

◆ Comic book hero Superman dies at the hands of the villain Doomsday in Superman No. 75. Later this year, the super-hero's editors find a way to bring him back to life.

◆ Honoring the memories of eleven million people killed systematically during the Nazi Holocaust (1933-1945), the United States Holocaust Memorial Museum opens in Washington, DC.

Masquerade Ball Barbie, *by Bob Mackie, haughtily poses with mask in hand.*

Charleston, anyone? It's the Roaring '20s, and ***Flapper Barbie*** *dances atop a fur stole as Rudy Vallee croons a tune.*

Factoid

Mattel sold more than 900 million fashions and one billion pair of shoes by 1993.

Bob Mackie had a huge hit with Masquerade Ball Barbie doll (#10803). The doll is dressed in a harlequin-pattern gown constructed with black and multi-colored bugle beads. Some dolls are known to have the Mackie fragrance infused in the doll; in addition, some dolls were packed with small flaçons of Mackie eau de toilette.

Mattel introduced the Great Era series with the Flapper Barbie doll (#4063) and the Gibson Girl Barbie doll (#3702). These dolls, aimed at the adult collector market, are recreations of important fashion eras.

The Australian Barbie doll (#3626) and the Italian Barbie doll (#2256) joined the Dolls of the World series in 1993. The Italian was a second edition after the first Italian Barbie doll introduced in 1980. This doll used the New Hispanic face mold, first found in the Teresa doll in 1992.

Sea Holiday Barbie (above) was dressed for a cruise and packaged for the international market. Australian Barbie (right) capitalized on Australian themes popular in U.S. cinema, clothing, food and drink.

1994
Mattel, Inc., says. . .

(Cover: Celebrating 50 years)

"The production of Barbie and other fashion dolls involves more detail than is readily apparent. The painting of the face, for instance, involves an average of 15 steps, and the doll's body is assembled from as many as 25 different parts. No one comes remotely close to the quantity of 90 million fashion dolls Mattel produces in a year, nor can any company match the high quality and low cost Mattel achieves in this category.

"The proceeds from the sale of the Dr. Barbie doll, combined with grants from the Mattel Foundation, resulted in a $2 million initiative supporting children's preventive health care facilities at federally-funded Head Start preschool locations."

(Source: 1994 Annual Report)

Mattel celebrated 35 years of the Barbie doll in grand style this year. The company issued a new line of Nostalgic Barbie dolls, kicking things off with a reproduction of the first Barbie doll (#11590 blonde and #11782 brunette). Donned in her zebra-striped swimsuit and sold with a reproduction box which replicated the original doll's packaging, the doll became

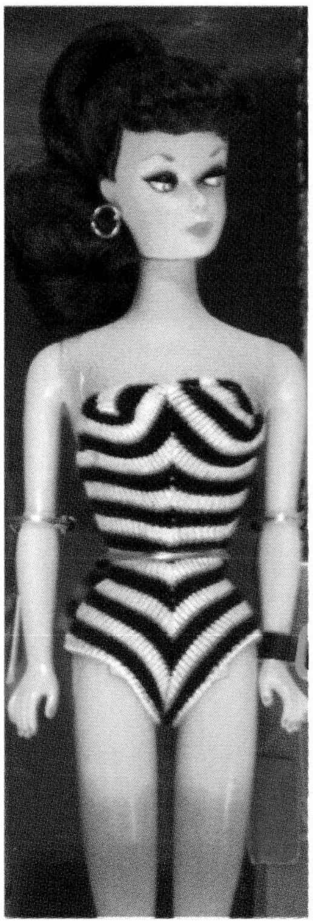

Mattel launched its successful Nostalgic Barbie line in 1994, with the 35th Anniversary Barbie dolls. Brunettes (left) were rumored to be in shorter supply than blondes (right). This giftset (center), only available in blonde to the mass market, was very limited. The package included reproductions of two of the most highly prized vintage outfits in Barbie's fashion history: Roman Holiday and Easter Parade.

*The **Gold Jubilee Barbie** continues to be a secondary market treasure due to its very limited production.*

an instant hit with collectors. In particular, the blonde doll packaged as a gift set (#11591) with two of the most rare costumes from 1960—Roman Holiday and Easter Parade—was very difficult to find.

The Barbie doll PR machine never worked as hard as when it cranked up to celebrate the doll's 35th anniversary. To mark the occasion, Mattel sponsored a bi-coastal celebration that brought out the stars. In the Los Angeles community of Compton, Jill Barad presented a $250,000 donation to actress Demi Moore on behalf of the Charles Drew Head Start Medical Clinic. Barad presented an additional check for $250,000 to actor/director Henry Winkler, founding president of the Children's Action Network, to support the organization's National Immunization Campaign. These contributions were part of Mattel's $1 million year-long campaign to support health care initiatives funded by the sales of the new Dr. Barbie doll and other Barbie products. On the day of these presentations, Ruth Handler appeared on the East Coast, at FAO Schwarz in New York City, for a doll signing event.

In honor of Barbie's 35th anniversary, Mattel released the brilliant Gold Jubilee Barbie doll (#12009), a limited and numbered edition of 5,000. There were an additional 2,000 units sold on the international market, and 200 dolls were produced for Mattel employees. The doll was made with Mattel's best "collector grade vinyl," described by Mattel as "porcelain vinyl." The doll was an immediate success with collectors. Its initial retail price of $295 was eclipsed, within weeks of the initial release, by a secondary market price as high as $1,000.

1994

◆ After many years away from the concert stage, Barbra Streisand mounts an international concert tour. The tour plays to sell-out audiences.

◆ Jacqueline Kennedy Onassis, 64, widow of U.S. President John F. Kennedy, died of cancer. Her clothing and hair styles were emulated by millions of women and the Barbie doll.

◆ South Africa holds its first universal suffrage elections. African National Congress President Nelson Mandela on May 2 proclaimed victory, declaring black South Africans "free at last."

◆ Israel and Jordan sign a peace treaty, formally ending 46 years of war and mistrust.

Dr. Barbie, in Black and Caucasian versions (#11814 and #11160, respectively), was released this year. As a symbol of Mattel's initiative to raise funds for children without access to health care, Dr. Barbie was a pediatrician. She was packaged with two newborn patients of different races (babies came as Black, Caucasian and Hispanic versions, which varied randomly by package). Dr. Barbie's magic stethoscope produced a heartbeat sound when pressed to the chest of her blanket-wrapped baby patient. Accessories included a doctor bag, pacifier, rattle, baby bottle, reflex instrument, and ear checker—details which were reminiscent of the Barbie doll's richly-accessorized medical costumes of the 1960's, such as Registered Nurse (#991) or Candy Striper Volunteer (#889).

One of 1994's greatest Barbie doll hits was the introduction of the Hollywood Legends Series, kicked off by the ultimate Hollywood Legend: Scarlett O'Hara of *Gone with the Wind* fame. There have been many versions of Scarlett dolls through

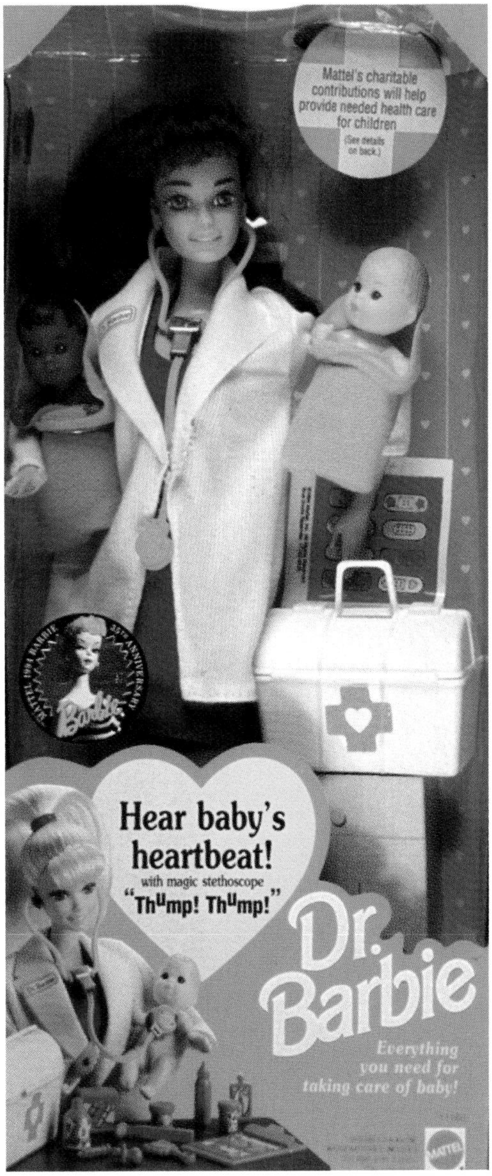

Dr. Barbie, *a pediatrician, came complete with patient and "working" stethoscope (left). The brunette variation of the 1994 doctor (right) was exclusively available at the Barbie Festival sponsored by Mattel in Orlando.*

The Scarlett and Rhett dolls from Gone with the Wind *were welcomed by collectors.* **Barbie as Scarlett** *dressed in her black and white honeymoon dress was a favorite among many collectors.*

the years including, but not limited to, Cissettes, Alexanders, and Franklin Heirlooms, among others. However, none to date have been as authentically and meticulously detailed as Barbie as Scarlett. Mattel offered four versions of Barbie as Scarlett O'Hara: Scarlett in her white and green barbecue dress (#12997); Scarlett in green velvet drapery dress with braided gold and green belt (#12045); Scarlett in red velveteen gown with beads and feather accents (#12815); and, Scarlett in her black and white honeymoon dress from her marriage to Rhett Butler (#13524). Speaking of Rhett, the Ken doll was also dressed as Scarlett's groom in black tuxedo and cape (#12741). Arguably the most remarkable aspect of these dolls is the authentic costume detail, in which every feature faithfully reflects the original movie costumes designed by Walter Plunkett.

Attention to detail was no more apparent than in this iconic dress (left) from GWTW, allegedly sewn in desperation from the drapes that hung in Tara. Remember when Scarlett in red velvet (center) looked askance as she wore this dress? Ken, as Rhett (right), looked dashing in his morning suit, complete with top hat.

The film's story line was even depicted on Barbie boxes such as the green barbeque dress box (left). The dolls also appeal to collectors of Hollywood and movie memorabilia, as well as Civil War junkies.

Factoid

By December 31, 1994, Mattel had established a total of sixteen Barbie Boutiques in FAO Schwarz toy stores, including the "Barbie on Madison" boutique at the FAO Schwarz *flagship store in New York City. By late 1995, the New York boutique had expanded to two stories.*

Customized Barbie dolls were hot in 1994. One of the most important designer dolls in *Contemporary BARBIE* doll history was Bloomingdale's Savvy Shopper Barbie designed by Nicole Miller. According to Bloomingdale's management, the doll could not be kept on the shelf. The doll is dressed in a quintessential Nicole Miller outfit: black velvet short cocktail dress with a black silk overcoat bearing a colorful tiny print typical of Miller. Miller also designed a series of people-sized silk accessories to celebrate the 35th anniversary of the Barbie doll. (For more on Nicole Miller, see Chapter 5, Pure Couture).

Another favorite customized doll was the Hallmark Victorian Elegance Barbie doll (#12579), first in a series of Hallmark-commissioned Barbie dolls. Hallmark had successfully launched its first Barbie doll Christmas ornament in 1993 with a miniature replica of that year's Happy Holidays Barbie doll, along with a Nostalgic #1 Barbie doll ornament. 1994's introduction of Hallmark's first actual Barbie doll has led the company to commission additional holiday Barbie dolls.

Barbie's successful career as an Astronaut was repeated this year in a celebration of the Apollo mission's 25th anniversary. Astronaut Barbie doll (#12149 Caucasian, and #12150 Black) came dressed in astro gear, including space helmet and a flag to plant on the moon. Was that, "One small step for womankind. . . ?"

FLO-JO'S INTO BARBIE

"Long before 'the fastest woman alive' won five Olympic medals, married gold-medalist Al Joyner, co-chaired the President's Council on Physical Fitness and Sports or ran her own business, Florence Griffith was a little girl who played with Barbie dolls in the L.A. projects.

"'I had 10 brothers and sisters, and my parents divorced when I was six,' says Flo-Jo, now 34. 'My sisters and I would pretend that Barbie and Ken were Mom and Dad. We'd put the dolls together, hoping our parents would get back together too.'

"They didn't. But Flo-Jo's childhood games led to an enduring passion for sewing and fashion. 'We couldn't afford Barbie clothes, so my mother taught me to make them. That was such a joyful time for me—doing something creative that we both loved.'

"She still designs for Barbie, but now with her daughter, four-year-old Mary (dubbed Mo-Jo by the press). 'We have close to a thousand dolls between us, and she always begs to sew for them.'

"Flo-Jo also makes garments for far bigger bodies. She has designed the Indiana Pacers' uniforms and women's athletic clothing sold in Japan. But her dream is to design uniforms for a U.S. Olympic team."

SOURCE: *Life*, August 1994, page 79

New Dolls of the World included Chinese Barbie (#11180), Dutch Barbie (#11104), Kenyan Barbie (#11181), and the second Native American Barbie doll (#11609). Kenyan Barbie used the new Nichelle face mold first employed in 1991 (and used extensively in Mattel's Shani line of dolls). The Kenyan figure was the first Barbie doll to have flocked hair (à la the earliest Ken dolls). Mattel also packaged the Chinese, Dutch and Kenyan Barbie dolls together in a Dolls of the World Giftset (#12043).

***Dutch Barbie** (above) from Dolls of the World in 1994, reminded vintage Barbie collectors of the Barbie in Holland outfit offered in 1963 as part of the Travel Costume Series (#0823).The second African Barbie doll (top right), **Kenyan Barbie,** used the beautiful Nichelle face mold (from the Shani line) and had close-cropped hair. **Chinese Barbie** (bottom right) was the first issue Chinese Barbie doll.*

1994 saw new innovations in marketing the Barbie doll. The cable television shopping channel, QVC, began to sell Barbie dolls that year. (The Home Shopping Network had successfully sold Barbie dolls, as well.) Dolls featured on QVC's hour-long Barbie doll program often sell out within the hour. The new distribution channel of home shopping for Barbie dolls expanded Mattel's access to new potential collectors; at the time of this writing, QVC was available in over 50 million U.S. homes.

A second emerging growth area impacting Barbie doll collectors was the entire field of licensing. Shady Character signed a license with Mattel in 1994 to manufacture men's and women's pajamas and lounge wear under the Nostalgic Barbie label. Their varied selection included six designs from the 1959 to 1964 Barbie period, such as knit and woven boxer shorts, nightshirts and other lounge wear categories. These were available through the QVC channel, at FAO Schwarz stores, and through a variety of other retail outlets. (For more on the subject, see Chapter 6, Custom Made).

Cynthia Young remembers Solo in the Spotlight. . .

Cynthia Young

Both Cynthia and I are among the earliest generation of Barbie doll collectors. I asked her about her favorite vintage Barbie doll memory. She responded instantly with this nostalgic, sweet story: "As a child, my favorite Barbie doll was Solo in the Spotlight. I remember one night when my parents went out for the evening. They left my sister and me with our grandmother. When they picked us up at 10 p.m., we were asleep and so we thought it was the middle of the night. After they woke us up, our parents gave each one of us a Barbie doll case, with the doll packed inside wearing Solo in the Spotlight, and all these Barbie doll clothes hung up on their little hangers in the case. We were still half asleep! This gift was not for any occasion. When I woke up in my own bed, the doll case, doll and costumes were on a table in my bedroom. I thought it was a beautiful dream. . . ."

This nostalgic memory is what drives many adult collectors to open themselves up to the Barbie doll. . .déja vù all over again!

SOURCE: Author's interview with Cynthia Young, August 1995.

1995

Based on Mattel's 1994 success with the kickoff of the Nostalgic line of Barbie dolls, the company introduced Solo in the Spotlight® Barbie doll (#13534) with a blonde ponytail—a reproduction of the iconic fashion sold between 1960 and 1964. The doll also came in a brunette version (#13820). Solo in the Spotlight had been one of the best-selling outfits from the vintage era. Busy Gal (#13675) reproduced a brunette Barbie doll in one of the most popular fashions from the early 1960s: Barbie doll as fashion designer, including period-perfect red suit and a portfolio of fashion sketches.

Mattel brought out its second in the Nostalgic series of Barbie dolls in 1995. ***Solo in the Spotlight*** *wore one of the most popular outfits from Barbie's vintage era. She came in blonde and brunette variations.*

The third Nostalgic Barbie doll was ***Busy Gal.*** *She wore the vintage costume of the same name, which was the outfit of an early 1960s fashion designer. The doll was packaged with fashion portfolio and drawings, and had black glasses akin to the ones worn by Edith Head.*

1995

◆ Shannon Faulkner makes history by becoming the first woman to enroll in the Citadel—a Charleston, SC, military school with a 152-year history of single-gender education. She drops out after one week.

◆ Mega media deals abound: Walt Disney Company buys Capital Cities/ABC; Westinghouse makes a bid for CBS; and Seagrams acquires MCA.

◆ The University of Connecticut men's and women's basketball teams are both ranked number one in their respective AP polls, marking a first in NCAA history. The women's team reached the top of the polls on January 17, one day after beating Tennessee, 77-66.

The porcelain doll celebrating Mattel's 50th anniversary wore a red and gold Fortuny pleated gown.

The eagerly awaited Christian Dior Barbie doll (#13168) from the Designer series was a favorite among many collectors. The doll wore the first replica from the couture house of Dior. A design by Gianfranco Ferré, the doll wore a two-piece beaded, brocade costume, studded with gold beads on a rich tapestry background. Her hair, coiffed by Alexandre of Laurent, was up in (appropriately enough) a French twist, reminiscent of Catherine Deneuve. Perhaps, that's because this doll used the popular 1987 SuperStar face mold, and Deneuve is one of cinema's global superstars.

In 1995, customized dolls proliferated in both volume and scope. Of particular note were the Bloomingdale's Donna Karan Barbie doll, issued in both blonde and brunette versions; and the Wessco International Travel Barbie doll. Both dolls, which were designed by Ann Driskill's group reflect a tailored suited look.

The Hollywood Legends Series presented its second and third releases in the form of Barbie as Dorothy in the *Wizard of Oz* (#12701) and Barbie as Maria in *The Sound of Music* (#13676). The Maria doll used the 1977 SuperStar face mold.

Mattel Toys celebrated 50 years of business in 1995. The company commemorated the golden anniversary with a special porcelain doll: the 50th Anniversary Barbie doll (#14479). The blonde doll wore a red velvet gown with a gold pleated metallic fabric in Fortuny pleats at the bottom. Fifty red roses, each accented with a sequin and bead, adorned her neckline, shawl and hairpiece. The doll wore a gold tone bracelet with the Mattel logo on one side and "50 Years" on the other.

Bob Mackie offered yet another stunning example of his sequin-and-bead artistry: Goddess of the Sun. The doll's costume and headdress are reminiscent of Mackie's very popular Neptune Fantasy, but instead of teal blue, the ensemble is gold. "Sunrays" of sequins and gold fan behind her torso, and rich gold beading is worked in a vertical design on the skirt of the floor-length gown.

Popular culture has always influenced Barbie doll marketers and designers. For the first time, the Barbie doll was matched with a television program. The popularity of the television show "Baywatch" married nicely with the popularity of the Barbie doll and resulted in the Baywatch™ Barbie doll (#13199). The doll's dolphin friend made realistic sounds and helped to present an ecological message. In addition, Baywatch Barbie can be viewed as a career doll since she performs the role of lifeguard. Furthermore, based on the popularity of the show's star, David Hasselhoff (especially in Europe, and particularly Germany), Baywatch Barbie and friends could be seen as global dolls. While Mattel claimed that the doll bore no likeness to any of the show's cast members, many believed that she strongly resembled Pamela Anderson Lee, the blonde lead actress in the cast. Mattel also put together a variety of cross-promotional deals for girl's apparel, swimwear and accessories.

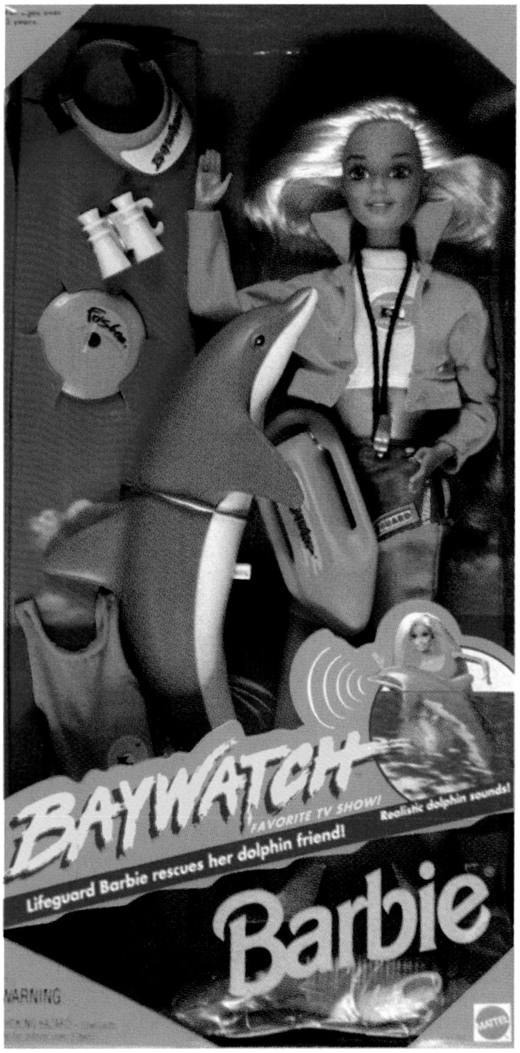

Mattel paired Barbie with the popular "Baywatch" television series. Many observers believe that the doll was modeled after Pamela Anderson Lee (but perhaps Pamela Anderson Lee has modeled herself after Barbie?).

Teacher Barbie doll (#13914) and Black Teacher Barbie doll (#13915) added an important career to Barbie doll's resumé. The doll was packaged with a boy and girl student in a classroom with a real chalkboard, bell, clock and pencil sharpener. In 1995, Mattel also marketed the Caring Careers™ Fashion Giftset, which added the jobs of firefighter, teacher and veterinarian to Barbie's 35 years of work experience.

Mattel packaged three career outfits in the Caring Careers set (below): firefighter, teacher and veterinarian. ***Teacher Barbie*** *(right), initially praised, encountered some problems in the children's market since the doll was not wearing underwear (as is the case with nearly all Barbie dolls!).*

The Renaissance of Dorothy

Abbe Littleton recalled the story of her early designs for the Barbie doll. "When I first came to Mattel in 1983, my supervisors told me to design what I wanted. I thought Barbie should be a movie star. Through being a movie star, she could play characters that allowed her to be a mermaid, a Fifties girl, or Marilyn Monroe. I finally sketched Barbie as Dorothy from the Wizard of Oz. That was in late 1983.

"Eleven years later, my boss said, 'We're thinking of testing a Wizard of Oz theme for Barbie.' I pulled out my old doll and doctored her up. I put a Little Debbie head on the body and turned her hair into braids. We tested the prototype and all of the adults loved it. She really looked like Dorothy.

"Then we took her and adapted the doll to Barbie's style: we added white eyelet fabric and gave her a fuller dress. She came out very sweet looking."

SOURCE: Author's Interview with Abbe Littleton, November 1995

Mattel kicked off two new collector's series for children. The American Stories Collection dolls reflected American historical periods and included Colonial Barbie (#12578), Pilgrim Barbie (#12577) and Pioneer Barbie (#12680). The Children's Collector Series featured the Rapunzel Barbie doll with her down-to-the-floor hair (#13016).

The American Stories Collection kicked off in 1995 with these three dolls: ***Colonial*** *(far left),* ***Pilgrim,*** *and* ***Pioneer Barbie,*** *which appealed to both younger and adult collectors.*

1995

◆ POG collecting becomes the rage among elementary-school-aged boys and girls, a reincarnation from their past lives as milk-bottle caps.

◆ Internet surfing goes mainstream with a product offering called, "Internet in a Box."

◆ Donna Karan celebrates 10 years in the fashion biz.

◆ Radio call-in talk shows create a new form of electronic populism.

*The **German Barbie** doll (left) from the Dolls of the World Series of 1995 was the second issue German, following the first offered in 1987. Instead of wearing white tights, her legs were painted white. Mattel offered the second **Irish Barbie** doll (center)—the first was available in 1984. She was very popular with collectors, and had the red hair of a typical Irish "Colleen." The same year also brought the **Polynesian Barbie** doll (right) to the Dolls of the World series. She was clad in "grass" skirt and came complete with lei.*

"Barbie Elevated to Doll Royalty"

"It is not clear what the Emperor Franz Josef would have made of it. His descendants, Austria's illustrious Habsburg clan, are marketing Barbie dolls to make ends meet.

"At a ceremony in the marble palace of the Habsburgs' imperial villa last week, doll collectors were invited to pay £3,000 (about US$4,500) for the "Archduchess Barbie," one of a rare and regal set of Barbie dolls produced in collaboration with Archduke Markus von Habsburg-Lothringen and the American toy company Mattel.

"The archduke makes no bones about welcoming a plastic doll into the family; proceeds from the sales of the 12in *(sic)* Barbies bedecked in silk and tiaras will go towards restoring the Kaiservilla, the Habsburg summer residence at Bad Ischl, a retreat favoured by Emperor Franz Josef at the turn of the century. The income from opening the building to the public has so far proved a disappointment, but the 10 Barbie dolls on offer were snapped up in an instant. . . .

"Mattel made a limited edition of Habsburg Barbie [dolls] modelled on Empress Sissy, wife of the Emperor Franz Josef. The venture has been so successful that the Archduke is contemplating giving permission for a Barbie version of Franz Josef himself.

"'Although the price of £3,000 per model was high, I thought there would be enough people in Austria who would want to buy it, and there were,' said the Archduke. 'I think we could have sold another 10 at the same price.'

"It could be the start of a regal Barbie explosion. Mattel is now considering approaching royal families throughout Europe."

SOURCE: *The London Sunday Times,* 30 July 1995

New Dolls of the World included the German Barbie doll (#12698) first introduced in 1987; Irish Barbie doll (#12998), first introduced in 1984; Polynesian Barbie doll (#12700); and the third Native American doll (#12699).

Since the introduction of Teen Talk Barbie in 1992, kids and collectors alike anticipated the arrival of another contemporary talking Barbie. It came in the form of 1995's Super Talk Barbie doll (Caucasian and Black versions, #12290 and #12379, respectively). Of the Super Talk costume that she designed, Cynthia Young said: "I tried to do something that was trendy and denim, stylish and fitted. I liked to blend denim and gold, to achieve an effect of 'opposites'."

Thanks to new technology not available for the 1992 Teen Talk, Super Talk has 100,000 phrases available to her. But based on Mattel's lessons from Teen Talk's "math class is tough" remark, the company carefully screened every single phrase for Super Talk. John Amerman, Mattel CEO, was quoted in a 1994 *Los Angeles* Magazine profile titled "King Barbie," as saying that, in this age of political correctness, "we're bound to screw up on at least one of them!"

BARBIE DOES THE BOULEVARD MONTPARNASSE

In 1995, the Barbie doll made a very big impression in the City of Lights. At the Musée Grévin, Jill Barad, Mattel President and Chief Operating Officer, unveiled a replica of Barbie wearing the same design as a House of Christian Dior gown that appears in the museum, a French waxworks in Paris.

By sharing the stage at the Musée Grévin with waxen impressions of Bill Clinton, first feline Socks, Boris Yeltsin and Madonna, Barbie's role as an American cultural icon was confirmed. (For more on Ferré and the House of Dior, see Chapter 5, Pure Couture).

The second in the Winter Princess series, Evergreen Princess, *was issued in 1994.*

Contemporary Themes

One of the most impressive aspects of *Contemporary BARBIE®* is the doll's continual evolution of personalities and activities. By design since Barbie doll's inception, the doll changes with the individual who is playing with it. In 1995 alone, nearly 100 new issue dolls named "Barbie" were available on the (relatively) mass market. Given that large volume, collectors can shape their collections based on themes of dolls. While some collectors choose to acquire examples from every category available, others choose to focus their collections on a particular theme.

The major themes that *Contemporary BARBIE* reflects include:

career	**hair play**
bridal	**holiday**
special effects	**glamour**
athletic	**"foodie"**
global	**beach/sun worshipping**
trend	

◆ Career Barbie

In the contemporary era, Barbie has had careers from A to Z, from Astronaut (in 1985 and 1994) to zookeeper (as Animal Lovin' Barbie in 1989). She has had at least 100 careers since her birth. The careers span a broad range from the sciences (such as doctor) to politics (such as running for President and attending international political events for UNICEF and the Children's Summit), to the arts and athletics (as fashion designer and skater for the Ice Capades and the Olympics, respectively). Barbie has been an airline hostess for American Airlines, Braniff (now defunct), Pan Am (also defunct), and Singapore Airlines. And, in a 1984 issue of *Barbie* magazine featuring Day-to-Night Barbie on the cover, Barbie became the star of her own cooking show, the "Glamorous Gourmet."

The Barbie doll has also been designed as a professional shopper for several prominent merchants, including Bloomingdale's (twice), FAO Schwarz (twice), Meijer's and Spiegel, as well as for Benetton.

Over the years, the career-oriented Barbie doll has appeared both as a woman of color and as Caucasian. The 1984 seminal Day-to-Night Barbie doll, who Kitty Black-Perkins designed as a career "every woman," came in Black, Caucasian and Hispanic versions. By 1989 and 1990, respectively, the UNICEF and Summit dolls came in Asian, Black, Caucasian and Hispanic versions.

An early example of a career doll in the contemporary period, ***Doctor Barbie*** *came equipped with her medical bag and, prepared for a quick change, an evening dress.*

The 1988 glamour doll, ***SuperStar Barbie,*** *was a movie star who came complete with a changeable ensemble.*

Contemporary B*ARBIE* as career woman

Astronaut	1985
Day-to-Night Barbie	1985
Rocker	1986
Tennis Star	1986
Olympic Skater	1987
Rocker (Dancin' Action)	1987
Ballerina	1988
Doctor	1988
Environmentalist, zookeeper	1988
Sensations rock star	1988
SuperStar Movie Star	1988
Tennis Star	1988
Army Officer (American Beauties)	1989
Aerobics Instructor	1990
Air Force	1990
The Beat (rock star)	1990
Flight Time (pilot)	1990
Ice Capades (pro skater)	1990
Summit (diplomat)	1990
UNICEF (diplomat)	1990
Marine Corps Officer	1991
Navy Officer	1991
Army Officer (Desert Storm)	1992
Presidential candidate	1992
Air Force Thunderbirds	1993
Police Officer	1993
Rockette	1993
Astronaut (25th Apollo)	1994
Dr. Barbie	1994
Silver Screen (movie star)	1994
Circus Star	1995
Dr. Barbie	1995
Firefighter	1995
International Traveler	1995
Teacher	1995

Part of the Stars 'n Stripes series, ***Marine Corps Barbie*** *(left) wore her dress uniform in 1991. Is it Cagney or Lacey? No, it's Barbie doll (right) as the Toys 'R Us* ***Police Officer Barbie*** *in 1993.*

*In 1995, Barbie took on one of the most challenging careers in her history: fire fighting. Both Caucasian (top) and Black (above) Barbie dolls were **Fire Fighters,** and came complete with faithful dalmations at their sides.*

*Shopping Barbie dolls are popular among collectors, and this doll was no exception. In 1995, Spiegel quickly sold out of this **Shopping Chic** doll following the publication of its prototype photograph in* Miller's Barbie Collector.

Factoid

According to Jill Elikann Barad, Mattel Chief Operating Officer, little girls "always pick the wedding gown over anything." However, the one thing that Barbie will never get is married. "Little girls are marrying and unmarrying her all the time. If we were to officially set it, it would cut off some of the fantasy."

◆ Barbie the Bride

Collecting bride dolls is a favorite theme for many doll collectors, Barbie-focused or otherwise. Both young and older collectors appreciate the beautiful detail applied to Barbie bride dolls—the highly-prized Bob Mackie Empress Bride doll providing one notable example. In the *Contemporary BARBIE* doll era, the Barbie doll has come packaged solo and with entire wedding parties (such as Wedding Day for Midge in 1991). In addition, many bridal fashions have been packaged separately for Barbie.

Dream Bride Barbie, *1991, was typical of bridal Barbie dolls. She came complete with a Barbara Bush-style double-strand pearl choker reminiscent of the earliest Barbie bridal outfits.*

Barbie bride theme dolls in the contemporary era

Romantic Wedding Barbie	1987	
Wedding Fantasy Barbie	1989	(Caucasian and Black)
Wedding Party Barbie	1989	(Porcelain reproduction)
Dream Bride Barbie	1991	
Wedding Day for Midge (Barbie doll)	1991	
Bob Mackie Empress Bride	1992	
Romantic Bride Barbie	1993	(Caucasian and Black)
Wholesale Clubs-Wedding Fantasy Gift Set	1993	
TRU-Dream Wedding Barbie	1993	(Caucasian and Black)
My Size Barbie Bride	1994	(Caucasian and Black)
Star Lily Bride	1994	(Porcelain)
Wal-Mart Country Bride	1995	(Caucasian, Black and Hispanic)
Wedding Party Barbie	1995	(Caucasian and Black)

Here comes The Bride. . . . Both Bob Mackie Barbie doll collectors and bride doll collectors highly prize the ***Empress Bride*** *doll from Mr. Mackie. Among some Mackie collectors, this doll far surpasses all others of his designs.*

◆ SPECIAL EFFECTS BARBIE

Barbie first bent her legs in 1965, twisted and turned in 1967, and "spoke" in 1968 (in both English and Spanish). Since then, the *Contemporary BARBIE* era has seen Barbie dolls with amazing features, physical and otherwise. These features are especially exciting for young girls, and Mattel designers and engineers work hard to develop new and interesting features to add even greater dimension to the doll and longevity to the child's play cycle with it. Special effects encompass a variety of forms and features including lights, color, "disappearing acts" or "visual hide and seek," movement (á la Dance Action, Dance Moves, and Gymnast), hair play features and innovative materials (e.g., Bedtime Barbie). Some special effects dolls serve dual-duty: the Angel Lights Barbie, issued in 1992, serves as both a light-up doll and a holiday doll (it can be used as a Christmas tree topper).

*The **Locket Surprise** dolls, although not a huge hit among collectors, employed a new design that allowed the doll's chest cavity to be opened for storing small items.*

Contemporary BARBIE special effects dolls released to date

Year	*Doll*	*Special Effect*
1980	*Beauty Secrets Barbie*	Doll's arms moved by pressing her back
1981	*Western Barbie*	"Winks" with a press of her back
1981	*Magic Curl Barbie*	Curly hair would "uncurl" with spray of Magic Mist
1986	*Magic Moves Barbie*	Doll moves arms with touch of switch
1986	*Dream Glow Barbie*	Gown and parasol glow in the dark
1987	*Dancin' Action Rocker Barbie*	Arms move when waist tilts
1990	*Dance Magic Barbie*	Doll "dances"; icy water changes lip color
1990	*Wet 'N Wild Barbie*	Beachwear changes color in icy water
1991	*Bath Magic Barbie*	"Magical beads" become sponge fashion accessories when dropped into water
1991	*Lights & Lace Barbie*	"Jeweled" belt lit up
1992	*Rappin' Rockin' Barbie*	Boom boxes play rap rhythms
1992	*Rollerblade Barbie*	Skates flicker and flash as they roll
1992	*Teen Talk Barbie*	Doll "talks" (four sayings)
1993	*Angel Lights Barbie*	Fiber optics light; can be used as tree topper
1993	*Locket Surprise Barbie*	Doll's heart-shaped chest cavity opens
1993	*Secret Hearts Barbie*	Pattern in fabric can be temporarily "erased"
1993	*Twinkle Lights Barbie*	Fiber optics light up in the dark
1994	*Bedtime Barbie*	Innovative "cuddly" material
1994	*Bicycling Barbie*	Doll's legs bend to operate bicycle
1994	*Dance 'n Twirl Barbie*	Doll dances in response to music
1994	*Gymnast Barbie*	Doll bends in infinite ways
1995	*Hot Skatin' Barbie*	Poseable/bendable doll "skates"
1995	*Super Power Barbie*	"Magical power shield" lights when touched
1995	*Supertalk Barbie*	Doll "talks" (100,000 sayings)

Factoid

In 1992, Teen Talk Barbie doll could get a job at the Teen Talk Club (cover charge: about $100). This technologically wondrous disco was wired to make the dolls say things like, "Help me pick a hot dance tune!" and "Burgers and fries sound great!" These were just two of the 12 sayings spoken at the Club.

(SOURCE: 1992 Mattel Girls Toys Catalog)

***Twinkle Lights Barbie** incorporated fiber optic technology to glow in the dark.*

*In 1994, **Bedtime Barbie** was manufactured with a cuddly fabric that allowed her to be safely taken to bed by youngsters.*

***Ski Fun Barbie** hit the slopes in 1991*

◆ Athletic Barbie

Major themes for Barbie doll designers since 1959 have been sports, fitness and athletics. Collectors of vintage Barbie doll clothing highly treasure several such outfits, including "Tennis, Anyone," "Ski Queen," "Icebreaker" and "Ballerina," all marketed in the early 1960s. The athlete theme has thus resonated with collectors through the entire history of the Barbie doll.

In the *Contemporary BARBIE* era, the doll was featured as "Our U.S. Olympic Favorite!" Gold Medal Barbie in 1976 (similar versions were made for the Australian, Canadian, and Italian markets). Once again, Barbie will be an Olympian in 1996 to commemorate the Games in Atlanta.

But between the 1976 Olympian and the present day, the Barbie doll has partaken in nearly every sport available. . .with the exception of bungee jumping! She has rollerskated, in-line skated, hot skated, gymnasticated, bicycled, aerobicized, golfed, baseballed and skied. . .to name just a few.

Athletic dolls are highly popular, especially with younger collectors who wish to see the doll "do what I do," according to Black-Perkins. An example of this phenomenon was 1994's fantastically popular Barbie Gymnast doll—one of Mattel's most successful dolls to date in capturing the interests of younger collectors (see sidebar in Chapter 3 for insights into the evolution of the Gymnast Barbie doll).

Barbie took up aerobics in the early 1980s. The phenomenal rise of aerobics as a new fitness regime began in 1971 when Jacki Sorensen, a dancer from Malibu, led the first aerobics dance class of six students in a church basement. By the time the Barbie doll donned her Great Shapes spandex gear in the early 1980s, aerobics had become a whole culture unto itself.

*This **Hot Skatin' Barbie** doll used a jointed body so Barbie could perform ice skating and in-line skating.*

Contemporary BARBIE doll athletes

Rollerskating	1980	
Ballerina	1983	
Great Shapes	1983	
Tennis Star	1986	
Olympic Skating	1987	
Tennis Star Gift Set	1988	
All Stars (Aerobics)	1990	
Ice Capades	1990	
Ice Capades	1991	(2nd edition)
Ski Fun	1991	
Target Baseball	1993	
Target Golf Date	1993	
Bicycling	1994	
Gymnast	1994	
Hot Skatin'	1995	
Winter Sports	1995	(International)
Equestrienne Gift Set	1995	(International)

*This 1995 **Equestrienne Barbie** doll was released for the international market, but was available through select U.S. retail channels. Her riding jacket is reminiscent of Versace print designs.*

***Golf Date Barbie** (left) and **Baseball Barbie** (right) were customized dolls sponsored by Target. They carry out the Barbie-as-athlete theme which has been popular since Barbie first appeared in Ice Breaker and Tennis Anyone outfits in 1960.*

The greatest impact of aerobics, other than on circulatory systems and ideal body types, has been on fashion. The outfits people wear for aerobic dance classes once would have been taboo in public: too sloppy, or in some cases too revealing. But the new, hyper-oxygenated sense of leisure wear, favored now by lots of fashion-conscious people who might not ever dream of actually exercising, says it's fine to go almost anywhere dressed for the gym. Since 1982, when Jane Fonda urged viewers to "go for the burn," on her workout tape—one of the best-selling videotapes in history—it has become common to see women and men in malls, restaurants, and on trains and planes wearing exercise suits and Lycra capri leggings as tight and close-fitting as skin. So, quite naturally, both aerobics and the miracle fabrics of Spandex and Lycra have impacted Barbie doll fashions.

◆ GLOBAL BARBIE

This category of collectors bridges both the young and adult collecting segments. Global Barbie doll collectors tend to collect in one of two ways: Either they go for all of the International/Dolls of the World dolls, or they purchase those dolls representing nations the collector has visited or finds particularly intriguing. Many collectors also acquire Barbie and family dolls available on the international market. Popular editions include the dolls marketed in the Philippines, India, and throughout Europe (these dolls manufactured for the market outside of the U.S. are not detailed in this book; some are described in books listed in the bibliography). Holiday dolls available on the international market have attracted the growing interest of American collectors as well.

For global Barbie doll collectors, the magic year and product development story began in 1980 with the introduction of the Barbie International Collection. Between 1980 and 1984, 11 International dolls were available in the series. In 1985, the name of the line-up was changed to the "Dolls of the World Collection" (DOW), but many collectors still use the short-cut nickname, "Internationals."

At least two new International/DOW Barbie dolls have been made every year since 1980, with the exception of 1985. When the line's name changed that year, the only new doll was the Japanese Barbie.

Collectors often ask about the process used in determining which countries will be represented by DOW dolls in a particular year. Because there have been three DOW dolls produced annually in the latter part of the *Contemporary BARBIE* era, Mattel identifies at least one nation or region in which they have a production plant, subsidiary, or large or emerging collector population. Another of the

This booklet introduced Barbie to children around the world. The Dolls of the World have become one of the most sought after collections in the contemporary era.

three dolls might be a second edition of a previously-released International doll. A third doll will normally be from a country not previously released. In the case of the 1995 Dolls of the World, both the German and the Irish Barbie dolls were second editions; the "new" addition to the series was the Polynesian doll. A fourth doll considered to be part of the DOW line in 1995 was the third Native American Barbie doll.

So, Mattel. . .where are the Polish, French-Canadian, Welsh, Danish, and Hungarian Barbie dolls?

The 25 most prevalent ancestry groups in the United States

1. German
2. Irish
3. English
4. African-American
5. Italian
6. American
7. Mexican
8. French
9. Polish
10. American Indian
11. Dutch
12. Scotch-Irish
13. Scottish
14. Swedish
15. Norwegian
16. Russian
17. French-Canadian
18. Welsh
19. Spanish
20. Puerto Rican
21. Slovak
22. White (other ancestry not listed)
23. Danish
24. Hungarian
25. Chinese

SOURCE: U.S. Bureau of the Census 1990 data,

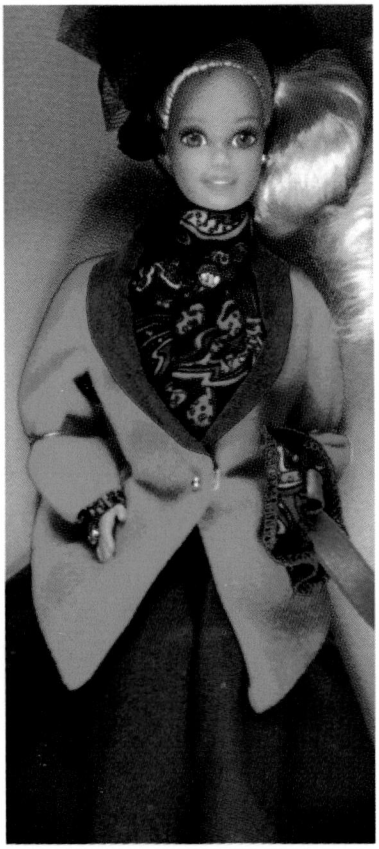

Barbie dolls representing three of the most prevalent ancestry groups in the U.S.—Irish, English and German.

International/Dolls of the World by Year and Mattel Stock Number

1980	*Parisian* (#1600), *Royal* (British, #1601), *Italian* (#1602)
1981	*Oriental* (#3262), *Scottish* (#3263)
1982	*Eskimo* (#3898), *India* (#3897)
1983	*Spanish* (#4031), *Swedish* (#4032)
1984	*Irish* (#7517), *Swiss* (#7541)
1985	*Japanese* (#9481)
1986	*Peruvian* (#2995), *Greek* (#2997)
1987	*German* (#3188), *Icelandic* (#3189)
1988	*Canadian* (#4928), *Korean* (#4929)
1989	*Russian* (#1916), *Mexican* (#1917)
1990	*Nigerian* (#7376), *Brazilian* (#9094)
1991	*Czechoslovakian* (#7330), *Malaysian* (#7329), *Scottish* (reissue, #9845), *Parisian* (reissue, #9843), *Eskimo* (reissue, #9844)
1992	*English* (reissue, #4973), *Spanish* (reissue, #4963), *Jamaican* (#4647)
1993	*Italian* (#2256), *Native American 1* (#1753), *Australian* (#3626)
1994	*Chinese* (#11180), *Kenyan* (#11181), *Dutch* (#11104), *Native American 2* (#11609)
1995	*Native American 3* (#12699), *Polynesian* (#12700), *Irish* (reissue, #12998), *German* (reissue, #12698)
1996	*Norwegian* (#14450), *Japanese* (reissue, #14163) and *Oshogatsu* (#14024), *Mexican* (reissue, #14449), *Indian* (reissue, #14451), *African*

Wal-Mart offered ***Country Bride Barbie*** *as its annual customized doll of 1995 in Caucasian, Black and Hispanic ethnic variations.*

◆ Barbie Doll as Trend-Setter

The Barbie doll, by definition and design, often takes a cue from leading-edge trends in the worlds of fashion, music and athletics. These dolls are especially attractive to younger collectors because they often reflect a fad or activity in which young people are involved. The production lead-times on these dolls are as much as one-half shorter, meaning that from the inception of the design through production, the time-to-market may be one year instead of the usual two.

The following sampling of trendy Barbie dolls reflects fads prevalent at the time of their release:

- Western fashion and music influences have been omnipresent since the advent of the Western Barbie doll in 1981 (#1757) through 1995's Wal-Mart Country Bride (#13614) Barbie doll in pink gingham wedding dress.
- POG Fun Barbie doll (#13239), a Toys 'R Us exclusive in 1994, capitalized on the POG collecting trend that emerged in 1993.
- Sunflower Barbie (#13488) of 1994 echoed the fashion trend of big yellow Van Gogh-inspired sunflowers in clothing, jewelry and interior decorating.
- Troll Barbie (#10257) borrowed the popular collectible gnome theme and translated it to Barbie doll's printed stretch pants, plastic earrings, and attachable troll hair ornaments.
- Rock music has provided the inspiration for several Barbie dolls in the 1980s. In 1988, Barbie and the Sensations (Barbie doll #4931) hearkened back to the Doo-Wop music of the 1950s (note Barbie's short circle skirts, sunglasses and ponytail). In 1986, Barbie and the Rockers (Barbie doll #1140 and #3055, second edition) were dressed in neon-colored spandex club outfits. And, in 1992, Rappin' Rockin' Barbie (#3248), reflected the street music innovated in urban areas of the country. These are far cries from the days when Barbie doll sang at the microphone, sultry and sophisticated, as Solo in the Spotlight (1960-64, #982)!

The limited edition ***Pog Fun Barbie*** *(right) played off on a current fad: pog collecting.* ***Sunflower Barbie*** *(center) combed the fashion magazines and found the sunflower motif popular in 1994.* ***Troll Barbie*** *(far right) capitalized on the resurgence of the troll fad of the 1960s.*

Rocker Barbie *(left) and* ***Barbie of the Sensations*** *(center) harmonize to the strains of their role models—pop divas like Vanessa Williams and Debbie Gibson. In 1995,* ***Dance Moves Barbie*** *(above) was a flashy disco diva, complete with microphone. Karaoke Disco, anyone?*

◆ Barbie as Hair Play Doll

Barbie doll designers have incorporated hair play features in the dolls since the 1970s, when focus groups revealed that hair play was a key dimension in play value associated with Barbie dolls. It is fair to say that most "main line" Barbie dolls, which are targeted to girls under 10 years of age, are hair play dolls (note that most dolls—even the adult-targeted Bob Mackie collector dolls—are packed with small plastic hair brushes). While hair play dolls are not meant to

*In 1993, **Hollywood Hair Barbie** broke the record for the longest-haired Barbie doll of all time. Needless to say, this quintessential hair play doll was very popular with young girls.*

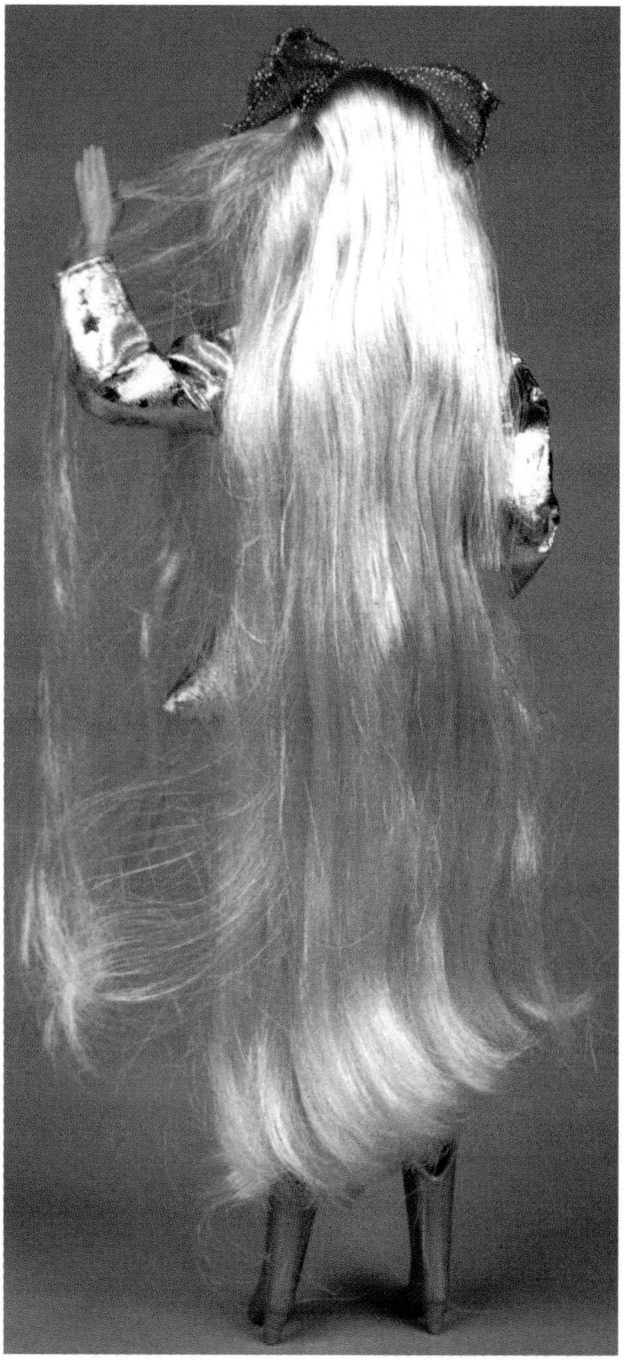

be adult-oriented collector dolls, some collectors acquire the dolls because they appreciate a particular face mold, hair style, or face painting colors, and they use them as mannequins for dressing up (I also know a hairdresser who owns every one of these dolls!).

Supermarkets and drugstore chains offered the **Schooltime Fun** doll in 1995. Befitting the school theme, she carried a backpack and wore flat shoes.

Hair play dolls in the *Contemporary BARBIE* doll era

Beauty Secrets Barbie	1980
Pretty Changes Barbie	1980
Golden Dream Barbie	1981
Magic Curl Barbie	1982
Twirly Curls Barbie	1983
Super Hair Barbie	1987
Perfume Pretty Barbie	1988
Style Magic Barbie	1989
Totally Hair Barbie	1992
Hollywood Hair Barbie	1993
Troll Hair Barbie	1993
Glitter Hair Barbie	1994
Cut 'N Style Barbie	1995

Factoid

Totally Hair Barbie was the most successful Barbie doll in Mattel's history with over 10 million dolls sold worldwide in 1992.

In 1990, ***Cool Looks Barbie*** *appealed to young girls and wore an orange, pink and black outfit that reflected the fad fashions of the time.*

This ***Paint 'n Dazzle*** *activity doll came packaged with fabric paints that could be used to decorate Barbie's denim outfit.*

◆ Holiday Barbie

The new Happy Holidays series, introduced in 1988, was not originally conceived as a series, but as a market test or pilot project. It was the first vinyl Barbie doll ever produced in the at-the-time stratospheric $20 price range, and she was glorious in her new display packaging. The doll was scarce. As Joe Blitman stated in his appearance in the Barbie-as-Scarlett infomercial with Leeza

Transforming Designs

Sometimes designs beget new designs. Kitty Black-Perkins created a unique Barbie doll for an AIDS benefit in Los Angeles in the late 1980s. The one-of-a-kind doll wore a black velvet gown with diamond-like crystals sewn all over it, and the gown lit up. Jill Barad appreciated this doll so much that two mass market versions of it were inspired and manufactured: the 1991 green velvet Happy Holidays (facing page) Barbie doll and the 1993 Angel Lights Barbie.

In 1994, this doll, the seventh in the Happy Holidays series, took the collector market by storm and shot up in value almost instantly. The fur-trimmed gown was an obvious attraction.

Clockwise from top: *The **1989 Happy Holidays Barbie** wore a fresh white dress trimmed with fur. The fuchsia-colored gown of **1990 Happy Holidays Barbie** was a surprise of color for the holiday season. The rich dark green velvet of the **1991 Happy Holidays** gown continues to be a favorite of many Barbie collectors. Among the more glamorous gowns, the **1992 Happy Holidays** version glistened with silver and glass beads. The **1993 Happy Holidays Barbie** doll brightly glowed in her red tulle gown.* (Dolls for these photos loaned by Sandi Holder of the Barbie Attic).

Gibbons, "Mattel didn't know what it had" in terms of sales potential. Only 300,000 units of the doll were produced, and they were sold in a retail-minute. (See the sidebar story about the Happy Holidays Barbie doll in Chapter 1, *Contemporary BARBIE* History).

There are a range of holiday-oriented Barbie dolls suited to every budget. The Happy Holidays Barbie dolls retailed for $30 beginning in 1988, and usually begin at $35 as current releases.

In addition to this line, however, Mattel manufactures a line of more main-line holiday dolls for supermarkets including: Holiday Hostess in 1993, Holiday Dreams in 1994, and Caroling Fun Barbie in 1995. Wholesale or warehouse clubs, such as BJ's Wholesale Club, Pace and Sam's Club, offer a line of holiday dolls that

By Christmastime the Caucasian version of the ***1995 Happy Holidays*** *doll was impossible to find and the Black version was very hard to find. Mattel announced a voucher campaign to give those who missed out a second chance to obtain the doll. . .around Easter 1996!*

The third in the Winter Princess series, ***Peppermint Princess,*** *was available for the 1995 holiday season.*

began with Winter Royale in 1993, continued with the popular Season's Greetings in 1994, and most recently featured the Winter's Eve Barbie in 1995—a doll that quickly disappeared from wholesale club shelves.

Mattel also offers the Winter Theme series of Barbie dolls. These have included: Winter Princess in 1993, Evergreen Princess in 1994, and Peppermint Princess in 1995.

Many collectors, both young and older, enjoy displaying these dolls at Christmastime because their design, colors and fabrications complement the red, green and gold themes of the holiday.

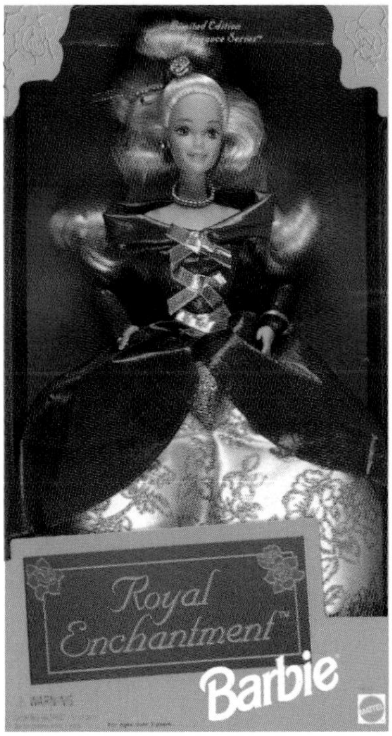

Top row, left to right: Wholesale clubs scored a major hit with this ***Season's Greetings*** *doll released for the 1994 holiday season. Her red velvet fitted jacket and red and green tapestry skirt scored high with adult collectors. A supermarket special from 1994, the* ***Holiday Dreams*** *doll was festive in her holiday-inspired sleepwear, nightcap and wrapped "gift." Wholesale clubs offered* ***Winter's Eve*** *in 1995, following up 1994's spectacularly popular Seasons Greetings. These dolls were whisked off store shelves and quickly increased in value. In 1993,* ***Holiday Hostess*** *was offered by supermarkets and drugstore chains.*

Bottom row, left to right: JC Penney's ***Royal Enchantment*** *was its 1995 customized doll offered for the holiday season. It won favor with many collectors who appreciated the gold and green gown that was priced within many collectors' budgets. Supermarkets and drugstore chains offered the* ***Caroling Fun*** *doll (far right) in 1995, following up the successful Holiday Hostess and Holiday Dreams dolls of the previous two years.*

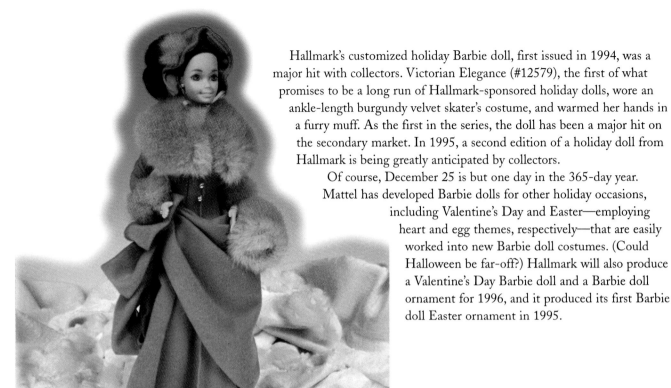

Hallmark's customized holiday Barbie doll, first issued in 1994, was a major hit with collectors. Victorian Elegance (#12579), the first of what promises to be a long run of Hallmark-sponsored holiday dolls, wore an ankle-length burgundy velvet skater's costume, and warmed her hands in a furry muff. As the first in the series, the doll has been a major hit on the secondary market. In 1995, a second edition of a holiday doll from Hallmark is being greatly anticipated by collectors.

Of course, December 25 is but one day in the 365-day year. Mattel has developed Barbie dolls for other holiday occasions, including Valentine's Day and Easter—employing heart and egg themes, respectively—that are easily worked into new Barbie doll costumes. (Could Halloween be far-off?) Hallmark will also produce a Valentine's Day Barbie doll and a Barbie doll ornament for 1996, and it produced its first Barbie doll Easter ornament in 1995.

Hallmark retailed its first customized Barbie doll in 1994, and it met with great success. ***Victorian Elegance Barbie*** *(left) wore an elegant burgundy velvet suit trimmed in fur, with details like a fur muff and ice skates completing the ensemble.*

Hallmark's second holiday offering, ***Holiday Memories,*** *was packaged like the first issue Hallmark doll. Her long skirted suit is trimmed in fur.*

JC Penney's ***Golden Winter Barbie*** *was greatly favored by collectors due to its opulent costume trimmed in fur.*

◆ Evening Gown Barbie Dolls

The roots of the Barbie doll are in the elegant gowns designers have conceived for the doll since 1959, many which were, in fact, inspired by couture designs from both U.S. and European fashion designers. Barbie doll collectors of all ages have always valued attention to evening gown details and the use of "real" fabrics like satins and silks. In the *Contemporary BARBIE* era there are scores of these dolls, favorites of both younger and adult collectors. Sometimes referred to as "glamour dolls," some collectors acquire the doll for the fantasy, others for the beautiful costumes. Regardless, these dolls comprise a large proportion of *Contemporary BARBIE*. Many of the retail store customized dolls, particularly those issued around the Christmas season, are evening-gowned dolls. Porcelain dolls that are not reproductions of vintage Barbie and family dolls can be considered evening gown dolls.

In addition to acquiring dolls wearing fabulous gowns, many collectors also highly prize evening gown fashions that are available in packages separately from the dolls, just as they were available in the 1960s. These would include the collections of fashionable outfits that are developed for both U.S. and foreign consumption such as the Private Collection, Haute Couture, Pret-a-Porter, and Beverly

Porcelain Barbie evening gown dolls

Blue Rhapsody	1986
Enchanted Evening	1987
Benefit Performance	1988
Wedding Day	1989
Solo in the Spotlight	1990
Sophisticated Lady	1990
Gay Parisienne	1991
Plantation Belle	1992
Crystal Rhapsody	1992
Silken Flame	1993
Royal Splendor	1993
Gold Sensation	1993
Silver Starlight	1994
Mattel 50th Anniversary	1995

The Art of Evening Gown Barbie

Barbie doll designer Janet Goldblatt has conceived some of Barbie's most glamorous and elaborate evening ensembles. Several of her personal favorites are Opening Night Barbie, Royal Splendor Barbie, Snow Princess Barbie, and the 1994 Happy Holidays Barbie. It's plain to see that Goldblatt's influences include Christian Lacroix, Valentino, Ungaro and Chanel. While harboring a passion for glamorous evening wear, Goldblatt, who has designed for Mattel for over 20 years, has also done dolls such as Bathtime Barbie, Western Fun Barbie and Animal Lovin' Barbie.

Janet Goldblatt, *Barbie doll designer*

*This ad for **Opening Night Barbie** promoted Janet Goldblatt, designer of the doll. Most advanced Barbie collectors are very familiar with, and highly value, Ms. Goldblatt's designs.*

Mattel is a savvy market-driven organization and has used print advertising to promote Barbie dolls throughout the Contemporary Barbie era. The porcelain dolls, in particular, benefited from this medium because they were targeted to adult collectors.

Hills fashion lines from the 1980s to the present day. Exciting fashion news for late 1995 was that Ann Driskill, Barbie doll and fashion designer at Mattel, had initiated the new Fashion Avenue line designed to be similar in feel to the internationally-distributed fashion lines. Based on early reviews from the Internet, they met with instant success.

Mattel, Barbie and McDonald's have enjoyed a cooperative relationship for several years. Here is their 1993 offering featuring Barbie holding a party for Stacie and Todd.

◆ Barbie Doll as "Foodie"

A trend in *Contemporary Barbie* involves cross-merchandising the doll with food companies. The Barbie doll has been paired with various food producers as both special edition dolls and as premiums. Food companies that have collaborated with Barbie and family dolls since 1980 include Coca-Cola, Kool-Aid, Kraft, Little Debbie, McDonald's, McGlynn's Bakery (and other regional bakeries), Pepsi and Pizza Hut. Most of these dolls tend to wear faddish fashions to appeal to younger collectors, although recently it is clear that some newer issues are targeted to the adult collector as well. This was the case with the Little Debbie Barbie, issued in 1993. Many adult collectors are interested in acquiring dolls through premiums, and many of the "foodie" Barbie dolls fall into that category.

◆ BARBIE THE SUN WORSHIPER

It can be argued that the Barbie doll has been a sun lover since her inception in 1959, since the first Barbie dolls were clad in a zebra-striped swimsuit, sunglasses and stiletto slides. For collectors, the "official" sun-loving era was commemorated in 1971 with the first Sun Gold Malibu Barbie, followed by Sun Set ("Today's Together Teens"), Sun Lovin' (from 1979 to 1981—the dolls with peek-a-boo tans), Sunsational ("She's got the California look!"), and Sun Gold Malibu Barbie dolls. The Sun Gold dolls were the last to incorporate the word "Malibu" in their name. In Barbie doll's sun-loving history, after Malibu came Tropicals, Island Fun, Beach Blast and Wet 'N Wild Barbie and friend dolls.

Some collectors call this theme the "swimsuit line." They tend to be among the least expensive dolls sold each year, having been designed for mass market consumption.

Sun, beach and water fun *Contemporary BARBIE* dolls

Sun Lovin' Malibu Barbie	1980
Sunsational Malibu Barbie	1981
Hawaiian Barbie	1982
Sun Gold Malibu Barbie	1984
Tropical Malibu Barbie	1986
Beach Blast Malibu Barbie	1988
California Dream Barbie	1988
Island Fun Barbie	1988
Wet 'N Wild Barbie	1990
Bathtime Fun Barbie	1991
Hawaiian Fun Barbie	1991
Mermaid Barbie	1991
Bath Blast Barbie	1992
Bath Magic Barbie	1992
Sun Sensation Barbie	1992
Glitter Beach Barbie	1993
Fountain Mermaid Barbie	1993
Sun Jewel Barbie	1994
Swim 'N Dive Barbie	1994
Baywatch Barbie	1995
Bubble Angel Barbie	1995
Tropical Splash Barbie	1995

*This **Sun Jewel Barbie** doll is typical of bathing beauty Barbie dolls that hearken back to Barbie's origins in her zebra-striped swimsuit.*

Barbie hits the big time in the Big Top as FAO Schwarz continued its popular customized Barbie line with Circus Star Barbie *in 1995.*

Chapter 6

Custom Made

Customized product is an area of Barbie® collecting that is growing every year and greatly contributes to the sheer volume of new dolls entering the market. Beginning in the early 1960s, retail giants have been working with Mattel to create Barbie dolls consistent with their stores' image and customer base.

In the vintage Barbie doll era, Mattel had product exclusives with Montgomery Wards (the 1962 Barbie Mix 'N Match Set, #861), Spiegel (the 1962 Barbie and Ken Tennis Set, #892), Sears (the 1966 Sears Color Magic Barbie Gift Set, #1043) and JC Penney (whose 1969 catalog showed Talking Barbie, available in a Pink Premier Gift Set).

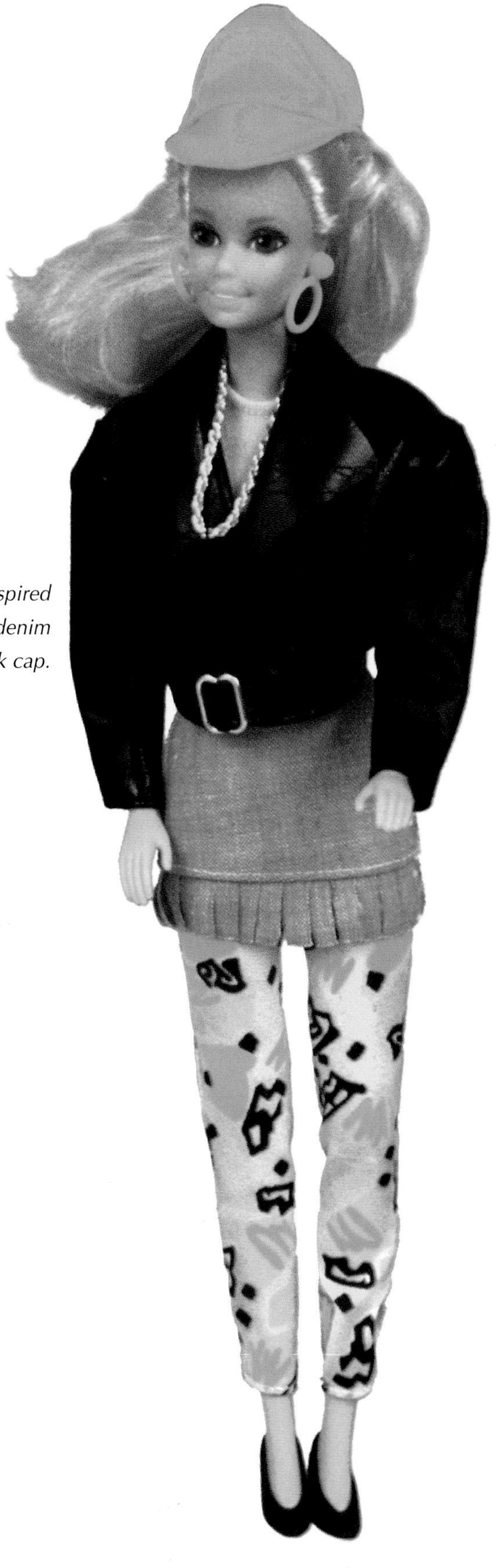

*In 1992, Target stores offered **Wild Style Barbie,** dressed in a Desperately Seeking Susan/Madonna-inspired combination of black "leather" jacket, print leggings, denim skirt, long gold chain and neon pink cap.*

*Target's **Steppin' Out Barbie** (left), the store's customized offering in 1995, wore a short fuchsia and black cocktail dress and was nicely accessorized. Hills offered this customized **Blue Elegance Barbie** doll in 1992 (right), dressed in a turquoise gown with dotted tulle and satin sleeves.*

By the 1980s, customized product development was a well-entrenched tradition between Barbie dolls and retail establishments. But only the largest retailers can take full advantage of customized editions since Mattel requires a minimum run before they will produce a special item. Many customized dolls are released in the fourth quarter of the year in anticipation of the holiday gift season.

FAO Schwarz
Silver Screen Barbie
from 1994.

◆ FAO Schwarz

The Barbie doll went "up-market" when FAO Schwarz got into the act. The store opened its first Barbie Boutique—the 1500-square-foot "Barbie on Madison Avenue"—at its New York flagship store in late autumn 1992.

The opening of the boutique was heralded by more than 100 journalists, Kathie Lee Gifford, and, of course, an appropriate and customized Madison Avenue Barbie doll (who, with her upswept blond hairdo, dark glasses, Chanel-inspired suit and ubiquitous shopping bag, broadly resembled Ivana Trump). The entire FAO Schwarz building was wrapped in a giant pink ribbon for the event, and pink carpet stretched from Fifth Avenue to the Madison Avenue entrance. Mattel announced at a ribbon-cutting event that $50,000 from the store's initial proceeds would be donated to the Pediatric AIDS Foundation, the national organization founded by Elizabeth Glaser to help children with AIDS and fight against prenatal spread of the disease from mother to child.

Early success of the Barbie on Madison Avenue boutique resulted in eventual expansion of the facility to a two-story "townhouse." A second Barbie Boutique was created at the FAO Schwarz store in San Francisco in 1993, and today there are special Barbie Boutiques in FAO Schwarz locales across the U.S. In addition, two Barbie Boutiques run in association with the Hudson Bay Co. retail chain are located in Canada.

FAO Schwarz also joined similar efforts launched by Bloomingdale's and Meijer's stores in coming up with an appropriately-clad version of a shopping Barbie doll. In 1994, Shopping Spree Barbie (#12749) made her debut. Wearing an FAO Schwarz oversized sweatshirt and purple stirrup pants, she carried the store's universally recognizable shopping bag. (The doll's packaging bore the words "Souvenir Edition," something never before seen on a Barbie doll box).

*This customized doll, **Shopping Spree Barbie,** from FAO Schwarz was popular with both young and older collectors. She came packaged with an FAO Schwarz shopping bag and was labeled a "souvenir" doll.*

Rockette Barbie *from FAO Schwarz practices her kicks in front of her stylized box.*

*This hard-to-find **Donna Karan Barbie** doll was a big hit with collectors. A brunette with sunglasses, and the second in Bloomingdale's customized series, she carries the famous "Big Brown Bag" from the store. . .Barbie-sized, of course!*

◆ Bloomingdale's

Hot on the heels of the FAO Schwarz up-scale shopping Barbie doll was Bloomingdale's Savvy Shopper from Nicole Miller, another customized success story involving Ann Driskill. According to Lisa McKendall of Mattel Toys, "1994 was the first year we did a special doll with Bloomingdale's: the Nicole Miller. The store could not keep them on the shelves; they sold out everything we could manufacture. Because Bloomingdale's had a long-term relationship with Donna Karan, the store decided to follow up Miller's success with Karan." Driskill recalled: "They [Bloomingdale's] sent us actual clothes [from Karan's studio in New York]. At first they didn't know if they wanted to do an outfit from her latest line. I found a pink jacket from the current collection that really was close to 'Barbie pink,' but the style didn't scream 'Donna Karan.' We made up a prototype of this, but we knew we wouldn't go in this direction. I went to New York on vacation and visited her studio. I met with her husband [Stephen Weiss] and a bunch of other people. So they set up some actual clothes and thought we should do something from her original collection as it was going to be her tenth anniversary in her own business. The consensus was that we should not do 'the pink.' For her tenth anniversary, we thought we'd do something quintessential Karan. Everybody remembers the original turtleneck body suits with the wrap skirt and the big shawl. So we worked that up, sent it to them and they approved it. It was really fun to work on."

Ann Driskill
Just Call Her "Ms. Customized Product"

I have to admit to gushing somewhat when I met Ann Driskill for the first time, but it is fair to say that the FAO Schwarz Madison Avenue Barbie is among my favorite Barbie dolls in the *Contemporary BARBIE* era. Driskill designed the doll. So how did the doll develop, anyway?

FAO Schwarz wanted a special doll to kick off the opening of the store's boutique—Barbie on Madison Avenue—in their New York flagship store. According to Driskill, "They [FAO Schwarz] wanted to see a New Yorker shopping in a realistic-type outfit. It was right up my alley because it was related to real clothes," Driskill explained. Her background was in fashion design, an area she was active in for several years prior to joining Mattel. The team at FAO Schwarz sent Driskill tear sheets of various designs from magazines. "I did lots of sketches," Driskill said, "and then we had to complete the final design in two days. It was one of the fastest development times of any doll, especially for a customized product. It was first of the series and different than anything else they had done before. . . ."

I asked Driskill about the doll's relationship to Ivana: art imitating life, or what? Driskill replied smartly, "We didn't plan it that way, but we always knew there would be an 'Ivana' connection, just as with Silver Screen Barbie, there was a 'Marilyn' connection."

SOURCE: Author's interview with Ann Driskill, August 1995.

◆ Toys 'R Us (TRU)

The leader in sheer volume for customized doll product every year is Toys 'R Us (TRU). Since the early 1980s, TRU has been associated with over 50 customized Barbie dolls.

In 1995, TRU introduced its most exclusive doll yet: Sapphire Dream Barbie (#13255), promising to be the first in a series called the Society Style Collection.

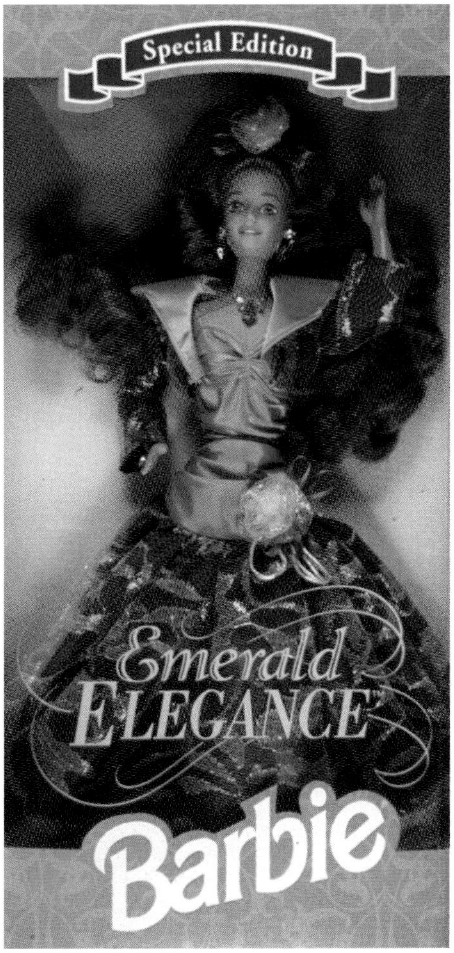

Toys 'R Us successfully appealed to adult collectors with this doll, ***Emerald Elegance*** *(above), probably because it featured rare red hair.*

Toys 'R Us offered both Caucasian and Black versions of this popular doll, ***Radiant in Red*** *(left), in 1992.*

Dressed in a rich blue velvet gown cinched at the waist with a gold and crystal brooch, her ensemble is topped with a sheer gold-painted wrap.

TRU has about 450 stores in the U.S. and, like Mattel, is optimistic about growth overseas. TRU currently operates in Canada, the United Kingdom, Germany, Singapore, Hong Kong, France and Japan, among other countries. It is likely that TRU's growing involvement as a major retail entity overseas will play a significant role in Barbie's presence in the global market.

See the Appendix for a complete list of customized TRU dolls, all identified with the prefix "TRU."

Barbie received her letter in fashion excellence in this ***Back to School*** *doll (top), offered through supermarket and drugstore chains in 1993. Toys 'R Us offered collectors the* ***Purple Passion*** *glamour doll (bottom) in 1995.*

In 1994 Mattel celebrated fifteen years of Hispanic Barbie-and-family dolls with the ***Quinceañera Teresa*** *doll. She features the Teresa face mold, a favorite among adult collectors.*

Toys 'R Us went up-scale with its first in a series called the High Society Collection in 1995. ***Sapphire Dream's*** *gown of royal blue velvet was warmly greeted by many adult collectors.*

◆ Sears

Sears was arguably the first department store to sponsor customized Barbie dolls in the contemporary era. The company marked its 100th anniversary with the Celebration Barbie doll (#2998) in 1986. According to that year's Sears Wish Book (the firm's holiday catalog), Barbie was dressed "in her most glamorous gown ever." The ensemble consisted of a long pink-and-silver skirt worn over a silver lamé jumpsuit. But this doll also wore something that hadn't been seen for a decade: a wrist tag. It read: "Celebration™ Barbie® doll Sears 100th Anniversary."

Sears offered an exclusive Black Barbie doll in 1990—Lavender Surprise Barbie (#5588). The company did not sponsor another Black exclusive doll until 1992, when Shani doll was offered in a gift set (#5882).

To celebrate the company's centennial in 1986, Sears commissioned this **Celebration Barbie** *doll. This custom would be repeated in future years by Wal-Mart, FAO Schwarz, and even Mattel itself in 1995.*

Sears' exclusive dolls

Year	Doll	Stock No.
1986	*Celebration Barbie*	2998
1987	*Star Dream*	4550
1988	*Lilac & Lovely*	7669
1989	*Evening Enchantment*	3596
1990	*Lavender Surprise* (Caucasian)	9049
1990	*Lavender Surprise* (Black)	5588
1991	*Southern Belle*	2586
1992	*Dream Princess*	2306
1992	*Blossom Beautiful*	3817
1993	*Enchanted Princess*	10292
1994	*Silver Sweetheart*	12410
1995	*Ribbons & Roses*	13911

◆ Other Stores

For the complete list of custom dolls by store, please refer to the Appendix: Comprehensive List of *Contemporary BARBIE* Dolls.

Barbie dolls have been sponsored by these retailers and other organizations

- Ames
- Applause
- Bloomingdale's
- Child World/Children's Palace
- Disney
- FAO Schwarz
- Hallmark
- Hills
- Home Shopping Club
- JC Penney
- Kmart
- McGlynn's Bakery
- Meijer's
- Mervyn's
- Osco
- Sears
- Service Merchandise
- Shop-Ko
- Spiegel
- Supermarkets nationwide
- Target
- Toys 'R Us
- Venture
- Wal-Mart
- Wessco
- Wholesale clubs (Sam's Club, Costco, BJ's Wholesale Club, Price Club)
- Winn-Dixie
- Woolworth

Wal-Mart's 1994 ***Country Western Star*** *(above) was done in Caucasian, Black and Hispanic (Teresa) variations. Service Merchandise store and catalog stocks of the 1995 customized* ***Ruby Romance*** *(right) were quickly depleted.*

In 1994, Service Merchandise scored a major hit with collectors with this ***City Sophisticate*** *doll, featuring a gold and black ensemble with velvet beret.*

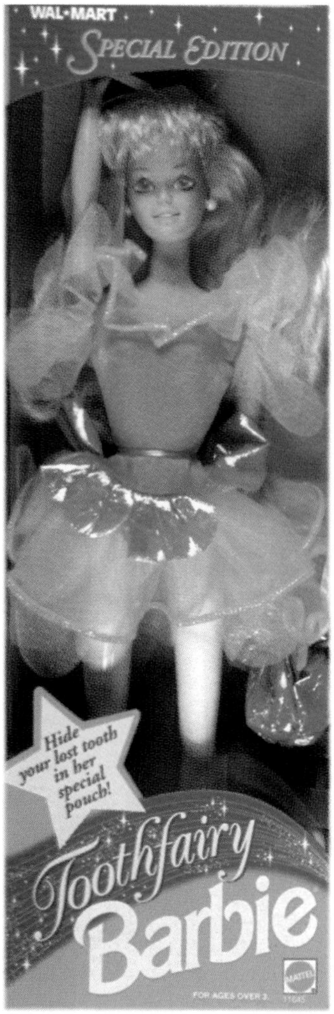

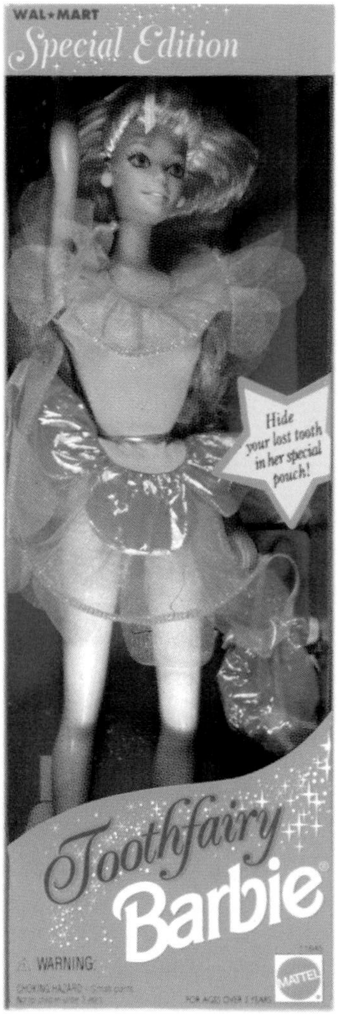

Wal-Mart's ninth customized Barbie doll, ***Toothfairy Barbie*** *(front of two box variations shown at left, and back of boxes depicted below), included a small bag in which a child could store a lost tooth while awaiting the Toothfairy.*

The first ***Disney Fun Barbie*** *doll from 1990 (right) was packaged with a mouse balloon and wore an outfit made with mouse-printed fabric. In 1993, Disney and Mattel paired up for a second* ***Disney Fun Barbie*** *doll (far right). This one came complete with Mickey Mouse ears (á la the Mouseketeers) and fabric printed with Mickey Mouse silhouettes.*

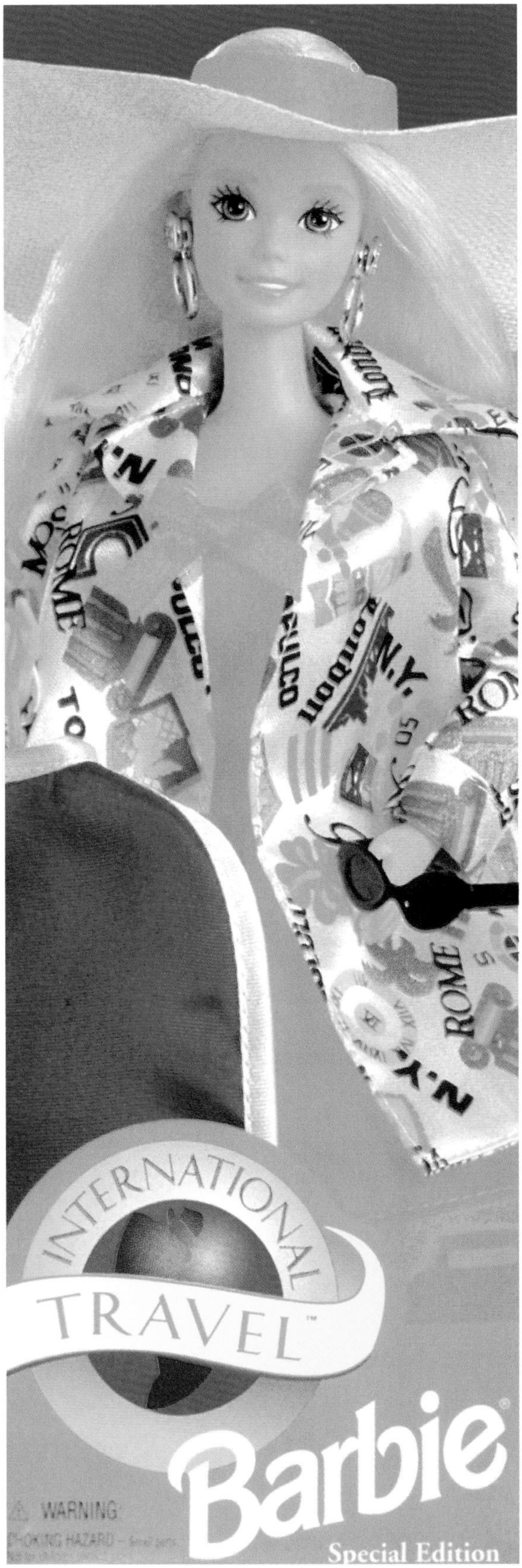

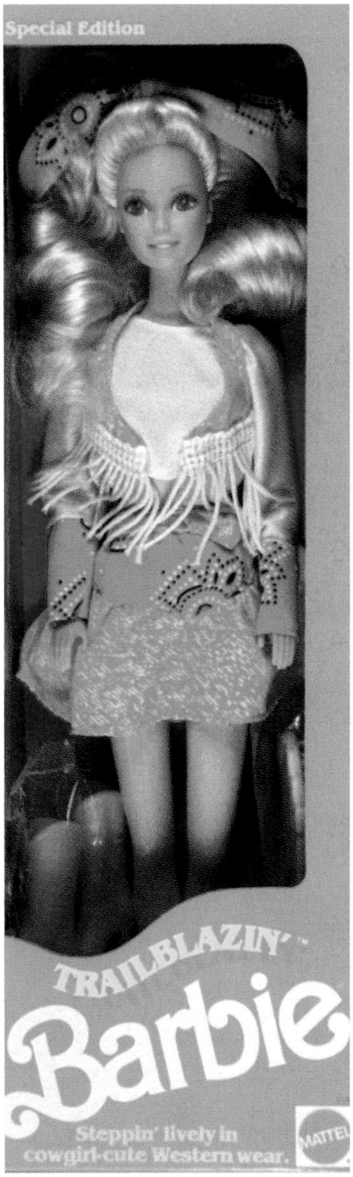

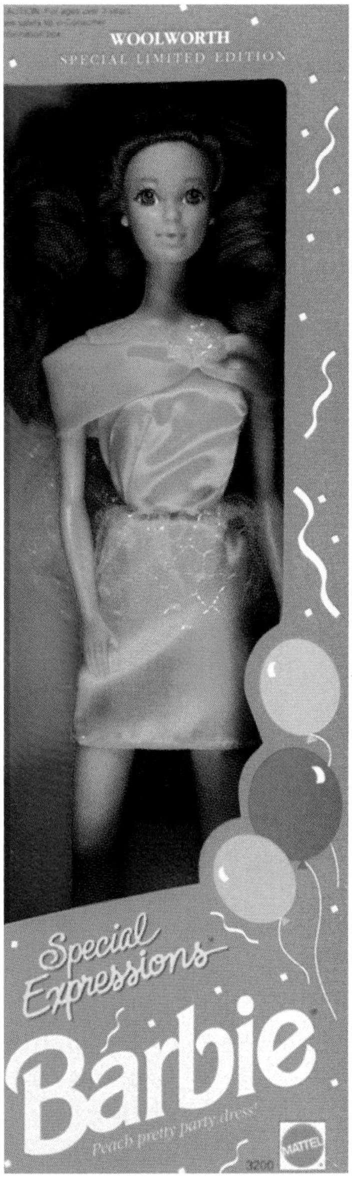

A so-called supermarket special in 1991, ***Trailblazin' Barbie*** *(above left) came dressed in a red bandana-print trimmed outfit and capitalized on the western fashion trend used throughout the* Contemporary Barbie *era. This first Hispanic doll for Woolworth's in 1992 (right) was from the store's customized* ***Special Expressions*** *series.*

Wessco sponsored the customized ***International Travel Barbie*** *doll, exclusively available through duty free airport terminals and through TWA.*

*JC Penney dazzled collectors with **Night Dazzle Barbie** in 1994 (right). Her costume was a variation based on a ready-to-wear outfit for the European market.*

*This 1993 example of a shopping Barbie doll, **Shopping Fun,** was customized for Meijer's, a Midwestern retail chain, and came complete with shopping bag. Later versions of similar shopping dolls, from Bloomingdale's to Spiegel, came with similar carry bags.*

*Hills **Polly Pocket** (left) was a surprise hit among collectors in 1994, incorporating the tiny Barbie-pocket-size dolls popular with young girls.*

◆ Premiums

Cross-merchandising the Barbie doll with other brands, primarily in the form of premiums, is not a story or technique exclusive to the contemporary era. The Barbie doll has worked with a range of consumer products and brands since the 1960s. Barbie's first premium, offered in 1962, was a free *Barbie* magazine earned with box tops from Kellogg's Corn Flakes. Another early Barbie doll premium was a tie-in with Carnation food products in 1963. The most famous premium campaign for Barbie in the vintage era was arguably the Twist 'N Turn Trade-In Barbie doll offered by Mattel in 1967. Regardless of source or type, contemporary era Barbie doll collectors have savored the opportunity to take advantage of a variety of premiums since 1980.

The majority of premium programs occurred between 1989 and 1992 via the "Pink Stamp" program. Regular Barbie merchandise and special items were available through the redemption of pink stamps found in select Barbie costume packages. The final version of the program offered five items for joining the program, a number of products in exchange for stamps alone, or a "speed plan" which was a combination of stamps and cash.

In 1989, Ralston-Purina, Inc. began a "Breakfast with Barbie" promotion. Each Breakfast with Barbie cereal box showed a 1989 Barbie doll next to a bowl of cereal. Featured dolls included SuperStar Barbie, Cool Times Barbie, Dance Club Barbie, Beach Blast Barbie, and the 1989 Happy Holidays Barbie doll.

Regional bakeries in 1991 offered a "Specialty Deco-Pak Barbie Doll," which was a ballerina Barbie that could sit (perhaps pirouette?) on top of a decorated cake (#1511 for the Caucasian doll, #1534 for the Black doll). They resemble 1991's My First Barbie doll, but differ in hairstyle, face paint and costume. In 1995, McGlynn Bakery also offered the doll as a premium.

Kraft General Foods, Inc., has offered Barbie doll premiums through its Kool-Aid Wacky Warehouse division. Kool-Aid's first special edition Barbie doll offering in 1993 was the so-called Collector's Edition Barbie Doll (#10309). A year later, Kool-Aid celebrated Barbie's 35th anniversary with a Kool-Aid Wacky Warehouse Barbie premium (#11763). The offer expired December 31, 1994, and required a completed form, 300 Kool-Aid points and $1.50 for postage and handling. (For readers who are not Kool-Aid fans, the "deal" equated to 200 quarts of Kool-Aid consumption, calculated at three points per two quart sugar-sweetened package). Seen another way, and based an average retail price of 50¢ for a one-quart packet of drink mix in 1993, the doll's cost would translate to $100 per doll. While this sounds unattainable, in fact the premiums were very successful.

Kraft Foods, Kool-Aid's parent company, offered a special edition Barbie doll (#11546) through the company's Kraft Treasures premium facility. This doll required 220 points, amounting to about 74 boxes of Kraft macaroni and cheese dinner, or an equivalent cost of about $50 per doll.

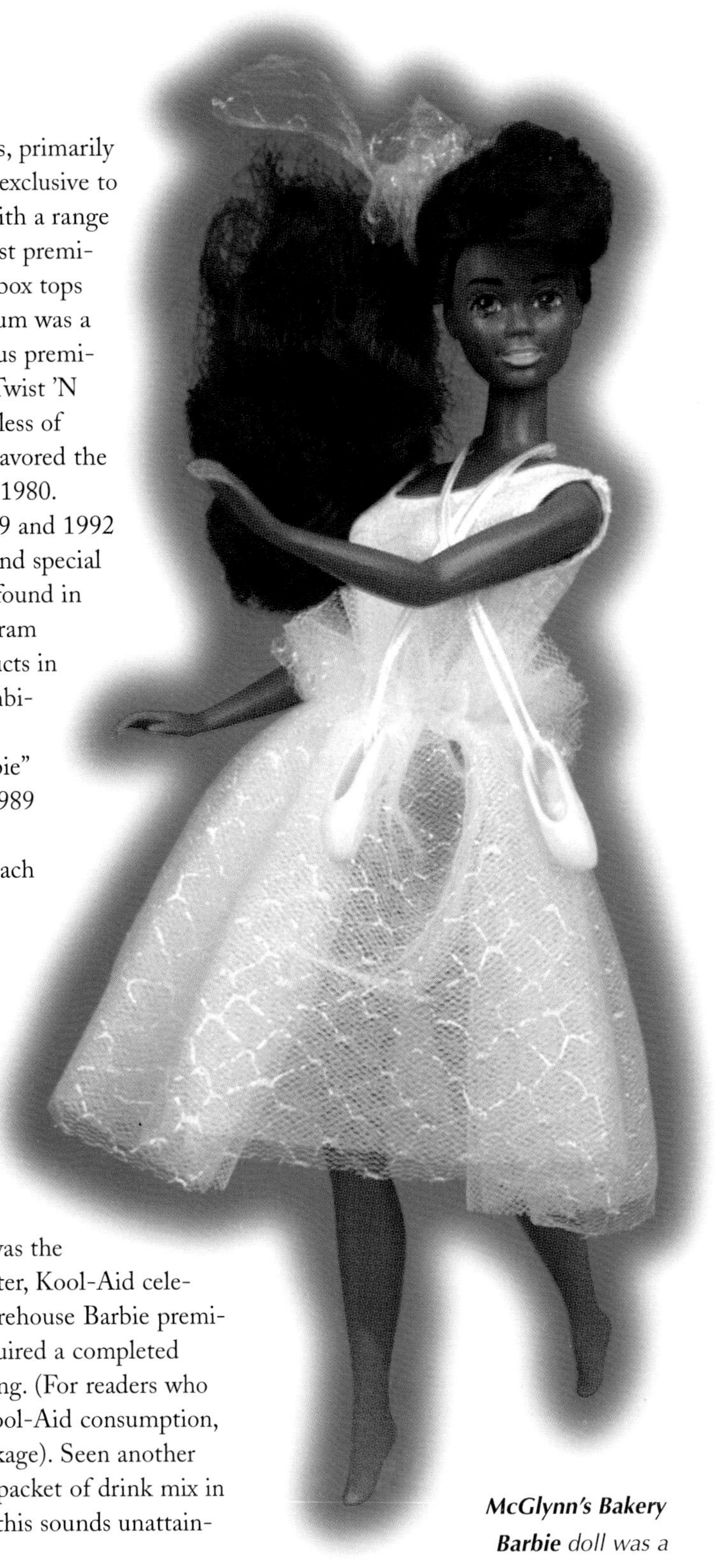

***McGlynn's Bakery Barbie** doll was a much sought-after doll in very limited distribution.*

(Sandi Holder, at The Barbie Attic, provided this doll for the photograph)

Barbie doll was paired with a favorite American snack food in this ***Little Debbie Barbie.*** *She was dressed in the costume of this longtime American icon. A second version is due out in 1996.*

McKee Foods Corporation holds the trademark on Little Debbie®—the snack line introduced in 1960, one year after Barbie doll entered the market. By 1993, both were mega-brands in their respective categories. When the two came together for a 1993 premium—Little Debbie Barbie (#10123)—the doll effectively captured the quintessential Little Debbie personality. She wore a blue and white checked dress and a sparkling-white apron customized with an iron-on Little Debbie label.

◆ Poetic License

In 1991, Mattel launched Barbie For Girls, an "umbrella concept" designed to expand the licensing potential of Barbie. Barbie Boutiques were set up with major retailers across the United States, providing a vehicle to promote and sell such licensed items as the World POG Federation's POG™ milk caps, Western Publishing's coloring books, Colorforms' stick-on books, Enesco's collectible figurines, and Wundies' sleepwear.

The licensing program has met with great success. The categories suitable for licensing arrangements with the Barbie doll brand are exploding, from publishing and fashion accessories to entertainment. The latter area even included the Barbie doll moving into a Nintendo game, not to mention a physical fitness exercise video.

To enforce licensee consistency in using the Barbie doll brand, Mattel publishes detailed annual style guides that assist licensees in packaging and promoting their products. Once a company has secured a license associated with the Barbie doll brand, they must follow through in a consistent way from the image of the product, the colors used, and the packaging that will contain the product. "Barbie pink" packages, for example, utilize very specific colors—combining a specified background color with accent colors in very precise proportions.

Companies that have licensed the Barbie brand

3M	Self-stick wall decorations
Abbeville Press	Books
American Postcard Company Inc.	Postcards
Anagram International, Inc.	Mylar balloons, balloon weights
The Ashton-Drake Galleries, Ltd.	3-D Holiday ornaments
Basic Fun, Inc.	Keychains
Best Personalized Books, Inc.	Personalized story books
The Bibb Company	Bedding
Borden Home Wallcoverings	Wallborders
The Bradford Exchange	Sculpted 3-D plates
Brookfield Athletic Company	Athletic goods
Buena Vista Home Video	Videos
Caboodles, Division of Plano Molding Co.	Plastic molded organizer cases
Chilton-Globe, Inc.	Playsets
Colorbok Paper Products	Stationery
Colorforms	Stick-on books, sewing cards
Craft House Corporation	Activity kits, arts and crafts kits

Designs from the Deep	Decoupage giftware
Disney Book Publishing, Inc. (FunWorks)	Hardcover interactive books
Enesco Corporation	Collectible giftware
ERO Industries, Inc.	Swimwear, slumber bags, luggage, playtents
Fisher-Price, Division of Mattel, Inc.	Outdoor playhouse
Fossil, Inc.	Watches
Franco Manufacturing Company, Inc.	Beachwear and related items
Franklin Mint	Collectibles
The Haddad Apparel Group, Ltd.	Outerwear
Hallmark Cards, Inc.	Greeting cards, giftwrap, stationery, calendars
Hamilton Lamp Corporation	Lamps, switch plates
Hope Industries	PVC jewelry and hair accessories, watches, clocks
i care International	Sunglasses
Imaginings 3/Diamond Publishing	Sticker books and stickers
Impact, Inc.	Bookpacks, shoulder bags, luggage
J.H. Design Group	Leather jackets, caps
Jerry Leigh	T-shirts, sweatshirts, shorts, denim jacket, caps
Kalimar, Inc.	Cameras, binocular, film, batteries
Kash 'N' Gold Ltd.	Telephones
Kentucky Derby Hosiery Company	Socks
KIDdesigns, Inc.	Children's electronics
KidNATION, Inc. (Pagoda Trading Co.)	Footwear
Knitwaves, Inc.	Girls apparel
Mamiye Brothers, Inc.	Swimwear
Marvel Family Publishing	Comic books, magazines
Matrix	Collectible giftware
Mattel, Inc.	Nostalgic Barbie Doll
MBI Inc.	Porcelain figurines
Meltzer Industries Corp.	Blanket sleepers
Michael Anthony Jewelers, Inc.	Precious metal jewelry
Micro Games of America	LCD handheld games
The Miner Group, Inc./Mello Smello	Stickers, sticker albums, sticker activities
Murat Caviale, Inc.	*Barbie Bazaar* magazine
Nicole Miller	Apparel
Peck-Aubry	Paper dolls
Power Wheels, Division of Mattel, Inc.	Battery-powered child-size vehicles
Rand International	Bicycles and accessories
Rubie's Costume Co., Inc.	Dress-up outfits, Halloween costumes, masks
Sara Lee Knit Products	Jersey tops and pants
Sara Lee Hosiery - L'eggs	Girls tights
Shadow Boxer NYC	Loungewear and pajamas
Simplicity Pattern Co., Inc.	Clothing patterns, iron-on transfers
Spectra Star, Inc.	Kites, yo-yos, flying discs
Tara Toy Corporation	Rubber stampers
The Thermos Company	Hard and soft-sided lunch kits
Tsumura International	Personal care products
Universal/Logo 7	Hats, caps, visors, gloves, scarves
Western Publishing Group, Inc.	Books, paper dolls, arts and crafts kits
Wilton Industries, Inc.	Bakeware
World POG Federation	Milk caps
Wundies, Inc.	Sleepwear
Zak Designs, Inc.	Tabletop items, bathroom accessories

SOURCE: Mattel, Inc. Marketing

Bob Mackie's 1995 offering, Goddess of the Sun, *had the golden sequins of the first Gold Mackie and the surreal "flames" reflected in Neptune Barbie's earlier mermaid costume.*

Chapter 7

Pure Couture

Not everyone can afford to buy full size original Bob Mackie, Christian Dior, or Nicole Miller ensembles, but buying these famous designs for the Barbie® doll is in the realm of financial possibility for many collectors. As Anne Parducci, marketing director of collectible Barbie dolls at Mattel, noted, "Barbie allows people to dream. We don't want to forget that she is about fashion, beauty and glamour. She allows a woman to dream about being in that gown. . . ."

Avid Barbie collectors highly prize the couture-designed evening gown dolls of the *Contemporary BARBIE* era. This segment of Barbie doll collecting generally represents the ultimate in terms of sophistication, attention to detail and, more often than not, price.

◆ Bob Mackie

To many collectors, Bob Mackie represents the créme de la créme in Barbie dolls. As of autumn, 1995, these high-end dolls were selling on the secondary market for as much as $1,000 for Mackie's first Gold Barbie doll, and over $1,000 for the Empress Bride Barbie doll. Mackie designs Barbie dolls and costumes consistent with his designs for Hollywood, Broadway, and the Follies Bergere.

As *People* magazine described in 1994, "Bob Mackie [has] worked with more stars than Carl Sagan." In fact, Mackie's exposure early in life to Hollywood movies and

Bob Mackie's Barbie doll designs to date

Issued	Doll	Stock No.
1990	*Gold*	5405
1991	*Starlight Splendor*	2703
1991	*Platinum*	2704
1992	*Empress Bride*	4247
1992	*Neptune Fantasy*	4248
1993	*Masquerade Ball*	10803
1994	*Queen of Hearts*	12046
1995	*Goddess of the Sun*	14056

Bob Mackie's ***Queen of Hearts.***

Every Bob Mackie Barbie doll comes packaged with a copy of Mr. Mackie's sketch of the doll. Mackie's ***Empress Bride Barbie*** *sketch is shown here.*

glamorous stars such as Betty Grable and Rita Hayworth are evident in his designs for the Barbie doll. After he attended Chouinard Art Institute in Los Angeles (which ironically was the alma mater of Charlotte Johnson, the first designer of Barbie doll outfits), Mackie was discovered by legendary costumer Edith Head in 1961 while working as a novice designer at Paramount Studios. He soon found himself designing for Marlene Dietrich, Mitzi Gaynor and Ann-Margret, and later for Cher, Diana Ross, Bernadette Peters and Carol Burnett. Mackie has won six Emmy Awards, plus Oscar nominations for *Funny Girl, Lady Sings the Blues* and *Pennies from Heaven.*

In a recent interview, Mackie talked about his showy fashion aesthetic. He said, "I'd rather be recognized for glitz than for khaki-colored canvas." Looking at his Barbie doll designs, Mackie should be a happy man. He is well-loved by legions of Barbie collectors.

◆ Nicole Miller

Barbie, the Savvy Shopper, was Nicole Miller's first Barbie doll design, created expressly for Bloomingdale's in 1994. Retail priced at $65, this doll has been a secondary market treasure, fetching between $90 and $120 in 1995. She is dressed in a prototypical Nicole Miller silk print coat (similar in lines to the navy taffeta coat from the highly prized 1960 ensemble, Easter Parade) and the proverbial "little black dress" in black velvet, complemented by matching velvet bag and fuchsia spike heels. Of course, she carries her Bloomie's shopping bag wherever she goes!

While her design for Bloomingdale's first Barbie doll exclusive was superb, Miller generally designs wonderful clothes and accessories for people substantially larger than 11½ inches. Her silk-based goods inspired by the Barbie doll include pajamas, vests, totebags and wallets, which Miller designed in both 1994 and 1995. The 1994 design commemorated the 35th anniversary and can sometimes be found on dealers' lists.

Miller is considered to be one of the most witty fashion designers practicing today. Her clients include Demi Moore, Meryl Streep and Linda Evans. She attended the prestigious Rhode Island School of Design before moving to New York City.

Thanks to Nicole Miller's Barbie doll, designer Barbie dolls have become big business at Bloomingdale's. The chain sold $1 million worth of the doll in 1994, excluding catalog sales. According to Bud Konheim, president of Nicole Miller, the company did about $3 million in full size ready-to-wear sales at Bloomingdale's chain-wide in 1994.

Nicole Miller has more Barbie projects in the works. According to Bloomingdale's, Mattel is creating a redheaded designer Barbie doll based on Miller, which will debut in 1996. The dolls will be distributed through 20 company-owned Nicole Miller boutiques, FAO Schwarz and Bloomingdale's.

***Savvy Shopper,** Bloomingdale's first customized Barbie doll, designed by Nicole Miller, was an instant hit. The doll wears a silk coat, in typical Nicole Miller style, over a little black dress. Of course, she carries her Bloomingdale's shopping bag.*

◆ BillyBoy*

"Le Nouveau Theatre de la Mode" was BillyBoy*'s special exhibit of international high fashion designers who each contributed a design for Barbie in 1985. BillyBoy* was one of the first Barbie observers to recognize and document the haute couture aspects of Barbie, as recorded in his book: *Barbie, Her Life and Times.* His two dolls created for Mattel include Le Nouveau Theatre de la Mode and the Feelin' Groovy (aka Glamour-a-Go-Go) Barbie. These are highly prized and valued on the secondary market. BillyBoy* subsequently left the Barbie doll behind to create an entire spinoff line of fashion dolls called "Mdvanii and Friends."

BillyBoy* began collecting Barbie dolls when he was 13. Ever joking, in an interview with *People* (December 2, 1985), BillyBoy* claimed to be "a product of the Flintstones and the Jetsons." In an interview with the Franklin Mint *Almanac* in 1987, BillyBoy* referred to Barbie as, "Nice and responsible and sweet and kind and loving...cool to the max, neat-o, snazzy, grooved out, hyper, ultra super stuff."

BillyBoy* is reputed to own 11,000 Barbie dolls and some 10,000 other dolls, along with a huge collection of couture garments from Elsa Schiaparelli, Dior, Chanel, Balenciaga, Patou, Lanvin, and other designers.

This ad for BillyBoy's* ***Feelin' Groovy Barbie*** *doll was based on bright, energetic colors and a dynamic layout to reflect the attitude of both designer and doll. It sharply contrasted with other ads in the 1986 doll magazine in which it was placed.*

BillyBoy* and Le Nouveau Theatre de la Mode

Le Nouveau Theatre de la Mode Barbie doll was designed for a major Barbie fashion show held in two railroad cars that toured France in 1985. The collection featured 600 Barbie dolls, many dressed in custom outfits from 70 top designers, including: Pierre Cardin, Hermes, Jacqueline de Ribes, Jean-Paul Gaultier, Yves Saint Laurent, Thierry Mugler, Frederic Castet, and Sonia Rykiel. Yves St. Laurent had his atelier craft a tiny version of the famous St. Laurent pea coat for BillyBoy*'s Barbie, as well as a replica of the safari outfit the model Verushka wore on a cover of *Paris Vogue* in 1968. The great Alexandre de Paris—Jacqueline Onassis' Paris hairdresser of choice—did Barbie's hair. Marc Bohan, of Christian Dior, created a lovely green and black strapless sheath for Barbie, an exact miniature of one he made for Princess Caroline of Monaco. Ungaro added four ensembles, Hanae Mori offered three, and Kenzo created a Japanese-style jacket with straight, wide pants and multi-colored straw hat. Andrée Putnam, interior designer, created a room exclusively for Barbie and Ken. The 400-piece Barbie exhibition was sponsored by Mattel, S.A., the French affiliate of Mattel Toys.

The exhibition also made a nine-city tour which started in New York in February 1985 and stopped in Chicago, Dallas and Philadelphia, among other cities. At a party in New York to celebrate the occasion, Andy Warhol unveiled his painting of Barbie and 1,300 guests danced until dawn to Barbie and the Rockers. Warhol was rumored to have given BillyBoy* the ubiquitous 1985 portrait of Barbie.

BillyBoy's* ***Le Nouveau Theatre de la Mode Barbie*** *poses on a Patron Original Christian Dior Paris design.*

◆ CHRISTIAN DIOR / GIANFRANCO FERRÉ

When Mattel announced at Toy Fair 1995 that a new Barbie doll would be on the market from Dior, many collectors immediately contacted their dealers. Within several months of the announcement, rumors spread that the doll was pre-sold out.

The Christian Dior Barbie doll was designed by Gianfranco Ferré, a favorite designer among many of Hollywood's fashion elite since the early 1980s. Gianfranco Ferré became the new designer at the House of Christian Dior in 1989, and all of Paris was struck by the irony that an Italian would be dictating French fashion. In protest, Princess Caroline of Monaco took her business elsewhere. So Ferré wears two hats, designing his own line of couture as well as providing expert direction for the House of Dior.

Ferré first burst into the Milan fashion scene in 1978. His trademark is using luxurious fabrics, such as silk organza and cashmere finished off with rich details and embroideries. Ferré's work for Dior tends to be cut in the elegant Dior mold, identified by big shoulders and cinched waists, but with a splash of wit.

Ferré's academic background wasn't in fashion, but architecture. He moved on to design jewelry and accessories for a friend and was "discovered" by the then-influential editor of Italian *Vogue,* Anna Piaggi. She liked his work, and asked him to make some baubles for a Vogue photo shoot. You've come a long way, Gianfranco!

◆ DONNA KARAN

Christian Dior and Gianfranco Ferré were not the only big-names in the world of fashion to design a Barbie doll in 1995. After the success of Nicole Miller's Barbie doll in 1994, Bloomingdale's did not have to think twice about commissioning a second exclusive. The retail giant chose a quintessential American fashion designer for Barbie number two: Donna Karan.

Based on the excellent sales results of the Miller Barbie doll the year before, Bloomingdale's bought two-and-a-half times as many of the Donna Karan dolls. Most of the

Released in 1995, the ***Dior Barbie*** *created by Gianfranco Ferré was based on an early couture design.*

dolls were already pre-sold prior to release in the fourth quarter of 1995.

Like the Nicole Miller costume, Karan's clothing is somewhat of a departure for Barbie. The outfit is more reminiscent of a tailored European Pret-a-Porter or Haute Couture Moderne fashion than a typical sequined or glittered outfit. Karan's Barbie is dressed in pieces from the first Donna Karan New York collection, introduced 10 years ago: a turtleneck bodysuit, black sarong skirt, red "cashmere" oblong scarf, gold jewelry, black beret and black faux crocodile belt and bag. The doll retailed for $65. She was available as both blonde and brunette; the brunettes were rumored to be more scarce.

One Bloomingdale executive was quoted as saying that, "Barbie is part of the Bloomingdale's theater. The Bloomingdale's customer is not interested in stores that, decor-wise, are glitzy, with tons of mirror and tons of chrome. She wants the excitement of theater. Theater is Donna Karan dolls."

Karan, a junior designer at Anne Klein early in her career, launched her own ready-to-wear line in 1985. She won an instant following by appealing to America's modern businesswoman—the exec with lots of cash, but little or no time to spare for shopping. Her clothes looked nothing like Brooks Brothers-for-women or John Molloy's model of dressing for success. She produced seven easy pieces that managed to be both professional and feminine. Her second line of comfortable sportswear—DKNY—included the kind of things every woman wants, but can rarely find: a faded pair of khakis, the perfect white T-shirt, and a boxy blazer. The idea for the clothes evolved, Karan says, because she was sick of wearing her husband's jeans.

In an interview in *Newsweek* magazine's issue of January 3, 1994, Donna Karan said, "The future of fashion will focus on technology—in fabric and personal electronics." So into the body skimmer, ladies, and strap on the info-wrist that contains an electronic Filofax and mobile telephone!

*Bloomingdale's second customized doll, the **Donna Karan Barbie,** inspired by Karan's earliest designs, was snapped-up by collectors directly via the store's toll-free telephone number. The brunette version is difficult to find.*
(For more information on the evolution of this doll, see Chapter 5, Custom Made).

◆ ERTÉ

While Erté's Stardust doll is not based on the Barbie persona, *per se,* she is nevertheless highly prized among many Barbie enthusiasts. Erté created magazine covers for *Harpers Bazaar* innovating the Art Deco style. Long famous for his fashion as featured in the Ziegfeld Follies, Erté's creations were also featured in the 1994 production of *Stardust* on Broadway. The dress worn by the doll was worn in the show. The doll stands about 13½ inches tall; has outstretched arms characteristic of Erté's mannequins; and features a fully hand-beaded dress with a headpiece in a star design. Each doll was numbered and retailed originally for $650.00.

*Erté's **Stardust** doll was the breathtaking physical incarnation of a two-dimensional Erté design originally created for a theatrical production. Below, typical Erté Art Deco fashion designs.*

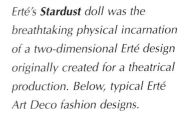

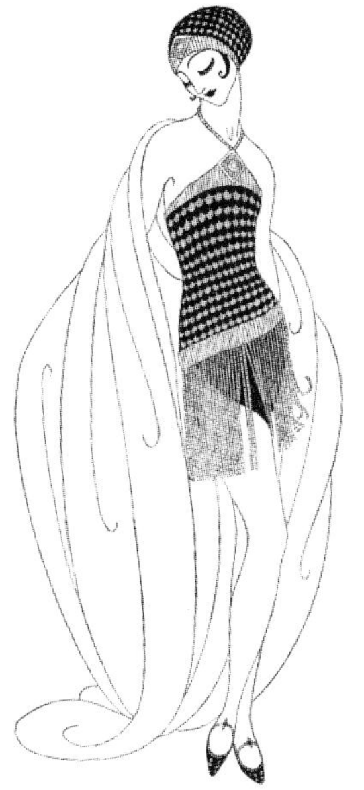

There's a first time for everything. Here are the "first" ethnic contemporary Barbie dolls for the mass American market. From left: Tropical Miko, Hispanic, Native American, Black and Hawaiian.

Chapter 8

COLOR ME BARBIE®

The *Contemporary BARBIE* doll continually evolves to reflect the times in which she is created. And, the times in the U.S. 'are a changin' insofar as American demographics are concerned. According to the U.S. Bureau of the Census, Hispanics will eclipse African-Americans as the nation's largest minority group in 2010. By 2050, the U.S. population will be just about evenly divided between its various minority groups on the one hand and non-Hispanic whites on the other. Beyond 2050, there may never again be a majority ethnic group in the United States.

Another way of looking at these numbers is that while the overall U.S. population is projected to grow by 15 percent by the year 2010, growth rates are projected to be much higher among minorities—22 percent for African-Americans, 56 percent for Hispanics, and 86 percent for Asians and Pacific Islanders.

Key features forecasted for U.S. ethnic diversity include:

- Hispanics, who represent 9 percent of the U.S. population today, will comprise 14 percent in 2010, and 23 percent in 2050.
- African-Americans, who represent 12 percent today, will represent 13 percent in 2010, and 16 percent in 2050.
- Asian-Americans will remain the fastest-growing minority group—increasing from 3 percent of today's population to 10 percent in 2010.
- The number of Native American Indians will double from 2.1 million today to 4.3 million in 2050, but their share of the total population will continue to hover at around 1 percent.
- As for non-Hispanic whites, their share of the population will drop from 76 percent today to 53 percent in 2050. Their actual numbers will grow from 188.6 million to 205.8 million in the period.

This special effect doll, ***Locket Surprise,*** *came in both Black and Caucasian versions in 1993.*

Growing ethnic diversity in the U.S. has played a role in the design of Barbie dolls since the mid-1960s. In 1967, "Colored Francie" (#1100) was presented as the first Black doll in the Barbie product line. Francie was the first so-called "colored" friend of Barbie (which is the way her ethnicity is treated on the doll's packaging).

In 1968, Mattel introduced two additional Black dolls to Barbie's world: Talking Julia (#1128) and Talking Christie (#1126). Talking Julia was based on a hit television series and was, according to the promotional booklet, endowed with "Diahann Carroll's lovely voice and starry-eyed looks!" Talking Christie was described as a "sweet talker [who] says many charming phrases." In 1977, Mattel presented Hawaiian Barbie (#7470), a new ethnic variation, complete with ukelele and windsurfer. The doll used the Steffie head mold.

*The first **Hispanic Barbie** doll was available in 1980, along with the first Black Barbie doll.*

Not until 1980 were Black and Hispanic dolls named "Barbie" introduced. Mattel implemented an advertising campaign for Black Barbie in targeted media, and this resulted in tremendous sales. This convinced Mattel of the market viability for the concept of Black fashion dolls. Black and Hispanic Barbie dolls were not made with the regular Barbie doll face mold; instead, they were constructed with the Steffie doll mold (as was the previously-noted Hawaiian Barbie). Steffie—one of Barbie's friends—was sold only from 1972 to 1973, but since then her head mold has often been used in Mattel's production of ethnic dolls.

Following the introduction of Black Barbie in 1980, Mattel continued to conduct focus groups with Black mothers and daughters and found that they felt "very underrepresented" and wanted more authentic African-American dolls. In 1991, Mattel introduced a new line of African-American fashion dolls led by Shani (the Swahili word for "marvelous"). Shani had two best friends: Asha and Nichelle. Each had a different skin tone, intended to reflect differences among African-American people. To promote Shani, Mattel tied into *Ebony* magazine's Fashion Fair, where three Black models wore replicas of Shani's outfits. Ads for the doll featured the headline: "Now here's a doll that can make a real difference in her life." Accessories included kente cloth outfits and other ethnic fashions. In place of Barbie's own signature fashion color—pink—the dolls featured a warmer gold. Based on Mattel's belief (supported by market research) that all little girls, regardless of race, love playing with hair, the dolls had long flowing hair.

The first Hispanic Barbie doll, issued in 1980, was dressed in what can be best described as a Mexican-style holiday outfit: white off-the-shoulder blouse, red skirt and black mantilla. Giving Mattel designers the benefit of the doubt, suffice it to say that she was dressed more as an International Barbie doll or Doll of the World than a Barbie doll that reflected the lifestyle of an American-Hispanic teenager. More mainstream Hispanic versions of the Barbie doll were welcomed by consumers later in the 1980s, with Sun Gold Malibu in 1984, Day-to-Night Barbie in 1985, and Dream Glow Barbie in 1986. By the mid-1990s, collectors grew to value the Hispanic doll, Teresa, as one of the most attractive friends in Barbie's world.

In 1993, Mattel issued the first Native American Barbie doll, followed by second and third issues in 1994 and 1995.

Ethnic dolls (including Asian, Black and Hispanic) named "Barbie" proliferated through the latter 1980s in the *Contemporary BARBIE* era. Given the reshaping of American demography, they should remain an evolving, integral component of Barbie's world.

*Toys 'R Us packaged a special **Fashion Brights Barbie** doll with a weekend of outfits in 1992.*

Ethnic dolls in the *Contemporary Barbie* era

Year	Doll	Stock No.
1980	*Black Barbie*	1293
1980	*Hispanic Barbie*	1292
1981	*Sunsational Malibu*	4970
1982	*Magic Curl Barbie* - Black	3989
1983	*Twirly Curls* - Black	5723
1983	*Twirly Curls* - Hispanic ("Ricitos")	5724
1983	*Spanish Barbie*	4031
1984	*Sun Gold Malibu*	4970
1984	*Crystal Barbie* - Black	4859
1984	*Great Shapes* - Black	7834
1984	*My First Black Barbie*	9858
1985	*Day-to-Night* - Black	7945
1985	*Day-to-Night* - Hispanic	7944
1985	*Dream Glow* - Hispanic	1647
1985	*Peaches 'n Cream*	9516
1986	*Magic Moves Barbie* - Black	2127
1986	*Tropical Barbie* - Black	1022
1986	*Hispanic Tropical*	1649

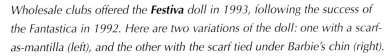

*Wholesale clubs offered the **Festiva** doll in 1993, following the success of the Fantastica in 1992. Here are two variations of the doll: one with a scarf-as-mantilla (left), and the other with the scarf tied under Barbie's chin (right).*

*Wholesale clubs offered the **Fantastica** doll in 1992, using the Teresa face mold.*

Factoid

Woolworth's 1992 Special Expressions Hispanic Barbie (#3200) was the first Hispanic customized Barbie doll.

Year	Doll	Stock No.
1985	*Dream Glow Barbie* - Black	2422
1985	*Astronaut Barbie* - Black	1207
1986	*Mi Primera Barbie*	5979
1987	*Jewel Secrets Barbie* - Black	1862
1987	*Super Hair Barbie* - Black	3206
1988	*Fun to Dress Barbie* - Black	1373 and 7668
1988	*My First Barbie* - Black	1281
1988	*My First Barbie* - Hispanic	1282
1988	*Perfume Pretty Barbie* - Black	4552
1988	*Animal Lovin' Barbie* - Black	4824
1989	*Feelin' Fun Barbie* - Black	4809
1989	*Feelin' Fun Barbie* - Hispanic	7373
1989	*SuperStar Movie Star* - Black	1605
1989	*Mexican Barbie*	1917
1989	*UNICEF* - Black	4770
1989	*UNICEF* - Hispanic	4782
1989	*UNICEF* - Asian	4774
1989	*Wedding Fantasy Barbie* - Black	7011
1989	*Woolworth Special Expressions* - Black	7326
1990	*Dance Magic Barbie* - Black	7080
1990	*Disney Barbie #1*	9835
1990	*Fashion Play Barbie* - Black	5953
1990	*Fashion Play Barbie* - Hispanic	5954
1990	*Flight Time Barbie* - Black	9916
1990	*Flight Time Barbie* - Hispanic	2066
1990	*Happy Birthday Barbie* - Black	9561
1990	*Happy Holidays Barbie* - Black	4543
1990	*Ice Capades Barbie* - Black	7348
1990	*Fun to Dress Hispanic Barbie*	7373
1990	*Sears - Lavender Surprise* - Black	5588
1990	*Summit Barbie* - Black	7028
1990	*Summit Barbie* - Hispanic	7030
1990	*Summit Barbie* - Asian	7029
1990	*Woolworth Special Expressions* - Black	5505
1991	*American Beauty Queen* - Black	3245
1991	*Bathtime Fun Barbie* - Black	9603
1991	*Bob Mackie Starlight Splendor*	2704
1991	*Costume Ball Barbie* - Black	7134
1991	*My First Barbie* - Black	9944
1991	*My First Barbie* - Hispanic	9943
1991	*Marine Corps Barbie* - Black	7594
1991	*Navy Barbie* - Black	9694
1992	*TRU - Barbie for President* - Black	3940
1992	*Bath Blast Barbie* - Black	3830

Year	Doll	Stock No.
1992	*Spanish Barbie*	4963
1992	*Bath Magic Barbie* - Black	7951
1992	*Fashion Play Hispanic*	3860
1992	*Birthday Party Barbie* - Black	7948
1992	*Birthday Surprise Barbie* - Black	4051
1992	*Kmart Pretty in Purple Barbie* - Black	3121
1992	*My First Barbie* - Black	3861
1992	*My First Barbie* - Hispanic	3864
1992	*Snap 'n Play Barbie* - Black	3556
1992	*Sparkle Eyes Barbie* - Black	5950
1992	*Army (Desert Storm)* - Black	5618
1992	*Army (Desert Storm) Gift Set* - Black	5627
1992	*Teen Talk Barbie* - Black	1612
1992	*Totally Hair Barbie* - Black	5948
1992	*Woolworth Special Expressions* - Hispanic	3200
1992	*TRU - School Fun Barbie* - Black	4111
1992	*TRU - Fashion Brights Barbie* - Black	4112
1992	*TRU - Cool 'N Sassy Barbie* - Black	4110
1992	*TRU - Radiant in Red Barbie* - Hispanic	4113
1992	*TRU - Spring Parade Barbie* - Black	2257
1992	*Woolworth Sweet Lavender Barbie* - Black	2523
1992	*Woolworth Special Expressions Barbie* - Black	3198

Mattel finally recognized the contributions of Native American women by issuing the ***Native American Barbie*** *dolls in 1993, 1994 and 1995 (left to right).*

This 1994 ***My First Black Barbie*** *doll was designed for a young girl's entry into the world of Barbie dolls.*

Year	Doll	Stock No.
1993	*Bedtime Barbie* - Black	11184
1993	*Classique - Evening Extravaganza* - Black	11638
1993	*Earring Magic Barbie* - Black	2374
1993	*Wholesale Clubs Festiva Barbie* - Hispanic	10339
1993	*Fountain Mermaid Barbie* - Black	10522
1993	*Happy Holidays Barbie* - Black	10911
1993	*Locket Surprise Barbie* - Black	11224
1993	*My First Barbie* - Black	2767
1993	*My First Barbie* - Hispanic	2770
1993	*Paint 'N Dazzle Barbie* - Black	10058
1993	*Romantic Bride Barbie* - Black	11054
1993	*Secret Hearts Barbie* - Black	3836
1993	*Fun to Dress* - Hispanic	2763
1993	*TRU - Dream Wedding Set* - Black	10713
1993	*TRU - Moonlight Magic Barbie* - Black	10609
1993	*TRU - Police Officer Barbie* - Black	10689
1993	*TRU - School Spirit Barbie* - Black	10683
1993	*Wal-Mart - Superstar* - Hispanic	10711
1993	*Twinkle Lights Barbie* - Black	10521
1993	*Western Stampin' Barbie* - Black	10539
1993	*Woolworth Special Expressions* - Black	10049
1993	*Woolworth Special Expressions* - Hispanic	10050
1994	*TRU - Astronaut Barbie* - Black	12150
1994	*Bicycling Barbie* - Black	11817
1994	*Birthday Barbie* - Black	11334
1994	*Camp Barbie* - Black	11831
1994	*Dance 'n Twirl Barbie* - Black	12143
1994	*Dr. Barbie* - Black	11814
1994	*Dress 'N Fun Barbie* - Black	11103
1994	*Dress 'N Fun Barbie* - Hispanic	11102
1994	*Glitter Hair Barbie* - Black	11332
1994	*Gymnast Barbie* - Black	12153
1994	*Happy Holidays Barbie* - Black	12156
1994	*My First Barbie Ballerina* - Black	11340
1994	*My First Barbie Ballerina* - Black	13065
1994	*My First Barbie Ballerina* - Hispanic	11341
1994	*My First Barbie Ballerina* - Asian	13064
1994	*My Size Bride Barbie* - Black	12053
1994	*Airforce Thunderbird Barbie* - Black	11553
1994	*Airforce Thunderbird Set* - Black	11582
1994	*Swim 'N Dive Barbie* - Black	11734
1994	*TRU - Emerald Elegance Barbie* - Hispanic	12353
1994	*Wal-Mart - Country Western Star* - Black	12096
1994	*Wal-Mart - Country Western Star* - Hispanic	12097
1995	*Baywatch Barbie* - Black	13258

Year	Doll	Stock No.
1995	*Birthday Barbie* - Black	12955
1995	*Birthday Barbie* - Hispanic	13253
1995	*Bubble Angel Barbie* - Black	12444
1995	*Butterfly Princess Barbie* - Black	13052
1995	*TRU - Fire Fighter Barbie - Black*	13472
1995	*TRU - Teacher Barbie* - Black	13915
1995	*Cut 'n Style Barbie* - Black	12642
1995	*Dance Moves Barbie* - Black	13086
1995	*Happy Holidays* - Black	14124
1995	*Hot Skatin' Barbie* - Black	13512
1995	*My First Barbie Princess* - Black	13065
1995	*My First Barbie Princess* - Hispanic	13066
1995	*My Size Princess Barbie* - Black	13768
1995	*Ruffle Fun Barbie* - Black	12434
1993	*Ruffle Fun Barbie* - Hispanic	12435
1995	*Slumber Party Barbie* - Black	12697
1995	*Wholesale Clubs Fantastica Barbie*	3196
1995	*Strollin' Fun Barbie & Kelly* - Black	13743
1995	*Supertalk Barbie* - Black	12379
1995	*Sweet Dreams Barbie* - Black	13630
1995	*Wal-Mart Country Bride Barbie* - Black	13615
1995	*Wal-Mart Country Bride Barbie* - Hispanic	13616

KITTY BLACK-PERKINS ON THE FIRST BLACK BARBIE DOLL

"The first Black Barbie that we did had short hair. She had on a red bodysuit with gold trim, and a long red wrap skirt. At that time one of my idols was Diana Ross. I really loved the way she dressed. When I designed the fashion for that doll, I thought 'this is the way to go,' the way that I would visualize Diana Ross if she were a Barbie doll.

"There was a lot of controversy about the color of the dress [red] and about the length of the hair [short], as well. I wanted to do something different than what we had done with Barbie's long hair before. I thought the short haircut was adorable. What I didn't know at the time, because at that time we didn't rely on a lot of market research, was that half of the play with the doll was [and still is] in the hair. What we know now through our market research is that it doesn't matter what color the child is, they like that long hair! That's one reason why a lot of Black kids will buy Barbie—for the length of the hair.

"A lot of the Black kids own white Barbies and a lot of white kids own Black Barbies. Color doesn't matter to a child.

"When we did Shani in 1991, we capitalized on some of the information from the research that we found when we did the first Black Barbie doll. That was the reason we opted to go with long hair instead of short hair. Another selling feature with Shani was that we did three different skin tones with her. We wanted the child to make a purchase that was most 'like me.' So, of course, Black people come in all different shades and colors. This was how we wanted our line to be reflected.

"Now Shani really is a part of Barbie's world. . .we have made her a part of the whole fashion doll world. Kids will mix Shani together with Barbie dolls. . .and that is one of the really neat things about watching them play. They don't have any problem with putting a ballerina Barbie with a Shani doll to go shopping or whatever. . . . It doesn't matter to them."

SOURCE: Author's interview with Kitty Black-Perkins, August 1995

Chapter 9

CYBERSPEAKING ABOUT BARBIE®

By the time of this book's publication, some fourteen years will have elapsed since IBM introduced the first personal computer. Since 1982, computers have become a ubiquitous feature of our daily lives at work, home and school. By 1994, two-thirds of American homes with incomes in excess of $75,000 had home computers. And today over 1 in 3 Americans age 3 and above have used a computer. Largely because they are more concentrated in occupations where computer use is high (in technical, sales, and administrative support jobs), women use a computer at work more than men.

And, by late 1995, millions of Americans, both male and female, were surfing the Internet.

Computer technology—indeed, technology in general—has impacted the Barbie doll since she first "spoke" in 1968 (thanks to a miniature tape player). While Talking Barbie (who spoke in both English and Spanish), Talking Christie, Talking Julia, and Talking Stacy (who spoke with a British accent) can still be found in dealers' lists to this day, most of the time these dolls are listed as being "mute." The first Talking Barbie uttered six different phrases, had bendable legs, and wore "real" eyelashes.

Throughout the years, Mattel's product developers have created a variety of talking Barbie and family dolls. However, not until the 1990s was the "talking" done by a computer chip. In fact, by the 1990s, the Barbie doll entered the cyber-world in several key ways:

- Computer chips were implanted into dolls such as Teen Talk Barbie, who spoke the controversial, "Math class is tough" and "Let's go shopping!" and the Supertalk Barbie, introduced at Christmas 1994, whose chip allowed Barbie to say at least 100,000 phrases.
- In 1991 Radio Shack, packaged an Earring Magic Barbie with software for becoming a "Barbie Fashion Designer."
- Computer chips were also implanted in Barbie allowing her to move in fairly random ways, such as the Dance Magic Barbie doll.

Things "cyber" that impact the Barbie doll will be played out in the following ways:

ON THE NET—As of September 1995, Barbie doll collectors were converging on various World Wide Web pages to communicate and educate. The Internet already links wired Barbie doll collectors globally, allowing cyber-savvy collectors to enact cross-border trades. For example, I have traded dolls unique to the American market with a Barbie doll "E-Pal" in France. This mode of communication and commerce will grow as more Barbie doll collectors become comfortable with navigating the Net. Other aspects of the Internet are being closely scrutinized by

*Radio Shack packaged the **Earring Magic Barbie** doll with Barbie Design Studio software, marking the first time a Barbie doll ever came packaged with software for the personal computer.*

Mattel, Inc. In 1995, an online Web magazine featured two Barbie dolls in a somewhat compromising position. Mattel issued a cease-and-desist order posthaste. The company will continue to monitor any potential violations of the brand image and name.

VIA THE INTERNET AND COMMERCIAL ON-LINE SERVICES—There are active Barbie doll collector bulletin boards on the largest commercial on-line services including America Online, CompuServe, Genie and Prodigy. As the Microsoft Network and EWorld increasingly penetrate homes, they undoubtedly will attract collectors. Collectors Net, an all-Barbie on-line service, achieved dramatic growth in its first year of operation in 1995, and attracted serious collectors and dealers to its ranks. Other more generic antiques and collectibles sites, such as *Antique Trader's* Collectors SuperMall home page, CSM OnLine (http://www.csmonline.com), have begun to emerge on the World Wide Web and are anticipated to continue to proliferate over the next several years.

ON CD-ROM—Various computer games are targeted to the younger Barbie doll consumer. Via the "Barbie and Her Magical House" CD-ROM, available in 1994, participants help Barbie decorate, cook, and move Ken's picture around the room. Also available that year, Nintendo's Game Boy Barbie Game Girl has her steer through a mall to meet Ken for a date, and search for fashion treasures for a fantasy ball. In a series of videogames available from Hi Tech Entertainment in 1995, Barbie mountain bikes, shops and performs other tasks. Mattel has licensed these and other vendors to create new computer games using the Barbie persona. Furthermore, Mattel plans to co-venture with a variety of technology companies to create innovative new approaches to Barbie-related games, both for pure fun and for education.

Internet Web Pages of Interest to Barbie Doll Collectors

South Bay Barbie Doll Collectors Club Home Page	http://www.primenet.com/~gambit/barbie.html
Plastic Princess Home Page	http://deepthought.armory.com/~zenugirl/barbie.html
FAO Schwarz Home Page	http://faoschwarz.com
Toys 'R Us Home Page	http://www.tru.com
Antique Trader *Home Page*	http://www.csmonline.com
Jennifer Warf's Home Page	http://silver.ucs.indiana.edu/~jwarf/barbie.html
Baddog's Home Page	http://www.interlog.com/~baddog
Royal-T Cleaners Home Page	http://www.primenet.com/~proclaim/royalt.htm
The Barbie Attic Home Page	http://tsdg.com/dollattc.html
Doll/Barbie Store Directory	http://205.199.112.103/barbie/
Kitty's Collectables Home Page	http://users.aol.com/kittyscol/kittys.htm
Barbie Info Home Page	http://users.aol.com/barbie747/barbie.htm
Those Swell Doll Guys Home Page	http://tsdg.com

List current as of February 1996

There is more to follow. As personal computers, online network subscribers, Internet surfers and specialty collecting networks proliferate the world over, the Barbie doll, too, will be taking her place on the cyber-stage. In 1994, Mattel hired a former executive of Sega of America, Douglas Glen, who will be developing computer-related products and services for the company. The Barbie doll and brand will inevitably be part of this plan. It is anticipated that education (and as it's known in media circles, edu-tainment) will be the core driving vision for many of these developments.

Mattel will work closely with other technology companies to put much of this together. Plans to develop Barbie doll adventures via virtual reality technologies are already under discussion. "The idea," Barad said in an interview with *Investor's Business Daily* in April, 1995, "is to bring value to where children will be spending their time and having her add value to their time. Those children on line or on the Internet will be able to interact with Barbie in very special ways." Such interactive "special ways" could include Barbie taking little girls on a journey, explaining new opportunities open to them as they travel in her world.

*"And I thought math class was tough!" complains **Teen Talk Barbie** as she learns how to surf the Net. She is pictured with her 1994 Home Office.*

Barbie at the Cybercafé

On November 10, 1994, at The Kitchen on West 19th Street in the Chelsea section of New York City, Barbie cyberhistory was made. The Kitchen joined cybersalons in far-ranging sites that included Santa Monica, Paris, Jerusalem, Tokyo, Berlin, Managua and Maui. This electronic café event, later called "Café Barbie—An Inter-Continental Salon," commemorated the 35th anniversary of the Barbie doll. Using state-of-the-art hardware largely donated by manufacturers and audio-visual communications lines installed by NYNEX, The Kitchen's performance space was fitted out as a balance of traditional café amenities such as espresso and biscotti completed by a computerized video installation. Speakers included a star-studded panel with personalities such as Betty Friedan, Lauren Hutton, Raquel Welch and Camille Paglia. Also on hand for the event was the Barbie Liberation Organization, the group notorious for entering toy stores and switching Barbie doll voice boxes with those of G.I. Joe.

Abbe Littleton's* Midnight Gala, *the sixth Classique doll in the series, was issued in 1995.

Chapter 10

"Mommy, Where Do Barbie® Dolls Come From?"

It is no small miracle that a Barbie doll ultimately finds its way to a toy store shelf. If you think the process begins and ends with the talented Barbie doll designers, you're mistaken. For each doll conceived by a designer, there is an extensive and dedicated team deployed that performs multiple functions and roles. The team works together to bring a beautiful, safe doll to the market.

According to Barbie doll designer Cynthia Young, a multidisciplinary team is involved with the designer from the initial concept. The team is "a wonderful blend of experts doing what they know best." Designers present ideas to the team and the group votes on which ones will work "best." Young described the complex, iterative brainstorming process: "The designer makes a Barbie sketch, drawing a picture like the Butterfly Princess dress, showing the butterflies and what the doll does. The group agrees that this is a good idea and recommends that a 3-D model be made up. The designer brings the model to the group's next meeting. The group critiques the model: 'Take off some butterflies, change the colors.' Designers and others at the team meeting have ideas about face paint, whether the doll's mouth should be open or closed. They will say things like, 'Don't use a closed mouth, the doll looks too serious. We want her to look younger.' Everyone adds all of their critiques, additions and edits. Then it goes back to the designer and she has to design it the way the group wants it. That's when she'll bring it back, when they say, hopefully, 'That's good. . .let's go for it'!"

The many individuals, sections and departments that have roles in the doll's development as it moves from concept through production include:

- *Manufacturing,* to determine the viability of producing the doll on time.
- *Costing,* to determine how the company will financially fare on the doll.
- *Time management and scheduling,* to calculate when the doll is needed for the market.
- *Chemical and Safety Laboratories*, to identify potential quality and health issues with the planned doll.
- *The Hair Department,* to work closely with the designer in creating an appropriate hair style for the doll, to be consistent with both the designer's vision and the various constraints set by costing, scheduling, and safety.
- *Face painting*, again to work closely with the designer to realize makeup that is consistent and complementary to the design.

- *Face sculpting,* to create a new head mold, or to select an existing head mold.
- *Engineers,* to provide input on technical aspects of the doll such as computer chips for speaking, pliability for bending the dolls, etc.
- *Textiles,* for designing and then sourcing the fabrics for the dolls.
- *Production pattern making,* to design the pattern for the costume.

Once the designer has conceptualized the [final] doll, she drapes, pins and sews fabric to it. Kim Burkhardt and her colleagues in the soft goods and fabrics area then have to actually produce the pattern for the gown. This is no easy task. Burkhardt, with a B.A. in Textile Science, has to carry through the designer's vision for the doll's costume, whether it's based on a fabric that wholesales for $80 per yard or is to be hand-painted. "We do whatever it takes to create the vision. Our job is to think about how to create the costume within a budget."

An example: For Barbie doll designer Abbe Littleton's popular 1995 Classique, Midnight Gala, Littleton had originally used gold metallic lace over the black velvet gown. However, the actual layout made the costume impossible to reproduce. As an alternative fabric, the textile engineer on the project, Wendy Wilson, worked out an engineered glitter print. After careful consultation with the designer, production, marketing and accounting team members, this was the resulting fabric for Littleton's doll. "We do our best to maintain the designer's vision, but a big part of our job is meeting marketing's product margin," Burkhardt explains.

"From the very start, we're working with another person on every single Barbie doll design. A production designer is looking at how we're putting the doll and costume together for production, and she is also responsible for putting together the patterns. Once we receive a doll design, we know fairly quickly how we're going to approach the product. We do a lot of 'translating' of fabric. The designer will layer up several fabrics, but we have to figure out how to make it into one layer of fabric," Burkhardt described.

The Hollywood Legends doll—Barbie as Maria in *The Sound of Music*—provides an example of this process. The designer, Janet Goldblatt, originally had envisioned glitter on the skirt of the dress. On the bodice, Goldblatt used a novelty raw silk with a metallic yarn woven into it, "far more expensive than anything we could have chosen to use," Burkhardt said. "On the skirt, Goldblatt had used a very large human-sized tapestry pattern," Burkhardt continued. "The designer cut a segment out of the fabric that she thought looked best for the skirt. Our dilemma is that we can't get the feeling we wanted through repeating the pattern. The designer initially resisted the change, but they know there are certain elements that don't work. We have a group here that designs our textile art that designed the floral motif for Maria's dress. As we sent the fabric out to the vendor, our vendors in the Orient started working on it, and through some color adjustment and throwing glitter on the product, it worked. They hit the bodice with a golden metallic foil without using glitter, and this very effectively translated the designer's original feeling."

The textile designers are sensitive to Barbie doll collectors' wants. They understand that collectors want to see quality fabrics on the dolls. Burkhhardt said: "Collectors would enjoy seeing 'real' designer fabrics being used, not just our

How Abbe Littleton was Meant to Work at Mattel, Inc.

Abbe Littleton

"When I joined Mattel, it was like it was meant to be. I always loved to draw, and I loved fashion. Even as a kindergartner, I was attuned to what everybody wore. After completing design school, I did design in downtown L.A. in the garment industry. I worked there for five years. I saw an article about Carol Spencer in a magazine and thought, 'What a dream job!'

"I always loved dolls. My mother and I have always been into miniatures. I played with my Barbie dolls even when I was 19 years old. My girlfriends would make fun of me until I opened the case on the floor and then they would get into it, too.

"My very first job out of college was at the factory at Mattel. My mother worked at the factory when I was a little girl. I had a lot of Mattel inside of me! I knew who Ruth and Elliot Handler were as a kid. So I had a lot of exposure to the product and knew where she was made since I was a young girl.

"When I was working in the garment industry, I saw an ad in *Apparel News* for a job with Mattel. I went for a first interview at Mattel, and they gave me a naked doll and said, 'Bring the doll back dressed.' So I had designed my wedding dress, and I decided to do the same design in red. I used a Valentine theme and made a box of chocolate out of erasers that I painted red. I took a feather boa and cut out little tiny red hearts out of sequins.

"This doll got me the job! I later found out that Mattel was coming out with a Valentine themed doll, Lovin' You Barbie. I couldn't believe I got the job. It was so ironic, because when I was in Girl Scouts, the first badge I got was Toymaker for making a doll."

SOURCE: Author's interview with Abbe Littleton, November 1995

standard Barbie fabrics." Burkhardt believes that the upcoming 1996 porcelain Rose Bride doll will satisfy collectors' desires for beautiful "adult" fabrics on the Barbie doll. This doll was designed by Demaris Vidal, who happened to be a wedding gown designer prior to joining Mattel. "The original design for the doll was absolutely fabulous, but when we got done costing the doll, we couldn't make it as originally conceived," said Burkhardt. The original design used embroidered net covered in iridescent sequins with seed pearls. "There was no way it was going to happen with the budget that we had," Burkhardt added. "The production designer and I sat down and really looked at the doll. We glitter-flocked a net in an engineered pattern and created a very shimmery, very delicate fabric on the net so that it could take a scalloped edge. By doing this, we didn't have to put any sequins on it as the fabric was shimmering on its own. We did all of the appliques this way, allowing us to add back in a lot of rosettes, keep the faux pearls on the doll, use really nice jewelry. It was the first time we've ever approached doing an engineered print." The labor in this is enormous; Burkhardt noted. "In the case of these dolls, instead of laying-up 30 at a time, we have to lay them up one at a time."

When the group finally agrees on a design, it is transferred onto a Computer Design, Inc., CAD system. Once designed, the patterns are transferred to the product development department and from there to manufacturing support where Mattel makes certain that designs are ready to go to the overseas plants in Indonesia, Malaysia and the People's Republic of China.

The plants utilize high technology manufacturing equipment. A complicated dress design, such as the jewel-laden Christian Dior, relies on special machine attachments for creating intricate designs. The plant has a special attachment that combines the hemming of the doll's skirt with the joining of sequins at the very edge of the skirt. Then, production workers hand-sew small accents on clothing such as bead buttons. It is not surprising that turnaround time for doll clothing, from concept to store shelf, can take up to 24 months.

Paulette Bazerman of Mattel Toys, Hong Kong, oversees much of this process. "I am Barbie's stepmother," Bazerman proudly asserts. "The designer trusts me to be their eyes. I have to make sure that Barbie is well taken care of. Once Barbie leaves home, I am watching her through boarding school. Boarding school is when Barbie doll leaves California and lands in the Hong Kong office, our Asian headquarters. Our office supervises the manufacture of Barbie dolls which is done

Mattel's Barbie production plant in the Republic of China.

Barbie doll assembly line floor within the plant in the Republic of China.

in two factories in China, one in Malaysia and one in Indonesia. There are also fabric soft goods that get utilized in Italy and Mexico. Barbie doll's cars and vans, accessories, horses, and beds are all made in Italy and Mexico. These accessories need soft goods, such as the horse's blanket, pillows for the bed. . .these get made in China and are shipped. We just completed the My Size Barbie, which is made in Mexico with clothes made in China. The final assembly is done in either Mexico or Italy."

Bazerman is well prepared for this choreographed logistical dance. "My background is in the garment industry in New York City and Los Angeles, so I went from women's clothing to Barbie clothing. Now I watch over collector and customized Barbie dolls, as well as ensembles such as the Fashion Avenue line."

Bazerman's team consists of textile engineers and final pattern-makers that provide the sewing standards to the plants throughout Asia. "When the dolls arrive here in concept form from California, their ensembles have glued and pinned fabrics which might have come from somebody's sweater," she said. "These are not in a manufacturable form, either for the fabric or the pattern. So it's still in concept form when we receive them. I have a group of 14 sample makers and a manager who make the prototypes that we're doing. The sample makers hand-decorate [e.g, hand-glitter] and make the prototypes for packages, toy shows, catalogs and television commercials. Of the 320 different Barbie items, I get about half of them. I have a colleague that has the same responsibilities covering the other half of the items."

Through each step, Bazerman is there to manage the many "moments of truth" in the manufacturing process. More complex dolls, generally beloved by collectors, often require modifications along the way. Sometimes there have to be compromises. Bazerman has to make a "call" on budgets and timing, ensuring the high level of quality that the designer intended. "I always want to make it gorgeous," she

There are many small steps in the completion of a Barbie doll. The rooting of the Barbie head, shown at right, is one of the most time consuming and important.

noted. "It's easy when you have a lot of money. . .even on beaded costumes, you'd think that was easy, but it's not. . .every single one is hand done. . .that's difficult to control. It's fairly straightforward for 100 of them, but think about 50,000 units of a doll. No other garment manufacture makes as much clothing as we do."

Echoing Cynthia Young's description of the multi-disciplined group, Bazerman described the team as follows: "Everybody is a specialist. Think of the design center as doctors; the specialists are dermatologists who paint the dolls' faces. Then we transfer them out to sub-specialists. Hong Kong is the fabric costume specialist. Next door are the people who know how to find the vendors who make the fabrics. This is difficult, since 99% of these vendors make fabric for the garment (i.e., human-sized) industry. And we invent fabrics all the time. They figure out how to find the fabric in a back-and-forth dance with the vendors. This process alone can take four weeks or as long as a year."

Dolls that must be turned around quickly are particularly challenging. One of the quickest turnaround-time Barbie dolls was the Target Baseball Barbie. The designers in California wanted to capitalize on the baseball frenzy at the time (think *Field of Dreams,* and you get the idea). "We try not to put new fabrics [i.e., fabric requiring design "from scratch"] on a doll like this," Bazerman said. "We had to go into the open market and find some stripes to give it top priority and capitalize on the baseball trend. Now we're working on Olympic Barbie the same way. Baywatch Barbie also had a quick turnaround. In these situations, the whole team has to work fast, design fast."

All this activity would be fathomable for a few dolls at a time. However,

Just a few Barbie heads waiting for assembly.

Bazerman admitted: "We have 50 projects on our plate at any one time." How are all these balls juggled at once? "Everything is managed on a computer," she said. "My secretary prints out flow charts every Monday and we manage the various projects in real time. My bottom line is to get it done!"

Another way of fast-tracking dolls is by working very closely with the team. Bazerman said, "Ann Driskill is coming to Hong Kong in November with the team, including managers of marketing, costing and planning. We will lock ourselves in a room for two weeks and go from concept to approval in the office in real time. This is how to get things done!"

"We've come a long way since 1985 when there were only two textile people and three pattern people. Today we have 50 such professionals," Bazerman said from her sophisticated high-rise office on Canton Road in Kowloon, chock full of glitter. . . .

Now, fast-forward from the glitter in Hong Kong to the glitter back at Mattel's corporate offices in El Segundo, California. Once the dolls are manufactured in Asia in a first run-through, along comes Judy Schizas from the Corporate Product Integrity group (CPI). To prevent potential pitfalls along the way, CPI is involved throughout the process. This function fills the crucial safety and quality assurance (QA) roles. Each doll is tested for its age-grading and has to meet every requirement for that group. CPI's laboratory conducts all kinds of testing. The CPI engineers write specifications, instructing the manufacturing plants how to test the toys. Manufacturing plants located outside of the United States must meet all requirements established by Mattel's CPI group in El Segundo, CA. Once CPI receives the manufactured doll, they perform audits in the CPI lab.

It seems that there are more types of testing than there were variations of Teen Talk Barbie dolls. Tests include:

- *Transit tests,* where CPI puts doll packages on "shake machines" to simulate the workout that the boxes will get when packed and shipped.
- *Drop tests,* a series of different drops to see if earrings fall off, if hair covers the doll's face, if the doll breaks even though it is hooked down. Schizas described: "We drop the doll from different attitudes. . .on her head, her arms, her bottom!"
- *Aging tests,* where CPI puts the doll in an oven to determine shelf life.
- *Humidity tests,* where the doll is placed in an environmental chamber. One scenario in a humidity test is a Barbie wearing black trousers: if the doll gets damp, do her legs get stained black? "We try to figure this out before it happens by doing these little tests," Schizas said.

Another time consuming assembly step is the packaging of the Barbie doll and accessories.

- *Function tests,* where every doll's legs, head and arms have to move.
- *Abuse tests,* where both reliability and safety abuse are tested. Schizas emphasized: "When we say abuse, we mean *very* abusive abuse. We pull arms and legs off, to determine how secure they are. We do bite and hair-pull tests. We conduct abrasion tests to see if the paint comes off of the doll's face."
- *Heavy elements test,* where the face paints and other chemicals are checked for lead and other elements.
- *Flammability tests,* "from the doll figure itself to her underpants," said Schizas. Every piece of material has to burn at a slow rate.
- *Life tests,* where the doll's arms are rotated a certain amount of times, knees are bent a number of cycles, and heads are turned a prescribed number of cycles.
- *Chemical and biological testing,* where if a doll is designed to go into the water, it must meet chemical and biological testing. This test focuses on mold inhibitors.
- *Other safety and health issues:* Even feathers for Bob Mackie dolls are sent out to labs to be tested, to make certain that they contain no bacteria.

After all of that abuse, it is interesting to note that only about four percent of dolls go back to the drawing board for retooling. Not until every test is completed does the doll move ahead to the manufacturing line to be prepared for production. From there, everything is sent to Asia for mass production.

Barbie dolls have never been manufactured in the U.S. Since 1959, the dolls have been made overseas. Manufacturing has occurred in Japan, Singapore, Malaysia, Indonesia, Mexico and the People's Republic of China (PRC). Currently, Mattel operates two plants in Malaysia, two plants in the PRC, and one plant in Indonesia. Barbie dolls are also being made in a new world-class manufacturing facility in Jakarta, Indonesia. Managing the mix of dolls coming off the line is a challenge; just ponder for a moment the many distinctions—some obvious and others more subtle—between a porcelain evening gowned doll, a Mackie vinyl Barbie doll, and a main line hair play doll, and you begin to appreciate the logistical challenge.

Larry Morgan of Mattel International is responsible for overseeing Asian manufacturing operations. "A funny thing happened on the way to Indonesia," he told me. To establish the manufacturing plant in Indonesia, Mattel had to obtain approval from the country's investment approval board BKPM, which advises President Suharto. The Mattel team presented their business case to a huge group of people to review. "They didn't know who we were when we walked into the meeting," Morgan recalled. "As part of our presentation, we brought our toy catalogs, which we opened to illustrate our business. As soon as we opened to the first page, their eyes lit up. They said, 'Barbie! Barbie!' They knew who *she* was, even though they didn't know Mattel!"

1995 Happy Holidays Barbie *sold out so quickly that Mattel issued vouchers for additional dolls to be made available Spring 1996.*

Chapter 11

BARBIE® ECONOMICS

The Barbie doll is big business. In 1992, *Financial World* magazine calculated a market value for Mattel, Inc., of $2.3 billion. But the bean counters found that when the value of the Barbie doll brand name was factored in, the company's market value increased to $4.5 billion.

That kind of brand equity only happens through diligence, sound strategic planning and no small amount of luck. This chapter focuses on the business side of Barbie doll, including advertising and the globalization and management of the brand.

Factoid

Between 1988 and 1993, sales of Barbie dolls doubled, reaching nearly $1 billion in 1992.

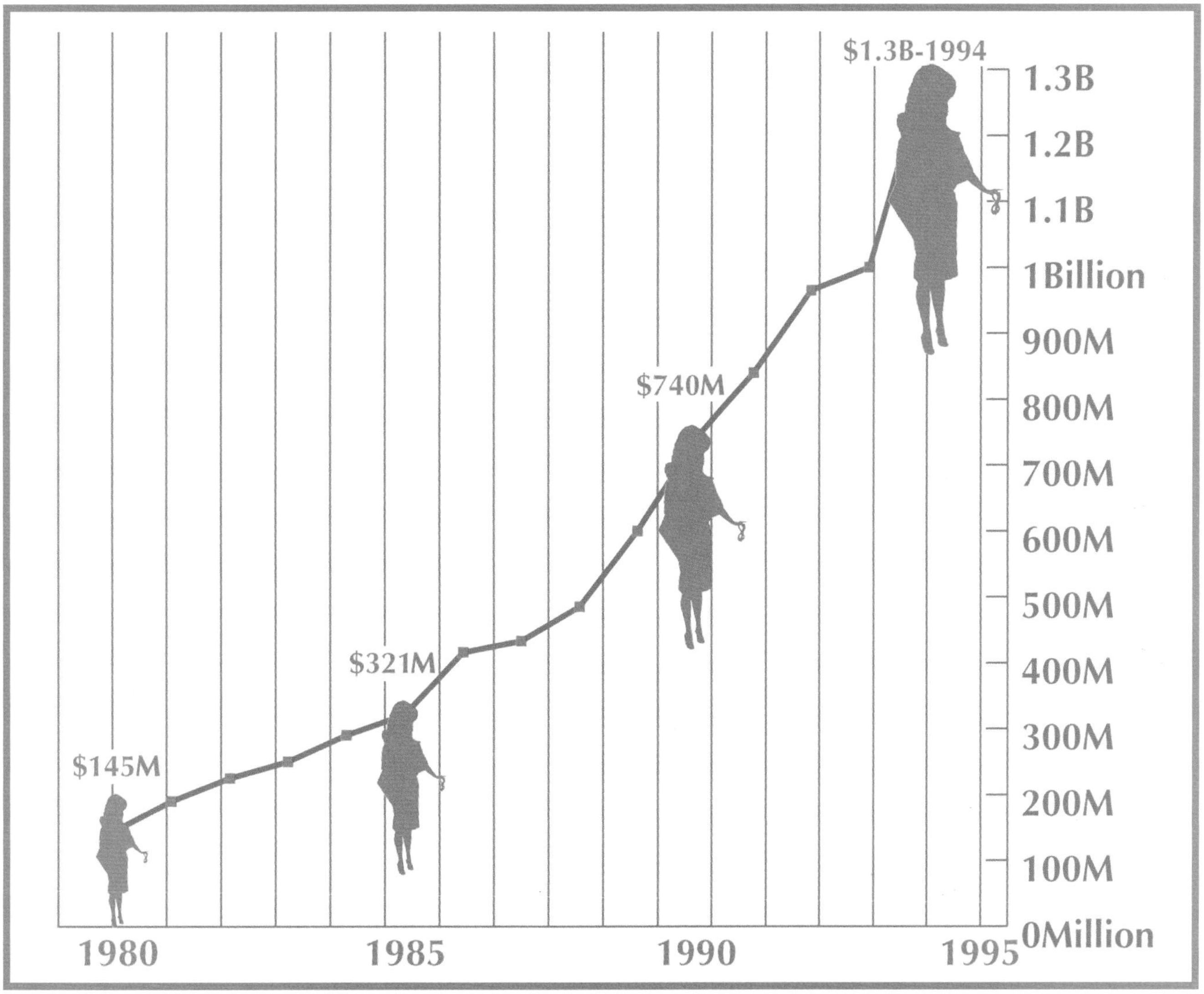

BARBIE WORLDWIDE SALES
1980—1994

Factoid

Barbie's last name, Roberts, derived from Mattel's first advertising agency for the doll, Carson Roberts.

◆ Advertising

One contemporary art medium is particularly relevant in a discussion about *Contemporary BARBIE*: the applied art of Madison Avenue known as advertising. Since the Barbie doll's introduction in 1959, advertising has played a key role in promotion of the doll. When the doll was first unveiled at New York Toy Fair in 1959, television advertising time was purchased during programs such as "The Mickey Mouse Club." In addition to TV ads, Barbie ads have been placed in print media—particularly magazines. Today, ads for the Barbie doll go well beyond traditional television and magazine promotions, and have evolved into thirty-minute infomercials and offers through electronic catalogs over on-line computer services, along with the proliferation of print catalogs.

It is informative to review Mattel's advertising for the Barbie doll since her inception. The changing ad campaigns reveal much about the language and social morés prevalent at any given time. In the course of compiling material for this book, I had the opportunity to review and analyze some sixty minutes of Barbie doll television commercials.

The Barbie doll was first advertised on television in 1960, back in the, "You Can Tell It's Mattel. . .It's Swell" era. The first commercial jingle was sung to the strains of an orchestra:

> Barbie you're beautiful
> You make me feel
> My Barbie doll is really real
>
> Barbie's small and so petite
> Her clothes and figure look so neat
> Her dancin' outfit rings a bell
> At parties she will cast a spell
> Purses, hats and gloves galore
> And all the gadgets gals adore
>
> Male voiceover: "Barbie dressed for swim and fun is only $3. Her lovely fashions range from $1 to $5. Look for Barbie wherever dolls are sold."
>
> Some day I'm gonna be
> Exactly like you
> 'Til then I know just what I'll do
> Barbie
> Beautiful Barbie
> I'll make believe that I am you
>
> Male voiceover: "You can tell it's Mattel, it's swell!"

Now fast-forward through years of Beach Boys/Jan & Dean-style surfing music, and Maureen McCormick (later famous as Marsha from the "Brady Bunch") promoting the New Living Barbie.

In 1972, the "Surprising Barbie" era of ads began. . .

> Hey! How can you make your Barbie's arms and legs move like that?
> Hey! You're making her walk!
>
> Meet new Walk Lively Barbie.
> She comes with her own walk and turn stand.
> Just put her in and push her along.
> Look, she even turns around.
>
> There's a Walk Lively Ken and Steffie, too.
> Now we can pretend she's going for a walk in the park with Ken.
> You can also make her walk off the stand.
> See how her head turns?
>
> [Song]
> With surprising Barbie there's always something new
> Lots of fun and surprising things to do
> Surprising Barbie. . . Barbie. . .Barbie. . .

Enchanted Evening Barbie *porcelain ad.*

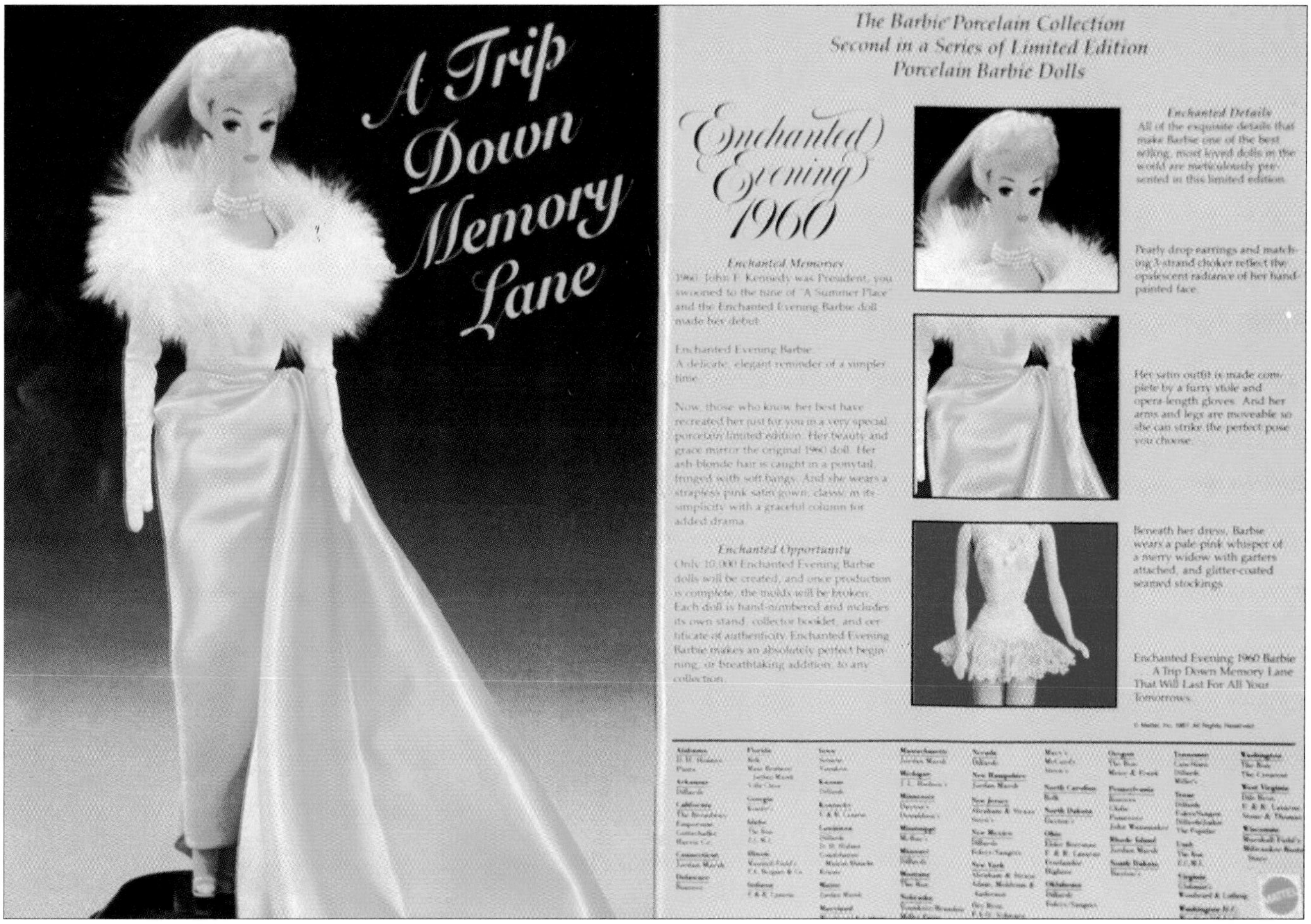

Then in a few years, Barbie promoted the "We Girls Can Do Anything" campaign. . .

> Here's Day-to-Night Barbie
> [Song]
> We girls make working lots of fun
> Right, Barbie?
> Day-to-Night Barbie
> We can work from nine to five
> And then change in a sec' for an evening with Ken
> Secret turnaround skirt, fabulous hair
> We girls can do anything
> Right, Barbie?
> Day-to-Night Barbie has a change-around outfit
>
> Ken doll sold separately.

Factoid

The "wall of pink" merchandising concept in retail stores began in 1991.

From "We Girls Can Do Anything," the ad campaigns shifted to, "We're into Barbie. . . ." This campaign was successfully and intensively used for California Dream Barbie, Island Fun Barbie, Perfume Pretty Barbie, Cool Times Barbie, Animal Lovin' Barbie, Doctor Barbie, Style Magic Barbie, Dance Club Barbie, Western Fun Barbie, Wet 'n Wild Barbie, Lights and Lace Barbie, Hawaiian Fun Barbie, and Costume Ball Barbie.

Then, rap music began to be used in some ads. . . .

> *[3 young girls rapping]*
> There's a brand new Barbie
> In a brand new mood
> She's a teenage Barbie
> With a cool attitude
> Feelin' fun is her name
> Havin' fun is her game
> Ooh, those clothes
> Ooh, that hair
> She's got friends everywhere
> She's where it's happening
>
> You put it together
>
> Feelin' Fun
> Feelin' Fun Barbie.

Factoid

In 1993, a typical American girl was exposed to 2,452 Barbie TV commercials a year.

The "You've Got Something Special Era," which began around 1991, has been the basis for ads for Totally Hair Barbie, Sun Sensation Barbie, Rollerblade Barbie and Sparkle Eyes Barbie.

The tone of child-directed ads radically shifted in 1994 to target adult consumers. Mattel's first Barbie doll infomercial was produced to promote the Classique line. The infomercial was hosted by Pam Dawber, of "Mork and Mindy" fame, hosting several Barbie collectors in the typical infomercial living room set-up. During the course of the infomercial, viewers are introduced to Janet

Goldblatt, Carol Spencer and Kitty Black-Perkins. The purchase offer included three Classique dolls with a bonus special gift—a Barbie collector's video filmed in part at the 1993 Barbie convention held in Baltimore, Maryland.

The second Barbie doll infomercial, which started airing in 1994, was the Scarlett Infomercial hosted by Leeza Gibbons, ex-"Entertainment Tonight" and current talk show host. Mattel credits these infomercials with very effectively attracting and communicating to new collectors. Count on seeing more of them in the future!

◆ Global Barbie

Mattel is more than a toy company: It's a global marketing company. It is clear that the company's major growth area looking to the year 2000 is outside of the United States. That's because there are twice as many children in Europe three times as many in South America and fifteen times as many in Asia as there are in the United States. In Europe, by the year 2000, more than 20 percent of the 40 million children in the European Community under the age of 10 will be living in the United Kingdom. And, Barbie already has a good start in Europe. Due to aggressive marketing efforts in the early 1990s, the typical girl in Italy had almost as many Barbie dolls (seven) as her American counterpart. In France and Germany, the average girl had five Barbie dolls.

Mattel maintains 34 marketing offices overseas. Further facilitating international expansion is the surging growth of Toys 'R Us into foreign markets. The huge toy chain has 234 stores from Germany to Malaysia, and plans to open at least 50 new stores overseas every year for the foreseeable future.

Factoid

In Sweden, more Barbie dolls have been sold than there are Swedes.

***UNICEF Barbie** dolls, like those shown here, helped to expand Barbie's global presence.*

One small step for Barbiekind....1994 and 1986 Barbie dolls on the moon....

Chapter 12

Reading the Pink Tea Leaves

Where do you want to see Barbie® in the year 2001? Given that the designers work on a two-year lead time, I didn't think the question would be too difficult for Barbie doll designers to forecast.

I asked everyone with whom I met at Mattel about the future of the Barbie doll. While Mattel designers cannot share specific plans, it is interesting to note the company-line response, which goes something like this: "Barbie will go places she's never gone before. . .places that haven't even been imagined yet." She could be in a movie, have her own theme park, and star in a Broadway musical. To those readers who may be cynical about such a possibility, ponder this: Who just a few years ago would have thought that Disney would ever consider refurbishing Times Square in New York to create a Disney neighborhood of attractions?

One intriguing possibility is that the Barbie character will be in a feature film. According to Mattel, they have been approached more than once to do a big-screen movie deal. But even with major studio interest over the years in the Barbie doll, Mattel has not yet received a satisfactory script. Even avid Barbie doll collector Demi Moore's production company, Moving Pictures!, has shown interest in a Barbie film project.

One certainty is that collectors will have a broad range of Barbie dolls from which to choose. . .and careful choosing is required. A glance at the *Contemporary BARBIE* doll list in the Appendix quickly reveals that the number of dolls named Barbie brought to market has grown each year—approximating 100 in 1995 alone. Given the cost of living indices for shelter, food and clothing, very few collectors can afford to buy, display or store every doll that comes on the market; nor is every doll available to every collector—limited editions being a case in point.

Mattel marketing management realizes that the collector market segment, particularly new collectors, is its fastest growing segment (domestically speaking). The Mattel team of designers, market management, engineers, production staff and accountants are working hard to attract new collectors, and to convert them to dedicated collectors. Their strategies are working; Mattel estimated that as of August 1995, there were well over 100,000 avid collectors with the following demographic characteristics:

- 90% of avid collectors are women (yes, Virginia, 10% are men).
- The median age of avid collectors is 40 years.
- Avid collectors buy more than 20 Barbie dolls each year.
- 45% of avid collectors spend upwards of $1,000 a year.

Mattel is working hard to attract new collectors to Barbie's world. Market research shows that there are some 28 million women between the ages of 25 and 45 who grew up playing with Barbie. This age group certainly represents many who are already avid collectors. The 35th anniversary, the success of the 1994 and 1995 releases of Nostalgic Barbie dolls, and the success of the Hollywood Legends Barbie as Scarlett series have demonstrated a fertile and as yet relatively-untapped market of baby boomers.

There are several ways that this phantom group might be enticed into the world of Barbie doll collecting. Here, for example, are just a few of the things we might expect:

- Mattel will further exploit direct mail, infomercials and home shopping via television. Some 19 percent of all collectible dolls were sold via direct mail in 1993, and 8 percent via home shopping. Collectors demand new retail channels for dolls. There are only 2,600 collectible doll stores in the United States, so the new distribution channels fill real needs and provide a level of service that collectors (particularly those working outside of the home) require.
- Mattel will continue to segment the Barbie doll market in a variety of ways. Dolls will be priced in every range for every taste.
- Barbie dolls will be "cross-germinated" with themes attractive to baby boomers, such as those with complementary collections (e.g., Star Trek, movie characters, and the like) or childhood memories and "tastes," via food tie-ins. Barbie dolls tie in well with adult brands such as Avon, Coca-Cola, Russell Stover and the like.
- Fashion fantasies and character dolls will be increasingly important in the future.
- Ethnic variations will continue to grow in importance given the changing demographics of the U.S. as well as the phenomenon of immigration on a global basis.

So, what's left for Barbie, the doll who seems to been "everywhere" and done "everything?" Well, not quite! The pink tea leaves reveal that Barbie will be more global, work at new careers, model fabulous new fashions, demonstrate even more interesting special effects, further exploit computer technology, and have the potential to eat into every collector's retirement funds if they don't strategically plan their Barbie doll collections.

As Kitty Black-Perkins told me, "Barbie in the year 2000 is not too far away. We're thinking about a lot of opportunities where she could go. . .but they take her to another level, to a broader range of people who love her. Now that we've had a generation of people who have played with her and love her, there are so many different ways to enjoy Barbie. It can be as a child, or it can be as an adult. There's a lot of room for loving her. . . ."

Porcelain Silken Flame Barbie

Comprehensive List of *Contemporary Barbie*® Dolls and Values

This chapter presents a comprehensive list of all Barbie dolls issued since 1980. The list is organized by year and includes the name of the doll, the Mattel stock number, the variation where it is appropriate, and an estimate of the value of the doll, Never Removed From Box (NRFB), with the box in flawless condition. Also included in the list is a photo reference page number if a picture of the doll was used in this book.

Estimates of the NRFB value have been derived from the following sources as of January 1996:

- Results of Barbie doll auctions as published in auction house "prices realized" lists
- Price lists published by six large national Barbie doll dealers
- Prices gleaned from individual sales on computer bulletin boards listing items for sale that have been successfully sold.

These values represent what the buyer would have to pay, and not what a seller of a doll to a dealer could fetch. Typically, a dealer would offer the seller a wholesale price for the doll (e.g., up to 50 percent less than the collector might realize in selling the piece directly to another collector).

Items in less than NRFB condition (that is, mint in box, excellent or lesser condition) would almost always be valued lower than the NRFB values. The discounted value would be a function of the rarity and condition of the doll, as well as the buyer's willingness to acquire the doll. Many buyers who wish to fill in an incomplete collection are sometimes willing to pay substantially more than the average market price.

This list is provided only as a general guide. Readers of *Contemporary Barbie* should educate themselves by collecting and analyzing all price information available in the market to become savvy Barbie doll consumers. Only then will the market for secondary Barbie doll collectibles work as well as it can.

***Barbie as Scarlett**, part of the Hollywood Legends Series, was creatively packaged in a gold foil box with a star cutout.*

CONTEMPORARY BARBIE 1980-1995

Latest Revision — February 1996

DOLL	MATTEL NO.	VARIATION/COMMENT	NRFB VALUE	BOOK PAGE
◆ 1980				
Beauty Secrets Barbie	1290	Blonde	$65	
Beauty Secrets Pretty Reflections Giftset	1702	Blonde	95	
Black Barbie	1293	First Black Barbie	70	8, 10, 142
Hispanic Barbie	1292	First Hispanic Barbie	65	142, 144
International - Italian	1601		225	
International - Parisian	1600		155	5, 19
International - Royal	1602		225	
Kissing Barbie	2597		40	
Pretty Changes Barbie	2598		45	
Rollerskating Barbie	1880		40	182
Sun Lovin' Malibu Barbie	1067		25	
◆ 1981				
Golden Dream Barbie	1874	Blonde	55	12
Golden Dream Barbie	1874	Blonde "big hair"	95	12
Golden Dream - Glamorous Nights Set	3533	w/fur coat	95	12
Happy Birthday Barbie	1922		25	12, 14
International - Oriental	3262		175	19
International - Scottish	3263		155	19
My First Barbie	1875		40	12, 13, 15
Sunsational Malibu Barbie	1067	Blonde	20	
Sunsational Malibu Barbie	4970	Hispanic	20	
Western Barbie	1757		35	13
◆ 1982				
Fashion Jeans Barbie	5313	Black	45	
Fashion Jeans Barbie	5315	Blonde	40	
Hawaiian Barbie	7470		40	18, 142
International - Eskimo	3898		135	16, 19, 105
International - India	3897		250	19
Magic Curl Barbie	3856	Blonde	40	
Magic Curl Barbie	3989	Black	40	16
Pink & Pretty Barbie	3554		50	12
Pink & Pretty Modeling Set	5239		55	

DOLL	MATTEL NO.	VARIATION/COMMENT	NRFB VALUE	BOOK PAGE
◆ 1983				
Angel Face Barbie	5640		$50	
Ballerina Superstar Barbie (Mervyns)	4983	Blonde	75	
Ballerina Superstar Barbie (Mervyns)	4984	Black	65	
Barbie & Friends Gift Set	4431	Blonde	95	
Barbie & Ken Camping Out Giftset	4984	Blonde	75	
Dream Date Barbie	1982		40	
Fashion Play Barbie	7193	Four outfit variations	20	
International - Spanish	4031		145	19, 20
International - Swedish	4032		145	19
Loving You Barbie	7583		60	
My First Barbie	1875		20	
Party Time Barbie	4798		25	
Playtime Barbie	5336		20	
Twirly Curls Barbie	5579	Blonde	45	
Twirly Curls Barbie	5723	Black	30	
Twirly Curls Barbie ("Ricitos")	5724	Hispanic	50	
Twirly Curls Gift Set	4097	Blonde	50	
◆ 1984				
Crystal Barbie	4598	Blonde - 25th anniversary	35	22
Crystal Barbie	4859	Black - 25th anniversary	35	
Great Shapes Barbie	7025	Blonde	25	182
Great Shapes Barbie	7834	Black	25	
Happy Birthday Barbie	1922		30	
Happy Birthday Gift Set	9519		85	
International - Irish	7517		165	19
International - Swiss	7541		135	19
Loving You Barbie	7072		55	
My First Barbie	1875	White	25	
My First Barbie	9858	Black	35	
Sun Gold Malibu Barbie	1067	Blonde	20	
Sun Gold Malibu Barbie	4970	Hispanic	15	
Sun Gold Malibu Christie	7745	Black	20	
TRU - Dance Sensation Gift Set	9058	Blonde	45	
◆ 1985				
BillyBoy* Le Nouveau Theatre de la Mode	6279		250	25, 138
Day to Night Barbie	7929	Blonde	35	24
Day to Night Barbie	7944	Hispanic	40	24

DOLL	MATTEL NO.	VARIATION/COMMENT	NRFB VALUE	BOOK PAGE
Day to Night Barbie	7945	Black	$30	24
Dreamtime Barbie	9180	Pink and Blue versions	40	
Happy Birthday Barbie	1922		15	
International - Japanese	9481		175	
Music Lovin' Barbie	9988		35	
Peaches 'n Cream Barbie	7926	Blonde	75	
Peaches 'n Cream Barbie	9516	Black	55	

◆ 1986

DOLL	MATTEL NO.	VARIATION/COMMENT	NRFB VALUE	BOOK PAGE
Astronaut Barbie	1207	Black	90	29, 170
Astronaut Barbie	2449	Blonde	90	29
Dream Glow Barbie	1647	Hispanic	35	31, 32
Dream Glow Barbie	2248	Blonde	30	31, 32
Dream Glow Barbie	2422	Black	30	31
Fabulous Fur (Mervyns)	N/A		55	
Gift Giving Barbie	1922		20	
International - Greek	2997		125	30
International - Peruvian	2995		125	
Magic Moves Barbie	2126	Blonde	30	28
Magic Moves Barbie	2127	Black	40	
My First Barbie	1788	Blonde - Pink Tutu	20	
My First Barbie	1801	Black - Pink Tutu	20	
My First Barbie	5979	Hispanic - Pink Tutu	35	
My First Barbie Gift Set	1879	Pink Tutu	25	
Porcelain - Blue Rhapsody	1708		750	
Rocker Barbie	1140		50	107
Sears - 100th Anniversary Celebration	2998	Blonde	100	126
Tennis Star Barbie	1760		25	
Tropical Malibu Barbie	1017	Blonde	25	
Tropical Malibu Barbie	1022	Black	25	
Tropical Malibu Barbie	1646	Hispanic	35	
Tropical Malibu Deluxe Gift Set	2996	Blonde	45	
Vacation Sensation Barbie	1675	Blue Set - First Edition	35	
Vacation Sensation Barbie	1675	Pink Set	45	

◆ 1987

DOLL	MATTEL NO.	VARIATION/COMMENT	NRFB VALUE	BOOK PAGE
American Beauties Mardi Gras Barbie	4930		150	
BillyBoy* Feelin' Groovy	3421	aka Glamour-a-Go-Go	250	37, 138
Cool Times Barbie	3022		30	
Dancing Action Rocker Barbie	3055		40	33
Fashion Play Barbie	9429		30	

DOLL	MATTEL NO.	VARIATION/COMMENT	NRFB VALUE	BOOK PAGE
Fun Time Barbie	1738	Blonde in blue w/watch	$25	
Fun Time Barbie	1739	Black in pink w/watch	20	
Fun Time Barbie (w/watch)	3718	Blonde in pink w/watch	20	
Fun Time Barbie (w/watch)	3717	Blonde in lavender w/watch	20	
Gift Giving Barbie	1205		20	
International - German	3188		115	
International - Icelandic	3189		115	
Jewel Secrets Barbie	1737	Blonde	30	36
Jewel Secrets Barbie	1756	Black	35	
Olympic Skating (Calgary)	4549		60	
Porcelain - Enchanted Evening	3415	1960 Barbie reproduction	500	167
Sears - Star Dream Barbie	4550		75	
Star Dream Barbie	4550		60	
Super Hair Barbie	3101	Blonde	20	
Super Hair Barbie	3206	Black	25	
Wal-Mart - Pink Jubilee	4589		85	

◆ 1988

DOLL	MATTEL NO.	VARIATION/COMMENT	NRFB VALUE	BOOK PAGE
Animal Lovin' Barbie	1350	Blonde	35	41
Animal Lovin' Barbie	4824	Black	35	
Beach Blast Malibu Barbie	3237	Blonde	20	
Beach Blast Malibu Christie	3253	Black	20	
California Barbie	4439		45	42
Doctor Barbie	3850		95	93
Fun to Dress Barbie	1372	Blonde	10	
Fun to Dress Barbie	1373	Black	10	
Fun to Dress Barbie	4558	Blonde	10	
Fun to Dress Barbie	7668	Black	10	
Happy Holidays Barbie	1703		700	39
International - Canadian	4928		85	42, 105
International - Korean	4929		85	
Island Fun Barbie	4061		15	
My First Barbie	1280	Blonde - White Tutu	20	
My First Barbie	1281	Black - White Tutu	20	
My First Barbie	1282	Hispanic - White Tutu	25	
Perfume Pretty Barbie	4551	Blonde	30	40
Perfume Pretty Barbie	4552	Black	30	
Porcelain - Benefit Performance	5475	1967 Barbie reproduction	450	116
Sears - Lilac & Lovely Barbie	7669		75	
Sensations Barbie	4931		75	107

DOLL	MATTEL NO.	VARIATION/COMMENT	NRFB VALUE	BOOK PAGE
SuperStar/Movie Star Barbie	1604	Blonde	$25	94
SuperStar/Movie Star Barbie	1605	Black	25	
TRU - Show 'N Ride Gift Set	7799		45	
TRU - Tennis Star Gift Set	7801	Barbie & Ken	50	
Vacation Sensation Gift Set	1675		25	
Wal-Mart - Frills & Fantasy	1374		40	

◆ 1989

DOLL	MATTEL NO.	VARIATION/COMMENT	NRFB VALUE	BOOK PAGE
American Beauties Army	3966		45	46
FAO Schwarz - Golden Greetings	7734		250	
Feelin' Fun Barbie	1189	Blonde	20	
Feelin' Fun Barbie	4808	Blonde - second issue	20	
Feelin' Fun Barbie	4809	Black	20	
Feelin' Fun Barbie	7373	Hispanic	20	
Garden Party Barbie	1953		30	
Happy Holidays Barbie	3253		250	111
Hills - Party Lace Barbie	4843		40	
International - Mexican	1917		50	
International - Russian	1916		85	46, 105
Kmart - Peach Pretty Barbie	4870		55	
Porcelain - Wedding Party Barbie	2641	1959 Barbie reproduction	695	
Sears - Evening Enchantment	3596		65	
Style Magic Barbie	1283		30	
Target - Gold 'n Lace Barbie	7476		35	
TRU - Denim Fun/Cool City Blues Gift Set	4893		50	
TRU - Party Treats Barbie	4885		25	
TRU - Pepsi Spirit Barbie	4869		75	
TRU - Sweet Roses Barbie	7635		45	
UNICEF Barbie	1920	Blonde	30	45, 169
UNICEF Barbie	4770	Black	30	26, 45, 169
UNICEF Barbie	4774	Asian	30	45, 169
UNICEF Barbie	4782	Hispanic	30	45, 169
Wal-Mart - Lavender Looks Barbie	3963		55	
Wedding Fantasy Barbie	2125	Blonde	40	
Wedding Fantasy Barbie	7011	Black	40	
Wedding Fantasy Gift Set	9852	w/6 dolls	100	
Winn Dixie - Party Pink Barbie	7637		25	
Woolworth - Special Expressions	4842	Blonde	25	
Woolworth - Special Expressions	7326	Black	25	

DOLL	MATTEL NO.	VARIATION/COMMENT	NRFB VALUE	BOOK PAGE
◆ 1990				
All Stars Barbie - Aerobics	9099		$20	182
Applause - Style Barbie	5313		40	
Barbie & the Beat Barbie	2751	Blonde	35	
Bob Mackie Gold Barbie	5405		850	52, 54
Cool Looks Barbie	5947		20	109
Dance Club Barbie	3509		35	51
Dance Club Hot Dancin' Gift Set	4917	w/cassette player	75	
Dance Magic Barbie	4836	Blonde	25	
Dance Magic Barbie	7080	Black	25	
Dance Magic Gift Set	5409		95	
Disney Fun Barbie	4385	Blonde - First in series	60	128
Disney Fun Barbie	9835	Black - First in series	60	
FAO Schwarz - Winter Fantasy	5946		350	
Fashion Play Barbie	5766	Blonde	20	
Fashion Play Barbie	5953	Black	10	
Fashion Play Barbie	5954	Hispanic	10	
Flight Time Barbie	2066	Hispanic	50	
Flight Time Barbie	9584	Blonde	50	
Flight Time Barbie	9916	Black	45	49
Friendship Berlin Wall Barbie	5506	aka German Friendship	50	48
Fun-to-Dress Barbie	4808	Blonde	20	
Fun-to-Dress Barbie	4939	Black	20	
Fun-to-Dress Barbie	7373	Hispanic	20	
Happy Birthday Barbie	7913	Blonde	25	
Happy Birthday Barbie	9561	Black	25	
Happy Holidays Barbie	4098	Blonde	200	111
Happy Holidays Barbie	4543	Black	200	
Hills - Evening Sparkle Barbie	3274		45	
Home Pretty Barbie	2249		25	
Ice Capades Barbie	7348	Black	25	
Ice Capades Barbie	7365	Blonde	25	
JC Penney - Evening Elegance Barbie	7057		100	
Kmart - Fashion Friend	7019	Swimsuit version	25	
Kmart - Fashion Friend	7026	Party Dress version	25	
On the Go Barbie	1007		80	
Porcelain - Solo in the Spotlight	7613	1961 Barbie reproduction	295	
Porcelain - Sophisticated Lady	5313		250	
Sears - Lavender Surprise Barbie	5588	Black	50	
Sears - Lavender Surprise Barbie	9409	Blonde	50	
Summit Barbie	7027	Blonde	30	50

DOLL	MATTEL NO.	VARIATION/COMMENT	NRFB VALUE	BOOK PAGE
Summit Barbie	7028	Black	$30	
Summit Barbie	7029	Asian	30	
Summit Barbie	7030	Hispanic	40	
Target - Party Pretty Barbie	5955		40	
TRU - Winter Fun Barbie	5949		75	
Wal-Mart - Dream Fantasy Barbie	7335		55	
Western Fun Barbie	2930	Black	35	
Western Fun Barbie	9932	Blonde	35	
Western Fun Gift Set	5408	w/Horse Sun Runner	45	
Wet 'n Wild Barbie	4103		20	
Wholesale clubs - Party Sensation Barbie	9025		60	
Winn Dixie - Pink Sensation Barbie	5410		30	
Woolworth - Special Expressions	5504	Blonde	30	
Woolworth - Special Expressions	5505	Black	30	

◆ 1991

DOLL	MATTEL NO.	VARIATION/COMMENT	NRFB VALUE	BOOK PAGE
All American Barbie	3712	w/Barbie's horse/Gift Set	65	
All American Barbie	9423	w/Reeboks	15	
American Beauty Queen	3137	Blonde	35	
American Beauty Queen	3245	Black	35	
Ames - Hot Looks Barbie	5756		35	
Ames - Party in Pink Barbie	2909		40	
Applause - Beauty Belle	4553		35	
Applause - Holiday	3406		55	
Ballerina Music Box - Swan Lake	1648		300	
Bath Magic Barbie	5274	Blonde	15	
Bath Magic Barbie	7951	Black	15	
Bathtime Fun Barbie	9601	Blonde	15	
Bathtime Fun Barbie	9603	Black	15	
Bob Mackie Platinum	2703		700	55, back cover
Bob Mackie Starlight Splendor	2704	Black	700	
Costume Ball Barbie	7123	Blonde	25	57
Costume Ball Barbie	7134	Black	25	
Disneyland Visit Gift Set	3177	"Barbie, Ken & Skipper"	70	
Dolls of the World - Malaysian	7329		55	
Dolls of the World - Czechoslovakian	7330		150	58
Dolls of the World - Nigerian	7376		85	58
Dolls of the World - Brazilian	9094		85	
Dolls of the World - Parisian	9843		55	
Dolls of the World - Eskimo	9844		55	
Dolls of the World - Scottish	9845		55	

DOLL	MATTEL NO.	VARIATION/COMMENT	NRFB VALUE	BOOK PAGE
Dream Bride Barbie	1623		$50	96
Dream Wardrobe Gift Set	3331		40	
FAO Schwarz - Night Sensation	2921		225	
Friendship Berlin Wall	2080		25	48
Friendship Berlin Wall	3677	Red variation	13	
Happy Holidays Barbie	1871		85	111
Hawaiian Fun Barbie	5940		20	
Hills - Moonlight Rose Barbie	3549		45	
Home Shopping Club - Evening Flame Barbie	1865		175	
Ice Capades Barbie	9847	Second edition	20	
JC Penney - Enchanted Evening	2702		110	
Lights & Lace Barbie	9725		20	
McGlynn's Bakery - Barbie	1511	Blonde	50	

She can do anything! A representative assortment of popular athletic Barbie dolls.

DOLL	MATTEL NO.	VARIATION/COMMENT	NRFB VALUE	BOOK PAGE
McGlynn's Bakery - Barbie	1534	Black	$50	131
Mermaid Barbie	1434		25	60
My First Barbie	9942	Blonde	15	
My First Barbie	9943	Hispanic	15	
My First Barbie	9944	Black	15	
Porcelain Treasures - Gay Parisienne	9973	1959 Barbie reproduction	250	
Radio Shack - Earring Magic	N/A	Includes Software Pak	75	152
Rollerblade Gift Set	7142		35	
Sears - Southern Belle	2586		60	
Service Merchandise - Blue Rhapsody	1362		300	
Shopko - Venture - Blossom Beauty	3142		55	
Ski Fun Barbie	7511		35	100
Spiegel - Sterling Wishes	3347		175	
Stars and Stripes Air Force Barbie	3360		55	
Stars and Stripes Marine Corps Barbie	7549	Blonde	35	94
Stars and Stripes Marine Corps Barbie	7594	Black	35	
Stars and Stripes Marine Corps Gift Set	4704	Blonde, Barbie & Ken	50	
Stars and Stripes Navy Barbie	9693	Blonde	35	56
Stars and Stripes Navy Barbie	9694	Black	35	56
Supermarket - Sweet Spring Barbie	3208		35	
Supermarket - Trailblazin' Barbie	2783		35	129
Target - Cute 'n Cool Barbie	2954		50	
Target - Golden Evening Barbie	2587		50	
TRU - Sweet Romance Barbie	2917		25	
United Colors of Benetton Barbie	9404	First in series	50	57,187
Wal-Mart - Ballroom Beauty Barbie	3678		50	
Wedding Day for Midge - Barbie	9608		35	
Wedding Day for Midge - Gift Set	9852	Six doll set	255	
Wholesale clubs - Bathtime Gift Set	N/A		50	
Wholesale clubs - Jewel Jubilee Barbie	2366		75	
Winn Dixie - Southern Beauty Barbie	3284		35	
Woolworth - Special Expressions	2582	Blonde	35	
Woolworth - Special Expressions	2583	Black	35	

◆ 1992

Ames - Denim 'n Lace Barbie	2452		40	
Ballerina Music Box - Nutcracker	5472		350	
Bath Blast Barbie	3830	Black	15	
Bath Blast Barbie	4159	Blonde	15	
Birthday Party Barbie	3388	Blonde	30	
Birthday Party Barbie	7948	Black	30	

DOLL	MATTEL NO.	VARIATION/COMMENT	NRFB VALUE	BOOK PAGE
Birthday Surprise Barbie	3679	Blonde	$35	
Birthday Surprise Barbie	4051	Black	35	
Bob Mackie Empress Bride	4247		900	97,136
Bob Mackie Neptune Fantasy	4248		850	iii, 62
Caboodles Barbie	03157		25	
Classique - Benefit Ball Barbie	1521		175	194
Dolls of the World - English	4973		95	72, 104
Dolls of the World - Jamaican	4647		35	72
Dolls of the World - Spanish	4963		45	72
Fancy Frills Barbie	3474		40	
FAO Schwarz - Madison Avenue	1539		225	66, 187
Fashion Play Barbie	2713	Blonde	20	
Fashion Play Barbie	3860	Hispanic	20	
Fun to Dress Barbie	3240	Blonde	8	
Fun to Dress Barbie	4809	Hispanic	8	
Happy Holidays Barbie	1429	Blonde	125	111
Happy Holidays Barbie	2396	Black	125	
Hills - Blue Elegance Barbie	1879		45	118
Holiday Sensation Fashion Barbie	7809		75	
JC Penney - Evening Sensation Barbie	1278		75	
Kmart - Pretty in Purple Barbie	3117	Blonde	35	
Kmart - Pretty in Purple Barbie	3121	Black	35	
Meijers - Something Extra Barbie	863		35	
My First Barbie	2483	Blonde	10	
My First Barbie	2570	Black	10	
My First Barbie	3839	Blonde	25	
My First Barbie	3861	Black	25	
My First Barbie	3864	Hispanic	35	
My Size Barbie	2517	Blonde	175	
My Size Barbie	11212	Black	175	
Osco - Picnic Pretty	3808		25	
Porcelain - Crystal Rhapsody	1553		350	64
Porcelain - Plantation Belle Barbie	7526		200	
Pretty Surprise Barbie	9823		20	
Rappin' Rockin' Barbie	3248		45	68
Rollerblade Barbie	2214		45	70, 182
Sears - Blossom Beautiful Barbie	3817		250	
Sears - Dream Princess Barbie	2306		60	
Service Merchandise - Satin Nights Barbie	1886		100	
Sharin' Sisters Gift Set	5716		35	
Shopko-Venture - Party Perfect Barbie	1876		35	
Snap 'n Play Barbie	3550	Blonde	15	

DOLL	MATTEL NO.	VARIATION/COMMENT	NRFB VALUE	BOOK PAGE
Snap 'n Play Barbie	3556	Black	$15	
Snap 'n Play Gift Set	2262	Blonde	25	
Sparkle Eyes Barbie	2482	Blonde	30	70
Sparkle Eyes Barbie	5950	Black	30	
Spiegel - Regal Reflections Barbie	4116		175	
Stars and Stripes Desert Storm Army	1234	Blonde	25	69
Stars and Stripes Desert Storm Army	5618	Black	25	
Stars and Stripes Desert Storm Army Gift Set	5626	Blonde	50	
Stars and Stripes Desert Storm Army Gift Set	5627	Black	35	
Supermarket - Party Premiere Barbie	2001		25	
Supermarket - Pretty Hearts Barbie	2901		65	
Supermarket - Red Romance Barbie	3161		45	
Target - Dazzlin' Date Barbie	3203		35	
Target - Pretty in Plaid Barbie	5413		40	
Target - Wild Style Barbie	0411		40	119
Teen Talk Barbie	1612	Black	50	
Teen Talk Barbie	5745	Blonde	150	153
Totally Hair Barbie	1112	Blonde	30	71
Totally Hair Barbie	1117	Brunette	55	
Totally Hair Barbie	5948	Black	25	
Troll Hair Barbie	10257		20	106
TRU - Barbie for President	3722	Blonde	50	67
TRU - Barbie for President	3940	Black	50	
TRU - Cool 'n Sassy Barbie	1490	Blonde	20	
TRU - Cool 'n Sassy Barbie	4110	Black	25	
TRU - Fashion Brights Barbie	1882	Blonde	30	
TRU - Fashion Brights Barbie	4112	Black	30	144
TRU - Radiant in Red Barbie	1276	Caucasian	60	123
TRU - Radiant in Red Barbie	4113	Ethnic	60	123
TRU - School Fun Barbie	2721	Blonde	25	
TRU - School Fun Barbie	4111	Black	25	
TRU - Spring Parade Barbie	2257	Black	45	
TRU - Spring Parade Barbie	7008	Blonde	45	
United Colors of Benetton Shopping Barbie	4873	Second in the series	25	63
Wal-Mart - Anniversary Star Barbie	2282		50	
Wholesale clubs - Fantastica Barbie	3196	Hispanic	80	145
Wholesale clubs - Peach Blossom Barbie	7009		60	
Wholesale clubs - Rollerblade Gift Set	N/A		75	
Wholesale clubs - Royal Romance Barbie	1858		75	
Wholesale clubs - Sparkle Eyes Gift Set	7131		35	
Wholesale clubs - Sun Sensation Barbie Gift Set	1390		65	
Wholesale clubs - Very Violet Barbie	1859		85	

DOLL	MATTEL NO.	VARIATION/COMMENT	NRFB VALUE	BOOK PAGE
Woolworth - Special Expressions	3197	Blonde	$35	
Woolworth - Special Expressions	3198	Black	35	
Woolworth - Special Expressions	3200	Hispanic	35	129
Woolworth - Sweet Lavender Barbie	2522	Blonde	50	
Woolworth - Sweet Lavender Barbie	2523	Black	50	
◆ 1993				
Ames - Country Looks Barbie	5854		30	
Angel Lights Barbie	10610		150	
Barbie Loves to Read Gift Set	10507		45	
Bob Mackie Masquerade Ball	10803		500	74
Classique - City Style Barbie	10149		120	187
Classique - Evening Extravaganza Barbie	11622	Blonde	75	
Classique - Evening Extravaganza Barbie	11638	Black	150	
Classique - Opening Night Barbie	10148		100	115, 194
Disney Fun	10247	Second in series	50	128
Dolls of the World - Australian	3626		20	76
Dolls of the World - Italian	2256		25	
Dolls of the World - Native American I	1753		95	142, 147
Earring Magic Barbie	2374	Black	20	
Earring Magic Barbie	7014	Blonde	25	152
Earring Magic Barbie	10255	Brunette	35	
FAO Schwarz - Rockette Barbie	2017		200	121
Fountain Mermaid Barbie	10393	Blonde	20	
Fountain Mermaid Barbie	10522	Black	20	
Fun to Dress Gift Set	3826		25	
Sun Sensation Barbie	3602		10	2
Great Era - Flapper Barbie	4063		150	75
Great Era - Gibson Girl Barbie	3702		80	
Happy Holidays Barbie	10824	Blonde	125	111
Happy Holidays Barbie	10911	Black	125	
Hollywood Hair Barbie	2308		15	108
Home Shopping Club - Winter Princess Barbie	10655		500	
JC Penney - Golden Winter Barbie	10684		75	114
Kool-Aid - Wacky Warehouse Barbie	10309	First in series	75	
Little Debbie Barbie	10123		75	132
Locket Surprise Barbie	10963	Blonde	25	98
Locket Surprise Barbie	11224	Black	25	143
McDonalds Birthday Fun Set	11589		50	116
Meijers - Shopping Fun Barbie	10051		35	130,187
My First Barbie	2516	Blonde	13	

DOLL	MATTEL NO.	VARIATION/COMMENT	NRFB VALUE	BOOK PAGE
My First Barbie	2767	Black	$13	
My First Barbie	2770	Hispanic	15	
Naf Naf Barbie	10997		40	
Paint 'n Dazzle Barbie	10039	Blonde	25	
Paint 'n Dazzle Barbie	10057	Dark Auburn	25	
Paint 'n Dazzle Barbie	10058	Black	25	
Paint 'n Dazzle Barbie	10059	Brunette	25	109
Porcelain - Gold Sensation Barbie	10246		300	
Porcelain - Royal Splendor Barbie	10950		250	116
Porcelain - Silken Flame Barbie	1249		250	174
Romantic Bride Barbie	1861	Blonde	40	
Romantic Bride Barbie	11054	Black	40	
Sea Holiday Barbie	5471		60	76
Sears - Enchanted Princess Barbie	10292		65	

She's off to the mall! Shopping Barbies complete with the appropriate shopping bags. From left: ***Classique City Style Barbie, Benetton Shopping Barbie, Meijer Shopping Fun Barbie, FAO Schwarz Madison Avenue Barbie.***

DOLL	MATTEL NO.	VARIATION/COMMENT	NRFB VALUE	BOOK PAGE
Secret Hearts Barbie	3836	Black	$25	
Secret Hearts Barbie	7902	Blonde	25	
Service Merchandise - Sparkling Splendor	10994		75	
Sharin' Sisters Gift Set	10143		25	
Spiegel - Royal Invitation Barbie	10969		150	195
Stars and Stripes Air Force Barbie & Ken Set	11581	Blonde	35	
Stars and Stripes Air Force Barbie & Ken Set	11582	Black	35	
Stars and Stripes Air Force Thunderbirds	11552	Blonde	25	56
Stars and Stripes Air Force Thunderbirds	11553	Black	25	
Supermarket - Back to School Barbie	10217		35	124
Supermarket - Be Mine Barbie	11182		40	
Supermarket - Holiday Hostess Barbie	10280		75	113
Supermarket - Spring Bouquet Barbie	3477		50	
Target - Baseball	4583		35	102, 182
Target - Golf Date	10202		35	102
TRU - Dream Wedding Gift Set	10712	Blonde	50	
TRU - Dream Wedding Gift Set	10713	Black	45	
TRU - Love to Read Barbie	10507		30	
TRU - Malt Shoppe Barbie	4581		25	
TRU - Moonlight Magic Barbie	10608	Caucasian w/dark hair	90	
TRU - Moonlight Magic Barbie	10609	Black	95	
TRU - Police Officer Barbie	10688	Blonde	50	94
TRU - Police Officer Barbie	10689	Black	50	
TRU - School Spirit Barbie	10682	Blonde	25	
TRU - School Spirit Barbie	10683	Black	25	
TRU - Spots 'n Dots Barbie	10491		25	
Twinkle Lights Barbie	10390	Blonde	30	99
Twinkle Lights Barbie	10521	Black	30	
Wal-Mart Superstar Barbie	10592	Blonde	45	
Wal-Mart Superstar Barbie	10711	Hispanic	95	
Western Stampin' Barbie	10293	Blonde	35	
Western Stampin' Barbie	10539	Black	35	
Wholesale clubs - Beach Fun Gift Set	11481		35	
Wholesale clubs - Festiva Barbie	10339	Hispanic	75	145
Wholesale clubs - Hollywood Hair Gift Set	10928		35	
Wholesale clubs - Island Fun Gift Set	10379	Barbie & Ken	35	
Wholesale clubs - Paint 'n Dazzle Gift Set	10926		35	
Wholesale clubs - Secret Hearts Gift Set	10929		65	
Wholesale clubs - Wedding Fantasy Gift Set	10924		95	
Wholesale clubs - Winter Royale Barbie	10658		100	
Winter Princess Series - Winter Princess	10655		475	

DOLL	MATTEL NO.	VARIATION/COMMENT	NRFB VALUE	BOOK PAGE
Woolworth - Special Expressions	10048	Blonde	$25	
Woolworth - Special Expressions	10049	Black	35	
Woolworth - Special Expressions	10050	Hispanic	25	
◆ 1994				
Bedtime Barbie	11079	Blonde	15	99
Bedtime Barbie	11184	Black	15	
Bicycling Barbie	11689	Blonde	35	
Bicycling Barbie	11817	Black	35	
Birthday Barbie	11333	Blonde	30	
Birthday Barbie	11334	Black	30	
Bloomingdale's - Savvy Shopper Barbie	12152	Nicole Miller	150	137
Bob Mackie Queen of Hearts	12046		250	135
Camp Barbie	11074	Blonde	25	
Camp Barbie	11831	Black	40	
Classique - Uptown Chic Barbie	11623		65	
Dance 'n Twirl Barbie	11902	Blonde	65	
Dance 'n Twirl Barbie	12143	Black	65	
Dolls of the World - Chinese	11180		25	83
Dolls of the World - Dutch	11104		25	83
Dolls of the World - Kenyan	11181		25	83
Dolls of the World - Native American II	11609		20	147
Dolls of the World Giftset	12043		75	
Dr. Barbie	11160	Blonde w/baby (varied)	50	79
Dr. Barbie	11814	Black w/baby (varied)	50	
Dress 'n Fun Barbie	10776	Blonde	5	
Dress 'n Fun Barbie	11102	Hispanic	5	
Dress 'n Fun Barbie	11103	Black	5	
Easter Fun Barbie	11276		35	
Enchanted Seasons - Snow Princess Barbie	11875		200	
Erté Stardust	10993		475	141
FAO Schwarz - Shopping Spree Barbie	12749		40	120
FAO Schwarz - Silver Screen Barbie	11652		250	120, back cover
Glitter Hair Barbie	10965	Blonde	10	
Glitter Hair Barbie	10966	Brunette	10	
Glitter Hair Barbie	10968	Redhead	10	
Glitter Hair Barbie	11332	Black	10	
Gold Jubilee Barbie	12009	LE of 5,000	1,000	4, 78
Great Era - Egyptian Queen Barbie	11397		65	
Great Era - Southern Belle Barbie	11478		65	
Gymnast Barbie	12127	Blonde	20	
Gymnast Barbie	12153	Black	20	

DOLL	MATTEL NO.	VARIATION/COMMENT	NRFB VALUE	BOOK PAGE
Hallmark - Victorian Elegance Barbie	12579	First in series	$125	114
Happy Holidays Barbie	12155	Blonde	150	110
Happy Holidays Barbie	12156	Black	200	
Hills - Polly Pocket Barbie	12412		40	130
Hills - Sea Pearl Mermaid Barbie	13940		25	
Hollywood Legends - Ken as Rhett	12741		75	80, 81
Hollywood Legends - Scarlett - Drapery	12045		75	81
Hollywood Legends - Scarlett - Picnic/BBQ	12997		75	81
Hollywood Legends - Scarlett - Red velvet	12815		75	81
Hollywood Legends - Scarlett - White honeymoon	13254		75	80, 174
JC Penney - Night Dazzle Barbie	12194		75	130
Jewel & Glitter Barbie	11185		30	
Kool-Aid - Wacky Warehouse Barbie	11763	Second Kool-Aid	75	
Kraft Treasures Barbie	11546		75	
My First Barbie (Ballerina)	11294	Blonde	10	
My First Barbie (Ballerina)	11340	Black	10	
My First Barbie (Ballerina)	11341	Hispanic	10	
My First Barbie (Ballerina)	11342	Asian	20	
My First Barbie (Ballerina)	13064	Blonde	10	
My First Barbie (Ballerina)	13065	Black	10	148
My First Barbie (Ballerina)	13066	Brunette	10	
My Size Bride Barbie	12052	Blonde	150	
My Size Bride Barbie	12053	Black	150	
Nostalgic - 35th Anniversary Barbie	11590	Blonde	40	77
Nostalgic - 35th Anniversary Barbie	11782	Brunette	50	77
Nostalgic - 35th Anniversary Gift Set	11591	Blonde	150	77
Porcelain - Silver Starlight Barbie	11305		495	
Porcelain - Star Lily Bride	12953		300	
Quinceanera Teresa	11928		40	124
Sears - Silver Sweetheart Barbie	12410		50	
Service Merchandise - City Sophisticate Barbie	12005		75	127
Spiegel - Theatre Elegance Barbie	12077		175	194–195
Sun Jewel Barbie	10953		12	117
Supermarket - Holiday Dreams Barbie	12192		40	113
Swim 'n Dive Barbie	11505	Blonde	20	
Swim 'n Dive Barbie	11734	Black	20	
TRU - Astronaut Barbie	12149	Blonde - 25th Apollo	45	3
TRU - Astronaut Barbie	12150	Black - 25th Apollo	35	170
TRU - Emerald Elegance Barbie	12322	Caucasian	35	123
TRU - Emerald Elegance Barbie	12323	Hispanic	35	
TRU - Pog Barbie	13239	Blonde	25	106
TRU - Sunflower Barbie	13489		20	106

DOLL	MATTEL NO.	VARIATION/COMMENT	NRFB VALUE	BOOK PAGE
Wal-Mart - Country Western Star Barbie	11646	Blonde	$35	127
Wal-Mart - Country Western Star Barbie	12097	Hispanic	55	
Wal-Mart - Country Western Star Barbie	12096	Black	50	
Wal-Mart - Tooth Fairy Barbie	11645		35	128
Wholesale clubs - Seasons Greetings Barbie	12384		125	113
Wholesale clubs - Western Stampin' Gift Set	11020		55	
Winter Princess Series - Evergreen Princess Barbie	12123		150	92, 195

◆ 1995

DOLL	MATTEL NO.	VARIATION/COMMENT	NRFB VALUE	BOOK PAGE
American Stories - Civil War Nurse Barbie	14612		25	
American Stories - Colonial Barbie	12578		25	89
American Stories - Pilgrim Barbie	12577		25	89
American Stories - Pioneer Barbie	12680		25	89
American Stories - Pioneer Shopkeeper Barbie	14765		25	
Baywatch Barbie	13199	Blonde	20	2, 87
Baywatch Barbie	13258	Black	20	
Birthday Barbie	12954	Blonde	20	
Birthday Barbie	12955	Black	20	
Birthday Barbie	13253	Hispanic	20	
Bloomingdale's - Donna Karan Barbie	14452	Brunette	125	122
Bloomingdale's - Donna Karan Barbie	14595	Blonde	150	140
Bob Mackie - Goddess of the Sun	14056		200	134
Bubble Angel Barbie	12443	Blonde	18	
Bubble Angel Barbie	12444	Black	18	
Butterfly Princess Barbie	13051	Blonde	25	
Butterfly Princess Barbie	13052	Black	25	
Career Collection - Fire Fighter Barbie	13472	Black	30	95
Career Collection - Fire Fighter Barbie	13553	Blonde	30	95
Career Collection - Teacher Barbie	13914	Blonde	35	88
Career Collection - Teacher Barbie	13915	Black	35	
Children's Collector Series - Barbie as Rapunzel	13016	First in series	35	
Classique - Midnight Gala Barbie	12999		60	154
Cut 'n Style Barbie	12639	Blonde	25	
Cut 'n Style Barbie	12642	Black	25	
Cut 'n Style Barbie	12643	Brunette	25	
Cut 'n Style Barbie	12644	Red Head	25	
Dance Moves Barbie	13083	Blonde	15	107
Dance Moves Barbie	13086	Black	15	
Designer Series - Christian Dior Barbie	13168		165	91, 139
Dolls of the World - German	12698		25	90, 104

DOLL	MATTEL NO.	VARIATION/COMMENT	NRFB VALUE	BOOK PAGE
Dolls of the World - Irish	12998		$40	90, 104
Dolls of the World - Polynesian	12700		25	90, 105
Dolls of the World - Native American III	12699		25	147
Dolls of the World Giftset	13939		60	
Dr. Barbie	14309	w/3 babies	35	
Dr. Barbie	14315	w/3 babies	35	
Easter Party Barbie	12793		35	
Enchanted Seasons - Spring Bouquet Barbie	12989		150	
Evening Series - Starlight Waltz	14070		85	
Equestrienne Barbie	12456		50	101
FAO Schwarz - Circus Star Barbie	13257		100	118
FAO Schwarz - Jeweled Splendor Barbie	14061		400	
Flying Hero Barbie (Super Power Barbie)	14030	Blonde	15	
Great Era - Elizabethan Queen Barbie	12792		60	
Great Era - Medieval Lady Barbie	12791		60	
Hallmark - Holiday Memories	14106		75	114
Happy Holidays	14123	Blonde	40	112, 164
Happy Holidays	14124	Black	40	112
Hollywood Legends - Barbie as Maria	13676		60	
Hollywood Legends - Dorothy Barbie	12701		60	
Hot Skatin' Barbie	13511	Blonde	25	
Hot Skatin' Barbie	13512	Black	25	101
JC Penney - Royal Enchantment	14010		50	113
Mattel's 50th Anniversary Porcelain Barbie	14479		600	86
My First Barbie Princess	13064	Blonde	10	
My First Barbie Princess	13065	Black	10	
My First Barbie Princess	13066	Hispanic	10	
My First Barbie Princess	13067	Asian	10	
My Size Princess Ballerina Barbie	13767	Blonde	150	
My Size Princess Ballerina Barbie	13768	Black	150	
Nostalgic - Busy Gal	13675		50	85
Nostalgic - Solo in the Spotlight	13534	Blonde	45	
Nostalgic - Solo in the Spotlight	13820	Brunette	30	85
Ruffle Fun Barbie	12433	Blonde	15	
Ruffle Fun Barbie	12434	Black	15	
Ruffle Fun Barbie	12435	Hispanic	15	
Sears - Ribbons and Roses	13911		50	
Service Merchandise - Ruby Romance	13612		75	127
Sharin' Sisters Gift Set	10143		30	
Slumber Party Barbie	12696	Blonde	18	
Slumber Party Barbie	12697	Black	18	

DOLL	MATTEL NO.	VARIATION/COMMENT	NRFB VALUE	BOOK PAGE
Spiegel - Shopping Chic Barbie	14009		$125	95
Strollin' Fun Barbie & Kelly	13742	Blonde	25	
Strollin' Fun Barbie & Kelly	13743	Black	25	
Supermarket - Caroling Fun	13966		25	113
Supermarket - Schooltime Fun Barbie	13741		20	109
Supertalk Barbie	12290	Blonde	25	
Supertalk Barbie	12379	Black	25	
Sweet Dreams Barbie	13611	Blonde	35	
Sweet Dreams Barbie	13630	Black	35	
Target - Steppin' Out Barbie	14110		30	119
Travelin' Sisters Gift Set	14073		40	
Tropical Splash Barbie	12446		15	
TRU - Purple Passion Barbie	13554	Blonde	25	124
TRU - Purple Passion Barbie	13555	Black	25	
TRU - Sapphire Dream Barbie	13255	First in series	125	125, 194–195
Valentine Barbie	12675		50	
Wal-Mart - Country Bride Barbie	13614	Blonde	30	106
Wal-Mart - Country Bride Barbie	13615	Black	30	
Wal-Mart - Country Bride Barbie	13616	Hispanic	30	
Wedding Party Barbie Gift Set	13557		30	
Wessco - International Travel Barbie	13912		75	129
Wholesale clubs - Winter's Eve	13613		60	113
Winter Princess Series - Peppermint Princess	13598		75	112
Winter Sports Barbie	13516		40	

WATERFRONT
PLAYBILL
ARCADIA
Translations
PLAYBILL
PLAYBILL
PLAYBILL

New York Nights— Barbie dolls in gowns (left to right): *Classique* Opening Night Barbie, *Classique* Benefit Ball Barbie, *Toys 'R Us* Sapphire Dream Barbie, *Winter Princess* Evergreen Princess Barbie, *Spiegel* Royal Invitation Barbie *(front): Spiegel* Theater Elegance Barbie

BIBLIOGRAPHY

Advertising Age, "Barbie Grows Up," v63, p30, June 1 1992
Advertising Age, "Mattel Fashions Barbie Boutique," v62, p3, July 1 1991
AdWEEK, "Barbie to Petra: You're No Friend of Mine," v32, p16, August 15 1991
AdWEEK, "Ethnic Barbie Struts her Stuff on TV," v40, p4, July 23 1990
AdWEEK, "Mattel's Barbie Ties Charity Drive to Worldwide Summit," v40, p47, November 5 1990
AdWEEK's Advertising Week, "Barbie at 30," v30, p20, February 13 1989
Antiques and Collecting, "Barbie is Thirty," v94, pp22-5, September 1989
Architectural Digest, "BillyBoy in Paris," v46, pp94+, September 1989
BillyBoy*. *Barbie - Her Life & Times,* New York: Crown, 1987
Bryan, Sandra. Barbie-The Eyelash Era. Self-published, 1989
Business Week, "Looking for a Few Good Boy Toys," p116, February 17 1992
Business Week, "Why Do All Those Street Kids Love Mattel," p130, October 28 1991
Business Week, "Mattel Struggles," p76+, May 9 1989
Business Week, "Dollhouse in Order," p66-7, August 28 1989
Business Week, "Barbie Is Her Best Friend," p80, June 8 1992
DeWein, Sibyl St. John. *Collectible Barbie Dolls,* 1977-79
DeWein, Sibyl and Evelyn Ashabraner. *Barbie Dolls & Collectibles.* Collector Books, 1992
Eames, Sarah Sink. *Barbie Fashion, 1959-1972.* Collector Books, 1990
Education Digest, "Barbie Doesn't Add Up," v58, pp72-4, December 1992
Financial Times, "Why grown men dream of a future with Barbie," p13
Financial Week, "Eternally Yours, Barbie," v161, pp36-7, September 1 1992
Forbes, "Barbie Does Budapest," v147, pp66+, January 7 1991
Forbes, "Brink of Bankruptcy," v136, pp50-1+, August 12 1985
Forbes, "Is There a Doctor in the House?" pp218-220, May 28 1990
Forbes, "Stick With the Doll that Brung Ya," v145, pp218-19, May 28 1990
Forbes, "Barbie Does Silicon Valley," v 154, pp84-5, September 26 1994
Forbes, "Barbie at 30," v142, pp248-9, November 14 1988
Fortune, "Putting Barbie Back Together Again," v102, pp84-88, September 8 1980
Fortune, "Earring Magic," v126, p56, September 21 1992
Hobbies, "Barbie Doll Boom," v90, pp32-6, June 1985
Interview, "Our Barbies, Ourselves," v21, p36, December 1991
Investor's Business Daily - Executive Update, "What Makes Barbie A Girl's Favorite Doll?" April 12, 1995
Jacobs, Laura. *Barbie in Fashion.* New York: Abbeville Press, 1994
Los Angeles Magazine, "King Barbie," v39, pp62-8, August 1994
Mandeville, A. Glenn. *Doll Fashion Anthology.* Hobby House Press, 1993
Manos, Susan. *The Wonder of Barbie.* Collector Books, 1990

Manos, Susan. *The World of Barbie Dolls.* Collector Books, 1990
Marketing News, "Mattel Chief Followed Her Instincts and Found Success," v26, p15, March 16 1992
Marketing News, "Toy Companies Release 'Ethnically Correct' Dolls," v25, p1, September 30 1991
Money, "Barbie Looks Like A Billion Bucks," v22, p82, May 1993
Ms., "Is There a Barbie Doll in Your Past?" v8, p102, September 1979
New Republic, "Bedtime Barbie," v 212, pp12-13, January 9-16 1995
New Choices, "All Dolled Up," v31, pp93-4, April 1991
Newsweek, "Hot Date: Barbie and G.I. Joe," v113, p59, February 20 1989
Newsweek, "Barbie at 24," v102, p10+, September 12 1983
Newsweek, "Finally, Barbie Doll Ads Go Ethnic," v116, p48, August 13 1990
Newsweek, "Honey, They Blew Up Barbie," v120, p42, July 27 1992
New York Times, "Toy Makers Meet The Inner Child, Ages 21 and Up," p12, December 27 1992
People, "Barbie Turns 30," v31, p186-7, March 6 1989
People, "Volley of the Dolls," v36, p95, September 9 1991
People, "Barbie, Meet Brenda," v37, p120-1, February 17 1992
People, "Barbie Bashing," v40, p67, August 9 1993
Philadelphia, "Oh, You Beautiful Doll," June 1993, pp31-2
Playthings, "Mattel Brings In-Line Skating Fun to Doll Market," v90, p78, February 1992
Rana, Margo. *Barbie Exclusives.* Collector Books, 1994
Robins, Cynthia. *Barbie-30 Years of America's Doll,* Contemporary Books, 1989
Sarasohn-Kahn, Jane. "Barbie Goes to Work," *Barbie Bazaar,* September/October 1994
Sarasohn-Kahn, Jane. "Barbie in Cyberspace," *Miller's Barbie Collector,* November/December 1994
Sarasohn-Kahn, Jane. "Barbie 2009," You've Come a Long Way, Barbie, Baltimore National Barbie Convention, August 1993
U.S. News & World Report, "Mattel Gets All Dolled Up," v115, pp74-6, December 13 1993
U.S. News & World Report, "Teen Talk Barbie," v113, p25, September 12 1992
U.S. News & World Report, "Barbie's New World," v111, p22, September 30 1991
U.S. News & World Report, "Valley of the Dolls?" v109, pp56-9, December 3 1990
Utne Reader, "What a Doll!" p46+, March-April 1992
Wall Street Journal, "Barbie, Miss America Make Up and Settle Dispute Over Looks," pC18, August 27 1992
Wall Street Journal, "Educators Give Barbie a Good Dressing-Down," pB1, September 25 1992
Washingtonian, "Child's Play," pp149-150, December 1994
Westenhauser, Kitturah. *The Story of Barbie.* Collector Books, 1993
Working Woman, "Moving Beyond Barbie," v18, pp46-8, December 1993
Working Woman, "Mistress of the Universe," v10, p160, September 1983
Working Woman, "It's How You Play the Game," v15, pp88-91, May 1990
Working Woman, "When Toys Mean Business," v12, pp133-4+, May 1987

INDEX

Note: To easily locate photographs of specific Barbie dolls pictured in this book, please consult the Comprehensive List of Dolls and Values starting on page 174.

About the Author

Jane Sarasohn-Kahn has been writing since her mother bought a thirty-pound IBM Selectric typewriter for her to work with in 1964. When not collecting Barbie dolls, Jane is a management consultant and economist who works globally with organizations on matters relating to the future of health care and technology. She has published articles in more than 40 business journals and collectibles magazines on topics ranging from health care technology and global business to Barbie collecting. She also writes a monthly column "Notes from a Friend of the Barbie Doll," for *Toy Trader* magazine.

Jane holds an M.A. in Economics, an M.H.S.A. in Public Health, a B.A. in Economics and a B.A. in Journalism, all from the University of Michigan. For the past ten years she has been married to an international banker who lovingly brings her Barbie dolls discovered in the course of his worldwide travels.

Photograph by Michael